THE INTERIORS OF SOCIAL MEDIA

THE INTERIORS OF SOCIAL MEDIA

Architecture, Space, and Technology in the 21st Century

JAVIER FERNÁNDEZ CONTRERAS

BLOOMSBURY VISUAL ARTS
LONDON · NEW YORK · OXFORD · NEW DELHI · SYDNEY

BLOOMSBURY VISUAL ARTS
Bloomsbury Publishing Plc
50 Bedford Square, London, WC1B 3DP, UK
1385 Broadway, New York, NY 10018, USA
29 Earlsfort Terrace, Dublin 2, Ireland

BLOOMSBURY, BLOOMSBURY VISUAL ARTS and the Diana logo are
trademarks of Bloomsbury Publishing Plc

First published in Great Britain 2026

Cover design: Eleanor Rose
Cover image: © Saktanong Chaipanya/Alamy

A catalogue record for this book is available from the British Library.

A catalogue record for this book is available from the Library of Congress.

ISBN: HB: 978-1-3505-3744-6
      PB: 978-1-3505-3743-9
      ePDF: 978-1-3505-3745-3
      eBook: 978-1-3505-3746-0

Typeset by RefineCatch Limited, Bungay, Suffolk
Printed and bound in India

For product safety related questions contact productsafety@bloomsbury.com.

To find out more about our authors and books visit www.bloomsbury.com
and sign up for our newsletters.

CONTENTS

Foreword

Javier Fernández Contreras ix

1 **Instagram, Typology, and Architecture**

Javier Fernández Contreras and Paule Perron 1

2 **Screens Within Screens: The Interiors of Twitch**

Javier Fernández Contreras 25

3 **Rooms, Pins, and Boards: The Hyper-interiors of Pinterest**

Javier Fernández Contreras and Michela Bassanelli 45

4 **TikTok: Vertical Editing**

Javier Fernández Contreras, Camille Bodin, Annie Bornet, and Taiana Broillet 73

5 **Architecture, Humanitarianism, and Social Media**

Javier Fernández Contreras and Damien Greder 87

6 **Pet Influencers: Animal Portraiture and Mediated Domesticities**

Javier Fernández Contreras 121

7 Unboxing Roblox: Architecture, Urbanism, and Video Games

Javier Fernández Contreras 139

8 Porn Rooms: Ultimate Interiority

Javier Fernández Contreras and Vytautas Jankauskas 163

Afterword

Marina Otero Verzier 169

List of Contributors 173
List of Contributors (Full Credits per Chapter) 175
List of Figures 179
Index 185

WorldWideWeb: Summary

August 6, 1991, 16:00 (GMT)

The message "WorldWideWeb: Summary" was transmitted on August 6, 1991, by Tim Berners-Lee, the creator of the World Wide Web.[1] It was a post on the alt.hypertext Usenet newsgroup containing a hyperlink to the first website ever created, hosted on a CERN server in Geneva.[2] The website explained what the World Wide Web was and how to use it:

> The WorldWideWeb (W3) is a wide-area hypermedia information retrieval initiative aiming to give universal access to a large universe of documents.
>
> Everything there is online about W3 is linked directly or indirectly to this document, including an executive summary of the project, Mailing lists, Policy, November's W3 news, Frequently Asked Questions.[3]

Wikipedia: Social media

December 6, 2024, 09:43 (UTC)

> Social media are interactive technologies that facilitate the creation, sharing, and aggregation of content (such as ideas, interests, and other forms of expression) amongst virtual communities and networks. Common features include:
>
> — Online platforms that enable users to create and share content and participate in social networking.
> — User-generated content—such as text posts or comments, digital photos or videos, and data generated through online interactions.
> — Service-specific profiles that are designed and maintained by the social media organization.
> — Social media helps the development of online social networks by connecting a user's profile with those of other individuals or groups.[4]

[1] The original message can be consulted online on the World Wide Web Consortium (W3C) website (accessed July 28, 2025), https://www.w3.org/People/Berners-Lee/1991/08/art-6487.txt

[2] For more information about the developments that led to the creation of the first website, see: World Wide Web Consortium (W3C), "A Little History of the World Wide Web" (accessed July 28, 2025), https://www.w3.org/History.html

[3] Tim Berners-Lee, "World Wide Web," *alt.hypertext* (Usenet newsgroup) (accessed July 28, 2025), http://info.cern.ch/hypertext/WWW/TheProject.html

[4] "Social Media," *Wikipedia*, last edited on December 6, 2024, 09:43 (UTC), https://en.wikipedia.org/wiki/Social_media

FOREWORD

Javier Fernández Contreras

In 1991, the World Wide Web was launched in Geneva by computer scientist Tim Berners-Lee, revolutionizing the way people accessed, shared, and interacted with information. The internet had existed long before. In 1963, technologist Ted Nelson conceived of the idea of hypertext—a digital writing system composed of interconnected nodes of information—laying the conceptual groundwork for nonlinear reading. In 1969, the Advanced Research Projects Agency launched ARPANET, the first packet-switching network and a technological precursor to the modern internet. It connected four computers at different academic institutions: Los Angeles (UCLA), the Stanford Research Institute (SRI), Santa Barbara (UCSB), and the University of Utah. In 1971, the first email was sent by programmer Ray Tomlinson on ARPANET, revolutionizing communication. Yet, the World Wide Web (WWW) was different from previous protocols. Unlike ARPANET, which was primarily a network for data transfer and communication between closed circuits, the WWW allowed for easy navigation and access to information through web pages connected using hyperlinks. Additionally, while early systems focused on nonlinear text and complex linking, the WWW simplified this with the merging of a standardized Hypertext Transfer Protocol (HTTP), a Uniform Resource Locator (URL), commonly known as a web address, and a defined Hypertext Markup Language (HTML) for web browsing, making it accessible to all computers and enabling the internet to become a global platform for information-sharing.[1]

By the end of the 1990s, there were more than 3 million websites operating on the World Wide Web. Six Degrees, largely considered the first social media web application, was launched in 1997. Based on the concept of "six degrees of separation," the idea that everyone in the world is connected by no more than six steps, it allowed users to create profiles, list their friends, and interact with other users. LiveJournal, a blogging site to maintain journals or blogs, was launched in 1999. Friendster, a social networking site that allowed people to connect with friends, share updates, and engage with others, was founded in 2002. MySpace, one of the first widely used platforms to include image-sharing, appeared in 2003, popularizing the practice of users uploading photos (mostly from webcams) as part of their personal profiles. LinkedIn (CV-sharing) was launched in 2003, Facebook (social-networking) and Flickr (photo-sharing) in 2004, YouTube (video-sharing) in 2005, Twitter (sloganing), Roblox (video-gaming), and YouPorn (porn-sharing) in 2006, Justin.tv (streaming) and Tumblr (microblogging) in 2007, Grindr (dating) in 2009, Instagram (photo-sharing) in 2010, Pinterest (image-cataloguing) in 2010, and so on.[2]

This book proposes that social media platforms are changing the way space and architecture are shared, conceived, consumed, and designed. More importantly, it argues that online social networks are creating spatial types that deserve architectural attention. It posits, for instance, that the Twitch rooms of the most followed streamers worldwide are non-circadian, with bodies and objects artificially lit, whereas Pinterest spaces are mainly diurnal and bodyless. In user-generated video games such as those on Roblox, architectural types are linked to its game engine as much as to the chats within its developer forum—a blog-based platform where design is discussed and code shared. While the study of types and typology has experienced a revival in architectural theory in recent years, it can be argued that most publications have perpetuated a focus on programmatic, tectonic, and geometric elements through photography and printed plans, without addressing how digital platforms are influencing not only the discipline's contemporaneity but also its historiography.[3] As a parallel hypothesis, the book therefore also proposes that interior spaces are gaining unprecedented agency through social media. These are the interiors of both anonymous users and celebrities who regularly post their mediated selves on Instagram or TikTok from within their living rooms, bedrooms, or personal gyms as theaters of their staged domesticities. These are also the interiors of camming and porn platforms, in settings where eroticism is built through the insertion of bodies into spaces to be portrayed, filmed, and streamed. Expanding into the nonhuman realm, the research also analyzes the interiors of domesticated animals who become influencers on social media, with their portraits, smiles, and antics monetized by their human owners within domestic settings. At a time when the inhabitants of contemporary urban societies spend over 85 percent of their time indoors,[4] the interiors of social media transform architectural spaces into sites for consumerism, display, and mediatization.

Of course, the entanglements between architecture and social networks started long before the digital era. The iterative condition of pictures lies at the center of the relationship between architecture and image. In the Netherlands, the 17th century—the Dutch Golden Age— saw the production of more than 5 million paintings,[5] many of them portraits of individuals or families within domestic interiors. The construction of the pictorial transformed spaces themselves, with genre art depicting stereotypical scenes of a daily life where interiors were in many cases both inhabited rooms and visually appropriated decors.[6] As an exterior counterpart, in the 17th and 18th centuries, during the Grand Tour, different generations of travelers would look at the same ruins in Italy and iterate them in endless personalized installments, whether textual or pictorial.[7] Their drawings and records would circulate and impact architectural culture in England, France, and Germany—for, as much as images mobilize collective imaginaries, people like to share them. Embedded into the spaces of the ordinary and the extraordinary, anonymous people, too, learned to become the figurants of their own life in front of the camera. By the end of the 19th century, *La Sortie de l'Usine Lumière à Lyon* (1895), the first film by cinema pioneers the Lumière brothers, captured workers coming out of their factory and was recorded in three different versions. In the second one, the workers dressed up, for they understood that the video record would be a definitive testimony of their personas. Whether domestic portraits, drawings by travelers, or videos, these images reflect a curiosity for seeing and consuming through the eyes of others—something inherent to human nature.

Architecture is, as well, at the center of this curiosity to see through images. With the institutionalization of mass media in the 20th century, these concepts expanded to include mediated and multimedia spatial types, as explained by architectural theorists and historians such as Beatriz Colomina and Penny Sparke, who argue that mediums such as photography, cinema, and commercial catalogs created new spatial patterns that informed the architectural ethos and, in particular, the design of interior spaces.[8] In the second half of the 20th century, the expansion of television, and the invention of video games and the personal computer, would further disrupt the boundaries between leisure and monetization throughout domestic interiors. The number of television sets in the United States increased tenfold during the 1950s, giving way to new ways of neighborhood bonding and community interaction in mass-produced suburbs.[9] The new focus on television sparked efforts to capture and monetize viewer attention. As technologist James Bridle notes, in 1968, the Children's Television Workshop was established to create educational programming for kids, its most famous outcome being *Sesame Street*, which centered on measuring and boosting children's engagement through behavioral analysis. Similar research laid the foundation for attention-driven screen programming and evolved into today's "attention economy."[10] First theorized in the 1970s by scholar Herbert A. Simon,[11] this concept treats human attention as a scarce resource to be captured in an information-rich world—a notion that grew in importance with the rise of the internet in the 1990s, as companies started to view engagement as a finite and valuable resource in the face of overwhelming media choices. As architect Andrés Jaque explains, parallel to the American experiments, in Italy, Milano 2—a residential district in Italy promoted by businessman Silvio Berlusconi starting in the late 1960s—structured life around a private cable TV service, Tele Milano, which in the 1970s began to target specialized groups by tailoring content to distinct audiences, using different channels, programs, and time slots to reach them.[12]

The practice of associating segmented content with the monetization of attention through screens set the foundation for many commercial strategies that would later be incorporated into the internet. That interiors were at the center of this revolution became clear in the 1980s with the progressive introduction of the personal computer and video game consoles into the domestic sphere. The first advertisement for the Apple II—arguably one of the most important devices in popularizing home computing—appeared as a two-page spread in the magazine *BYTE* in 1977, displaying a couple inside a domestic space, namely an open-plan kitchen. Similarly, in the 1982 packaging of the Atari VCS game console, a family is seen playing *Space Invaders* in their living room. Both advertisements reflect the gender biases of their time by merging technology and domesticity. In the first image, the man is working on (supposedly his) personal computer while the woman prepares (supposedly their) food. In the second, the father and the child play with different joysticks—even though at the time only one person could play—while the mother and daughter watch and smile, seemingly hypnotized by the screen.[13]

As screens multiplied, they transformed interiors and incorporated cameras that look at us while we look at them, getting progressively closer to the human body. The first webcam, introduced in 1993 at the University of Cambridge, was created to monitor a coffee pot in the meeting room, allowing researchers to check if there was enough coffee without leaving their desks. That the first webcam was associated with an idea of surveillance, originally of an object, is very telling of what the further development of technology would be like. The first mobile phone to include a camera was the Kyocera VP-210, released in 1999 in Japan. Interestingly, it was a front-facing camera positioned alongside the screen. Although limited, it could make videocalls, sending two images per second through Japan's PHS mobile phone network system. A few years later, in 2006, Apple popularized the use of built-in webcams in laptops with the launch of the MacBook and MacBook Pro, although it had already used this technology in 2005 with the iMac G5, which featured an integrated iSight camera. This reversal, or duality, in the direction of observation amounts to a paradigm shift in the understanding of the surface of representation. As opposed to analogic imagery, like Diego Velázquez's painting *Las Meninas* (1656) or Jeff Wall's photograph *Picture for Women* (1979), where the respective surfaces of the canvas and the cibachrome could play with the ambiguity of the reversal of perception but actually not "look back" (at least technologically) at the individuals or objects depicted,[14] most 21st-century screens are equipped with integrated cameras and data surveillance systems designed to track human behavior in real time. These systems include eye-tracking technology and facial recognition, and monitor a range of user activities such as browsing history, app usage patterns, location data, typing speed, and other biometric information, offering an unprecedented level of data collection, and all serving as fundamental technologies in the interaction dynamics embedded in social media.

Interestingly, webcams have also reintroduced ornaments and decoration to serve new processes of economic profitability and identity construction, as explained by writer Nicholas Korody in his research on contemporary decoration.[15] In an essay on the interior architecture of the camming rooms inside Studio20 in Los Angeles, he explains how each room is a set, with one side dedicated to technical equipment such as cameras, lights, and a computer, while the other side is arranged with furniture and decor to resemble a bedroom. For Korody, "the webcam acts like a tether to the body, orienting and circumscribing potential movement as it divides a room into 'on-screen' and 'off-screen' zones."[16] One could also add another side of the screen, that of the audience, with all sides being essential in the construction of a new architectural mediatization. To that extent, Aneesh Chaganty's screenlife film *Searching* (2018) is a good example of how the story unfolds entirely on a laptop screen, which simultaneously overlays its content and the spaces recorded by its camera. As a father searches for his missing daughter, the film uses overlapping windows—from chats and video calls to web searches and social media—to create a dual-layered narrative. This approach embeds viewers within the protagonist's screen, making them feel as if they inhabit the spaces, chats, and windows represented, and, perhaps, as though they cannot escape being endlessly recorded. It is no wonder that the work of artists such as Hito Steyerl has built heavily on how to hide, and how to avoid the metrics of surveillance because, in the 21st century, becoming invisible, leaving no trace, no records, is hardly avoidable. In works such as *How Not to Be Seen: A Fucking Didactic Educational.MOV File* (2013), a satirical guide on how to avoid being seen in a world dominated by surveillance, Steyerl interrogates the nature of visibility in the age of digital media, exploring how individuals can become both visible and invisible within camera systems and raising important questions about agency, identity, and the politics of representation.

These developments have been matched by changes in the economic model of the internet, in which social media and social media-like strategies are now central to marketization and privatization. This model was reshaped at the beginning of the 21st century by the bursting of the dot-com bubble, a series of companies rooted in the Web 1.0 era. This crash laid the groundwork for what internet theorists later called "Web 2.0," a term coined by web expert Darcy DiNucci in 1999[17] and later popularized by author Tim O'Reilly, who organized the Web 2.0 Summit annually between 2004 and 2011 as a regular executive conference for technology and business leaders.[18] It is significant that his most influential essay on internet theory, "What Is Web 2.0," does not provide a synthetic, explicit definition, assuming instead that the concept "doesn't have a hard boundary but rather a gravitational core."[19] In a comparative diagram, O'Reilly illustrated the transition from the first era of the World Wide Web to the second with paired examples. In a retrospective definition, we could rephrase his diagram by saying that, back in 2005, Web 2.0 marked a shift toward a dynamic, participatory web where search engine technology revolutionized online advertising with targeted, cost-per-click models (Google AdSense), while photo-sharing services enabled users to upload, organize, and tag images (Flickr). Peer-to-peer file sharing changed how digital content was distributed through decentralized servers (BitTorrent, Napster), and user-generated knowledge platforms allowed for collaborative editing and information-sharing (Wikipedia). Online publishing gave individuals a platform for self-expression (blogging), paired with social event sites that facilitated the discovery and sharing of local events (Upcoming.org, EVDB). Search engine optimization (SEO) became crucial for improving website visibility, while wikis and tagging allowed users to collaboratively build and organize content ("folksonomy"). Finally, content could be shared across multiple platforms, keeping users informed with automatic updates (syndication).

Interestingly, the words "private" and "privatization" do not appear anywhere in the essay, and nor do "money" or "monetization." However, as early as the first Web 2.0 conference in 2004, in the preliminary set of principles, the first one was "the web as platform."[20] As a follow-up, the term "platform capitalism" was popularized in 2016 by political theorist Nick Srnicek, in a book of the same name, to examine the rise of digital platforms (like Google, Amazon, Facebook, and Uber) and how they have transformed the market economy, representing a new phase of its development, with business models that prioritize data collection, network effects, and monopolistic tendencies.[21] At the core of Web 2.0 are user-generated content, the monetization of attention, data surveillance, and the intensification of human activity. In 2017, Reed Hastings, CEO of Netflix—a film streaming company whose behavioral model builds heavily on data-driven personalization, user engagement, and content-recommendation algorithms—openly declared that "[w]e are competing with sleep, on the margin, it's a very large pool of time."[22] It is arguably one of the first times in modern economic history that human physiology has been bluntly identified as a more important competitor than other companies, supporting Professor Jonathan Crary's argument, in *24/7:*

Late Capitalism and the Ends of Sleep (2013), that the erosion of sleep is both the aim and the result of capitalism and the attention economy, where the pairing of technology and wakefulness drives profitability.[23]

The intersections between Web 2.0 and social media entail the privatization of a territory (the Internet), the monetization of its domains (platforms), and the behavioral alteration of its users (humans). In her book *After the Internet* (2022), media theorist Tiziana Terranova explains the "significant shift from the Internet as a set of interoperable network protocols governed by a series of public and/or voluntary non-profit organizations, to gated digital communities with strong ownership of data, software, and infrastructure."[24] These are privately owned online services that she calls the "Corporate Platform Complex (CPC)." In this ecosystem, Terranova explains, "the Web 2.0 included companies that will later be called social media (Friendster, Facebook, Flickr, Myspace, Second Life, and Blogger), but also applications such as Google, inasmuch as the latter is built on the successful capacity of its algorithms to harness and extract value out of the browsing practices of its users."[25] Similarly, the extractability of users' activities became central to the business models of later applications from the 2000s and 2010s. In front of the screen—the laptop, the mobile phone, or the headset—humans are simultaneously users, clients, consumers, and workers: "We would love to hear your feedback," "Please don't forget to evaluate your ride," "How would you rate our service?" In reviews for companies such as Amazon, Airbnb, Booking, and Uber, customers are providing quality-checking services for free, often happily, sometimes adding emojis to their comments, on platforms that rely heavily on social media strategies involving feedback, interaction, and marketization.

Architecture is at the center of this phenomenon. As a physically constructed and digitally connected environment, it is intertwined with how social media circulates, influences, and constructs contemporary spaces. Studies of social media are abundant, ranging from collections of essays to thematic publications analyzing it from the perspectives of technology, digital studies, social sciences, anthropology of media, and cultural analytics, to name a few. The literature examining how digital technology is transforming space is extensive, spanning scales from the planetary—where philosopher Benjamin H. Bratton illustrates how global-scale computation disrupts the sovereignty of nation-states[26]—to localized architectural processes of design and navigation, and extending to the impact of digital devices on the perception and use of space, as analyzed by scholar Richard Coyne.[27] Significantly, in recent years, there has been growing interest and awareness regarding the importance of dedicated studies at the intersection of architecture and social media. Beyond the authors already mentioned, the work of Davide T. Ferrando stands out for its relevance and comprehensive approach. His research analyzes both specific platforms (like Facebook and Twitch)[28] and broader phenomena, such as the influence of social media on contemporary domesticity and architectural criticism.[29] Additionally, scholars working on new media theory, such as Lev Manovich, have incorporated architecture into their analyses of the digital turn. This is exemplified in his book *Instagram and Contemporary Image* (2017), which examines millions of photographs from global cities, with specific sections focused on the perception and consumption of space.[30] Architecture institutions have also started incorporating online social networks into their research agendas, as illustrated by the 2023 conference *Architecture Archives of the Future* at the Jaap Bakema Study Centre, which dedicated a section to social media;[31] the 2024 exhibition *Madskills: Self-Documenting Construction on Social Media* at the Canadian Centre for Architecture;[32] and the 2024 exhibition *Private Lives: From the Bedroom to Social Media* at the Musée des Arts Décoratifs.[33]

The Interiors of Social Media is a further step in this line of research, offering a thorough examination of how the technology is transforming contemporary architecture. By analyzing the spatial dynamics of the most-followed accounts on Instagram, Twitch, Pinterest, and TikTok, as well as those on porn platforms, user-generated video games, imagery of humanitarian crises, and the domesticities of mediatized pets, the book sheds light on the ethical, political, and ecological implications of digital platforms. The research, primarily conducted with students in Interior Architecture at HEAD – Genève, focused mainly on analyzing the most-followed accounts, popular videos, liked posts, and widely circulated images per platform and topic over specific years, ranging between 2022 and 2025. No complex analytical tools—such as data scraping or big data—were used. As an exercise in technology accessibility and media studies, the project is based on the premise that any student or researcher can, through a structured analysis of the abundant content available online, develop a theory and critique applied to social media, space, and architecture. Relying on simple metrics, the book sheds light on the complexities that arise from the integration of technology, media, and architecture in shaping contemporary social interactions and spatial experiences. For example, it shows that Oh Joy!, Pinterest's top influencer, dedicates most of her boards to architecture and interior design, including "For the Home," "Retail Inspiration," and "Oh Joy! Builds a House," which documented the construction and decoration of her Los Angeles home, in collaboration with *Architectural Digest*, in 2020. It also reveals that Ninja, the world's most-followed Twitch streamer, regularly broadcasts his gameplay of video games such as *Fortnite* and *League of Legends* for hours on end from a room devoid of natural light, illuminated by blue LED lamps that suppress melatonin secretion and disrupt the need for sleep. The book also explores how pet influencers such as That Little Puff, the most-followed cat on TikTok, communicate exclusively from interior spaces, often dressed up and performing activities like life hacks or cooking, with fast-paced editing featuring shots lasting less than a second and stop-motion antics that conceal the human hands setting them up. Additionally, it examines how social media platforms covering the conflicts in the Democratic Republic of the Congo and the West Sahel region highlight gendered uses of space, portraying women in ephemeral, tent-like shelters that underscore their precarious existence amid conflict, and men in concrete buildings associated with diplomacy or healthcare, suggesting power and control while reflecting how architecture reinforces problematic gender roles and conveys political messages of power, vulnerability, resistance, and restriction. The fact that these references are randomly grouped in the same paragraph might seem shocking, much like the way people scroll, navigate, and click through random, often ethically contradictory, content on their smartphones.

Many architects have probably never heard of these references, just as most non-initiates have never looked at magazines like *El Croquis* or attended the Venice Architecture Biennale. This book is not about explaining why some online influencers have more impact than professional architects and curators in mediatizing the discipline. Instead, it seeks to understand how contemporary space and architecture are shaped and transformed by social media. As opposed to Hito Steyerl's didactics, it is an exercise in visibility. What to look at? Where to begin? The issue here is not the absence of information but its overabundance.

By organizing content into comparative grids based on simple criteria—such as image type (photographic, audiovisual), framing (horizontal–vertical, frontal–diagonal), bodies (human–nonhuman, number, position), circadianism (day–night), chromatic palette, and so on—the book makes visible spatial phenomena that traditional channels of the discipline such as schools, publications, exhibitions, and biennials have sometimes overlooked. It is structured into two series of chapters—two complementary and interconnected blocks, which are segmented either by social media platform or by topics that span multiple networks.

The chapters in the first block analyze applications that, for different reasons, are considered central because of their impact on contemporary architecture and interiors: Instagram, Pinterest, Twitch, and TikTok. As of 2024, Instagram is the world's third-largest platform after Facebook and YouTube,[34] and it has become inseparable from the understanding of spaces that are edited and aestheticized through its filters. Its adjectival form, "instagrammable," is the most frequently added social media-originated adjective to dictionaries worldwide, which typically pair their examples with notions of place and locus.[35] Pinterest, meanwhile, is the most important platform for curating and sampling spaces, where most content is synced from external sources and repinned in endless accumulations of boards that design aspirational futures, both by anonymous users and professionals alike.[36] Over the years, it has become a socially networked search engine, generating novel architectural constructs characterized by simultaneously individualized and hyperlinked rooms, detached from their original contexts and endlessly re-sampled without temporal or spatial boundaries. Twitch, though seemingly niche, has become a central hub for experimental lengthy and nonstop broadcast, with streamers often using their homes (or studio setups resembling teenage bedrooms) as backdrops, offering viewers a seemingly intimate look at new forms of domesticity. The platform blends architecture, live streaming, gamification, community interaction, and content creation, turning the medium into a territory where the screening of contemporary interiors unfolds. The block culminates with a visual chapter on TikTok, providing a grid of images and simple statistics, allowing readers to form their own hypotheses using this raw material. All of these chapters follow the same methodological framework: they analyze the ten most-followed accounts over the course of one year—2022 for Instagram, Twitch, and TikTok, and 2024 for Pinterest—providing a discrete stratum within a larger layering of data that nonetheless enables trends and patterns to be scrutinized.

The chapters in the second block examine multiple platforms, focusing on the ethical and political implications of topics at the intersection of architecture and social media, such as humanitarian crises, mediatized animals, user-generated video games, and porn sites. These topics, which might seem disconnected at first glance, turn out to share common threads when studied from the perspective of how bodies—or avatars—are inserted and edited within physical and digital spaces, addressing questions of agency, domination, intimacy, and the politics of representation. These chapters explore both human and nonhuman dimensions of space, namely human displacement, violence, and sheltering in the context of humanitarian crises, as well as animal lives that are mediatized and monetized within domestic settings. Additionally, the video game application Roblox is analyzed as a form of social network in which users are both players and designers of games that are created and edited on the platform. The block ends with a chapter on the interior spaces of porn sites, mainly Pornhub, that attract high levels of engagement in terms of visualizations, comments, and feedback. Methodologically speaking, the research is more diverse than in the first block. Humanitarian crises were analyzed per geographic region, with more than 200 accounts researched globally, comparing institutional narratives (NGOs, governments) with those of anonymous users, often victims. Animals that become online celebrities (pet influencers) were studied sequentially, tracing the evolution of the phenomenon through the dominant platforms of each era, from Facebook and YouTube in the 2000s to Instagram and TikTok in the 2020s. For Roblox, the ten most-played video games globally in 2024 were analyzed, comparing the most represented spaces with those that remain marginalized, and examining whether virtual architecture perpetuates the invisibility of traditionally overlooked spatial questions such as ancillary areas, basements, and accessibility routes. Finally, Pornhub, the world's most-visited adult website, was analyzed as a form of social media through the most-watched user-generated videos up to 2025, whose interiors were categorized as eroticized architectural types.

Data analytics were developed as short case studies with students across various modules: BA students from the module *Theory of*

Mediated Spaces, MA students from the module *Plural Bodies within Interiors*, and both BA and MA students from the *Semaine de Tous les Possibles* workshop at HEAD – Genève. Further methodological details are provided in the context of each chapter, and the students responsible for each analysis are credited accordingly. Some chapters are co-authored with fellow researchers (Paule Perron, Michela Bassanelli, Damien Greder, Vytautas Jankauskas) with whom I had the pleasure to collaborate, while others are authored independently. Some of them were previously published in journals like *KoozArch*, *e-flux Architecture*, *Burning Farm*, and *PLOT*, while others appear in this book for the first time. They have also been presented in lectures at international conferences, including the symposium *Architectures Archives of the Future*, organized in 2023 in Rotterdam and Delft; *Post Like*, the first edition of the Youth Architecture Biennial of Catalonia, held in 2023 in Barcelona; the 2024 edition of MMMAD—Madrid Urban Digital Art Festival; the 2024 edition of the NPATAK International Architecture Festival in Yerevan; and the 2025 Research Day at the Flanders Architecture Institute in Antwerp. They all serve as contributions to an ongoing conversation with peers, editors, and students on how social media is transforming contemporary architecture. Of course, the absences are larger than the presences. Most applications are American, most global influencers broadcast in English—with some exceptions in Spanish—and the Chinese internet is not addressed. Similarly, the impact of generative AI on interiors (largely absent from the analyzed accounts in the sampled years) is underrepresented, Web3 social media platforms— arguably the next step in this evolutionary process—are not included, and so on. This is not a treatise, but a book of fragments. In its very fragmentation, it hopes to open up new paths of research into the pictures, streams, likes, pins, comments, emojis, samples, filters, glitches, and on-and-offs of contemporary architecture.

Notes

1 The literature on the early history of the internet is abundant. See, for example: Christos J. P. Moschovitis, Hilary Poole, Tami Schuyler, and Theresa M. Senft, *History of the Internet: A Chronology, 1843 to the Present* (Santa Barbara: ABC-CLIO, 1999); Tim Berners-Lee, *Weaving the Web: The Original Design and Ultimate Destiny of the World Wide Web* (New York: Harper Business, 2000); Johny Ryan, *A History of the Internet and the Digital Future* (London: Reaktion Books, 2010); Leonard Kleinrock, "An Early History of the Internet [History of Communications]," *IEEE Communications Magazine* , no. 48(8) (August 2010), 26–36.

2 The literature on the early history of social media is abundant. See, for example: danah boyd and Nicole B. Ellison, "Social Network Sites: Definition, History, and Scholarship," *Journal of Computer-Mediated Communication*, no. 13(1) (October 2007), 210–230; Judy Malloy (ed.), *Social Media Archeology and Poetics* (Cambridge: MIT Press, 2016). For a broader historiography of the digital era, including social media, see: Alessandro Baricco, *The Game: A Digital Turning*, trans. Clarissa Botsford (San Francisco: McSweeney, 2020). First published in Italian as *The game. Storie del mondo digitale per ragazzi avventurosi* (Milan: Feltrinelli, 2018).

3 See, for example: Peter Ebner, Eva Herrmann, et al., *typology+: Innovative Residential Architecture* (Basel, Birkhäuser, 2009); Emanuel Christ, Christoph Gantenbein (eds.) *Typology, Hong Kong, Rome, New York, Buenos Aires. Review No. II* (Zurich: Park Books, 2012); Emanuel Christ, Christoph Gantenbein (eds.) *Typology, Paris, Delhi, São Paulo, Athens. Review No. III* (Zurich: Park Books, 2015); Andreas Lechner, *Thinking Design: Blueprint for an Architecture of Typology* (Zurich: Park Books, 2022); Rafael Luna and Dongwoo Yim, *A Language of Contemporary Architecture. An Index of Topology and Typology* (London: Routledge, 2023); Liliane Wong, *Adaptive Reuse in Architecture: A Typological Index* (Basel: Birkhäuser, 2023).

4 Neil E. Klepeis, William C. Nelson, Wayne R. Ott, et al., "The National Human Activity Pattern Survey (NHAPS): a resource for assessing exposure to environmental pollutants," *Journal of Exposure Science & Environmental Epidemiology*, no. 11 (2001), 231–252, https://doi.org/10.1038/sj.jea.7500165

5 Maarten Prak, "Painters, Guilds and the Art Market during the Dutch Golden Age," in Epstein, Stephen R. and Prak, Maarten (eds.), *Guilds, Innovation, and the European Economy, 1400–1800* (Cambridge University Press, 2008), 147.

6 Jean-François Staszak, Rémy Knafou. "Les figures du seuil dans la peinture hollandaise du XVIIe siècle," in B. Collignon and J.-F. Staszak (eds.), *Espaces domestiques. Construire, habiter, représenter* (Paris: Bréal, 2004), 46–64.

7 For a comparative study of the pictorial iterations of travelers visiting architecture (including the Grand Tour), see: Luis M. Mansilla, *Apuntes de viaje al interior del tiempo* (Barcelona: Fundación Caja de Arquitectos, 2001); Enric Miralles, *Cosas vistas a izquierda y derecha (sin gafas)* (PhD Thesis, 1987. Archive COAC Library, Barcelona).

8 See: Beatriz Colomina, *Privacy and Publicity: Modern Architecture as Mass Media* (Cambridge: The MIT Press, 1994); Penny Sparke, *The Modern Interior* (London: Reaktion Books, 2008).

9 Lynn Spigel, "The Suburban Home Companion: Television and the Neighborhood Ideal in Postwar America," in Beatriz Colomina (ed.), *Sexuality & Space* (Princeton: Princeton Architectural Press, 1992), 185–217.

10 James Bridle, *The Distractor,* installation at Kunsthaus Zurich, 2023 (accessed February 24, 2025), https://jamesbridle.com/works/the-distractor

11 Herbert A. Simon, "Designing Organizations for an Information-rich World," in Martin Greenberger (ed.), *Computers, Communications, and the Public Interest* (Baltimore: The Johns Hopkins Press, 1971), 37–52.

12 Andrés Jaque, "Transmedia Urbanism: Berlusconi and the Birth of Targeted Difference," *Perspecta*, no. 50 (September 2017), 243–251.

13 Mathieu Triclot, "Le salon, la télé, la princesse et maman," in *Philosophie des jeux vidéo* (Paris: La Découverte, 2011), 189–221.

14 Both artworks can be interpreted in terms of the multiplication of viewpoints and the reversal of perception.

—Writing about *Las Meninas*, philosopher Michel Foucault observed the canvas's capacity to embed multiple, overlapping spaces: "At the extreme right, the picture is lit by a window represented in very sharp perspective; so sharp that we can see scarcely more than the embrasure; so that the flood of light streaming through it bathes at the same time, and with equal generosity, two neighboring spaces, overlapping but irreducible: the surface of the painting, together with the volume it represents (which is to say, the painter's studio, or the salon in which his easel is now set up), and, in front of that surface, the real volume occupied by the spectator (or again, the unreal site of the model)." Michel Foucault, *The Order of Things: An Archaeology of the Human Sciences*, trans. Alan Sheridan (New York: Vintage Books, 1994), 5. First published in French as *Les Mots et les choses* (Paris: Gallimard, 1966).

—Writing about the mirror and questioning its presence in *Picture for Women,* writer and curator David Campany argued as follows: "Looking closely at *Picture for Women* in the retrospective at Tate Modern, I noticed a few 'reversals'. For example, the manufacturer's nameplate on the front of the camera (for the nerd, it is a Linhof Technika 4 × 5 monorail) reads backwards, as if in a mirror. However, this could be achieved by reversing a transparency or negative left-to-right. The idea is not as perverse as it seems. Consider how frequently painters traced off reversed camera obscura images, or how often slides are shown reversed in art history lectures and publications, or that the photographic daguerreotype produced reversed portraits of sitters close to their own mirror-images. Flipping a photographic image can be harnessed as a modernist gesture in its own medium-specific way. It can keep an image intact while fundamentally changing its relation to reality and foregrounding the picture plane. Just like a mirror, the flip is natural and unnatural, true and distorting, ordinary yet extraordinary (thus it tends a little toward the uncanny, showing us the 'familiar and agreeable' but in some way 'concealed and kept out of site' to paraphrase Sigmund Freud)." David Campany, "'A Theoretical Diagram in an Empty Classroom': Jeff Wall's *Picture for Women*," *Oxford Art Journal*, no. 30(1) (Jeff Wall Special Issue, 2007), 7–25.

15 Nicholas Korody, *Los usos de la decoración* (Madrid: RUA Ediciones, 2020).

16 Nicholas Korody, "Intimate Distance: The Technosexual Architecture of Camming," *e-flux architecture*, October 2019 (accessed November 13, 2024), https://www.e-flux.com/architecture/positions/280819/intimate-distance-the-technosexual-architecture-of-camming/

17 Darcy DiNucci, "Fragmented Future," *Print*, no. 53(4) (1999), 32, 221–222.

18 The 2004 and 2005 events were named the Web 2.0 Conference, later rebranded as the Web 2.0 Summit starting with the 2006 edition.

19 Tim O'Reilly, "What Is Web 2.0: Design Patterns and Business Models for the Next Generation of Software," Communications & Strategies, no. 1, (First Quarter 2007), 17, https://ssrn.com/abstract=1008839

20 Ibid.

21 Nick Srnicek, *Platform Capitalism* (Hoboken: Wiley, 2016).

22 Aatif Sulleyman, "Netflix's biggest competition is sleep, says CEO Reed Hastings," *The Independent,* April 19, 2017 (accessed February 24, 2025), https://www.independent.co.uk/tech/netflix-downloads-sleep-biggest-competition-video-streaming-ceo-reed-hastings-amazon-prime-sky-go-now-tv-a7690561.html

23 Jonathan Crary, *24/7: Late Capitalism and the Ends of Sleep* (London; New York: Verso Books, 2013).

24 Tiziana Terranova, *After the Internet. Digital Networks between Capital and the Common* (South Pasadena: Semiotext(e), 2022), 8–9.

25 Ibid., 46–47.

26 Benjamin H. Bratton, *The Stack: On Software and Sovereignty* (Cambridge: The MIT Press, 2015).

27 Richard Coyne, *The Tuning of Place: Sociable Spaces and Pervasive Digital Media* (Cambridge: The MIT Press, 2010).

28 See: Davide T. Ferrando, "Occupy Facebook! New Spaces for Architecture Criticism," in &beyond collective (ed.), *Archifutures Volume 2: The Studio* (Barcelona: dpr-barcelona, 2016), 146–159; Davide T. Ferrando. "The Streaming Room of Our Own," in Nina Bassoli (ed.), *Home Sweet Home* (Milan: Electa, 2023), 180–189.

29 See: Davide T. Ferrando. *City of Legends: Stanze, webcam e social network* (Brescia: Krisis Publishing, 2024); Davide T. Ferrando. "Architecture Criticism in the Age of Social Networks," in *Critic|all I International Conference on Architectural Design & Criticism*, Madrid, 12–14 June 2014, Digital Proceedings (Madrid: critic|all press, 2014), 422–431; Davide T. Ferrando, "Our House (in the Middle of the Web)," *Volume*, no. 56 (December 2019), 60–63.

30 Lev Manovich, *Instagram and Contemporary Image* (self-pub., 2017) (accessed November 13, 2024), https://manovich.net/index.php/projects/instagram-and-contemporary-image

31 *Architecture Archives of the Future,* international conference at the Jaap Bakema Study Centre, Delft-Rotterdam, November 22–23, 2023. *Social Media,* Proceedings (TU Delft, Nieuwe Instituut, 2023), 111–142.

32 *Madskills: Self-Documenting Construction on Social Media*, exhibition at the Canadian Center for Architecture, Montreal, June–October 2024.

33 *Private Lives: From the Bedroom to Social Media*, exhibition at the Musée des Arts Décoratifs, Paris, October 2024–March 2025.

34 Monthly active users (in millions), as of April 2024: Facebook (3,065), YouTube (2,504), Instagram (2000), in *Statista*, "Most popular social networks worldwide as of April 2024, by number of monthly active users (in millions)" (accessed November 24, 2024), https://www.statista.com/statistics/272014/global-social-networks-ranked-by-number-of-users/

35 See, for instance: Cambridge University Press, s.v. "Instagrammable," *Cambridge Dictionary* (accessed November 24, 2024), https://dictionary.cambridge.org/dictionary/english/instagrammable; Larousse, s.v. "Instagrammable," *Larousse Dictionnaires* (accessed November 24, 2024), https://www.larousse.fr/dictionnaires/francais/instagrammable/191125

36 "Gen Z-ers are making aspirational boards about houses they want to live in, places they want to visit, and even people they want to date." Sara Pollack, quoted in Adam Hoover, "Pinterest Is Having a Moment. Millennials may have popularized Pinterest, but Gen Z is pushing the platform to new heights," *Wired*, December 14, 2023 (accessed November 24, 2024), https://www.wired.com/story/pinterest-gen-z-future/

1
INSTAGRAM, TYPOLOGY, AND ARCHITECTURE

Javier Fernández Contreras and Paule Perron

To raise the question of typology in architecture is to raise a question of the nature of the architectural work itself. To answer it means, for each generation, a redefinition of the essence of architecture and an explanation of all its attendant problems. This in turn requires the establishment of a theory, whose first question must be, what kind of object is a work of architecture? This question ultimately has to return to the concept of type.[1]

RAFAEL MONEO, "On Typology," 1978

Few concepts reflect more accurately the ethos of architectural discourse throughout history than that of "type." From Quatremère de Quincy's and Jean Nicolas Louis Durand's emphasis on tectonic and geometric elements in the 19th century to Le Corbusier's functionalist approach and the cultural and historicist perspectives of Giulio C.

Figure 1.1 (following pages) Analysis of posts without explicit commercial purpose published by the eleven most-followed Instagram accounts worldwide in 2022. Age and follower count of each celebrity as of February 2023

@cristiano
Cristiano Renaldo
Soccer player
Portuguese
38 years old

@leomessi
Lionel Messi
Soccer player
Argentinian
35 years old

@kyliejenner
Kylie Jenner
Media personality, socialite,
and businesswoman
American
25 years old

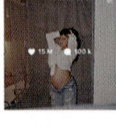

@selenagomez
Selena Gomez
Singer, actress, and producer
American
30 years old

@therock
Dwayne Douglas Johnson
Actor and former wrestler
American
50 years old

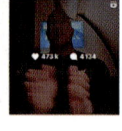

@arianagrande
Ariana Grande
Singer
American
29 years old

@kimkardashian
Kim Kardashian
Media personality, socialite,
and businesswoman
American
42 years old

@beyonce
Beyonce
Singer, songwriter,
and dancer
American
41 years old

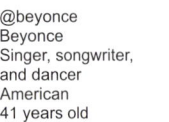

@khloekardashian
Khloe Kardashian
Media personality, socialite,
and businesswoman
American
38 years old

@justinbieber
Justin Bieber
Singer
Canadian
28 years old

@kendalljenner
Kendall Jenner
Model, media personality,
and socialite
27 years old

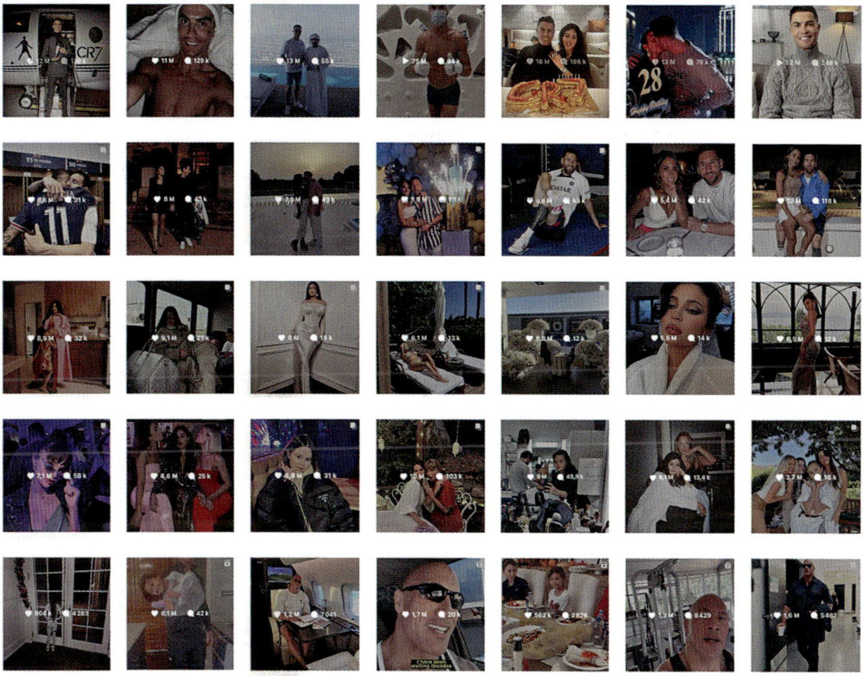

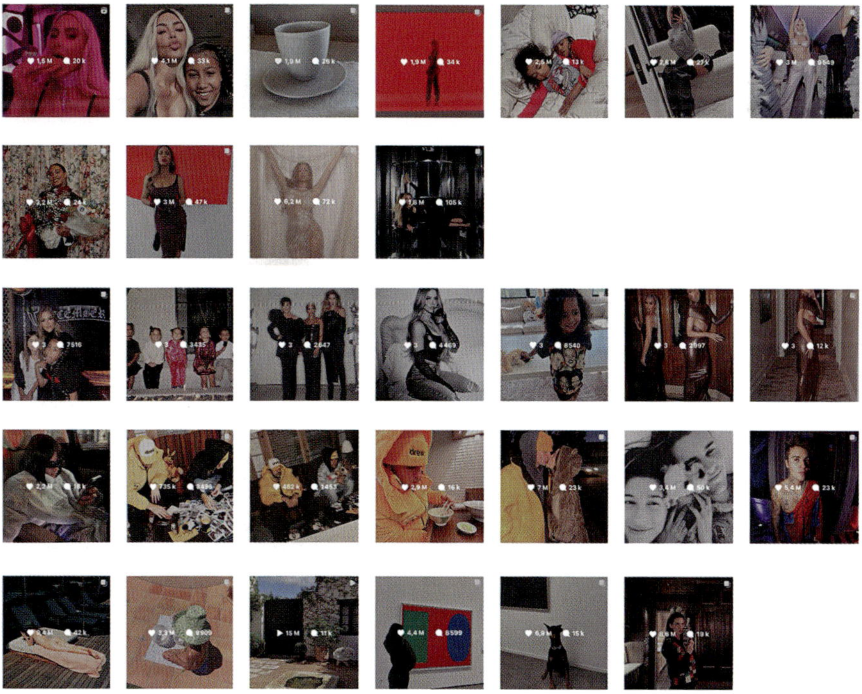

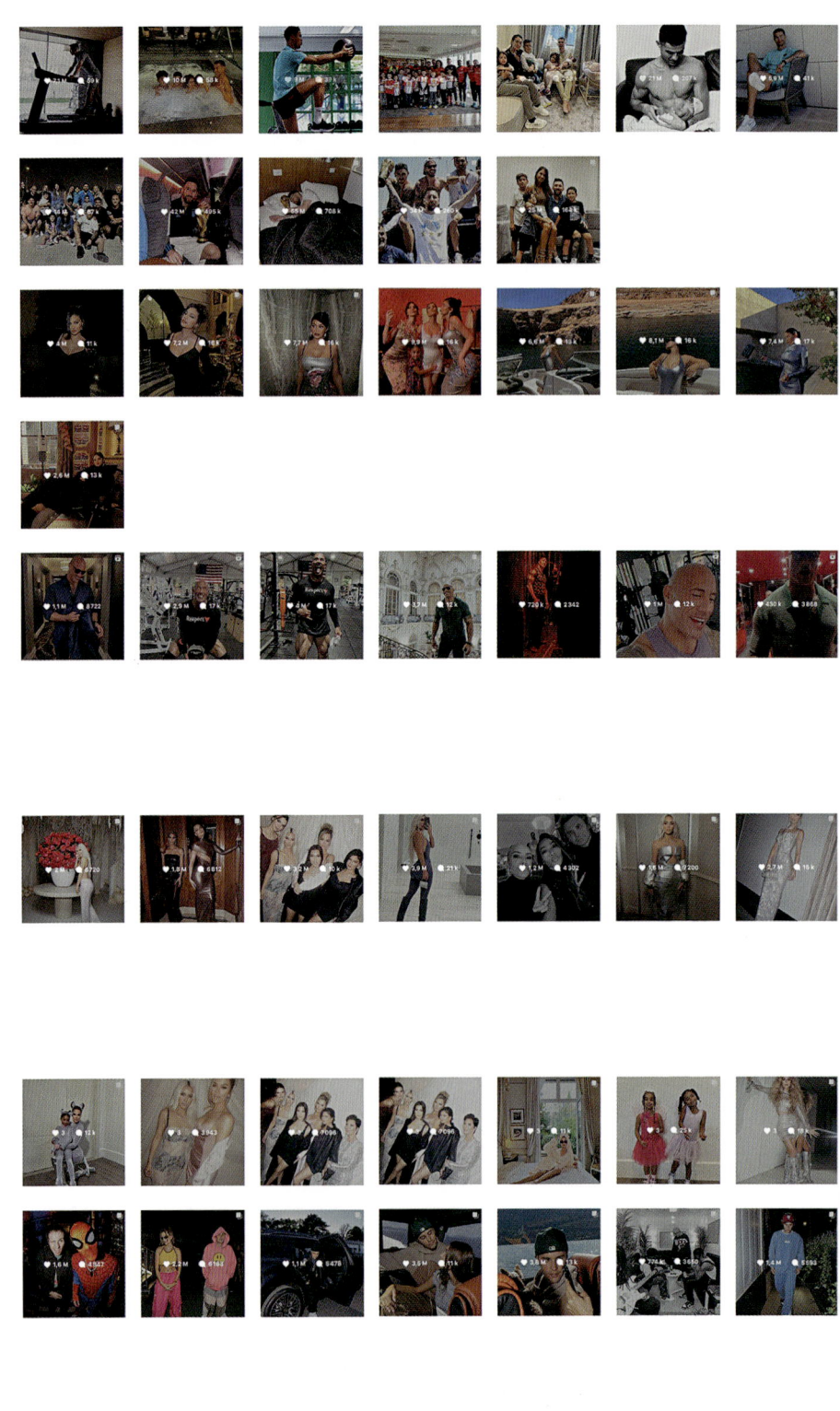

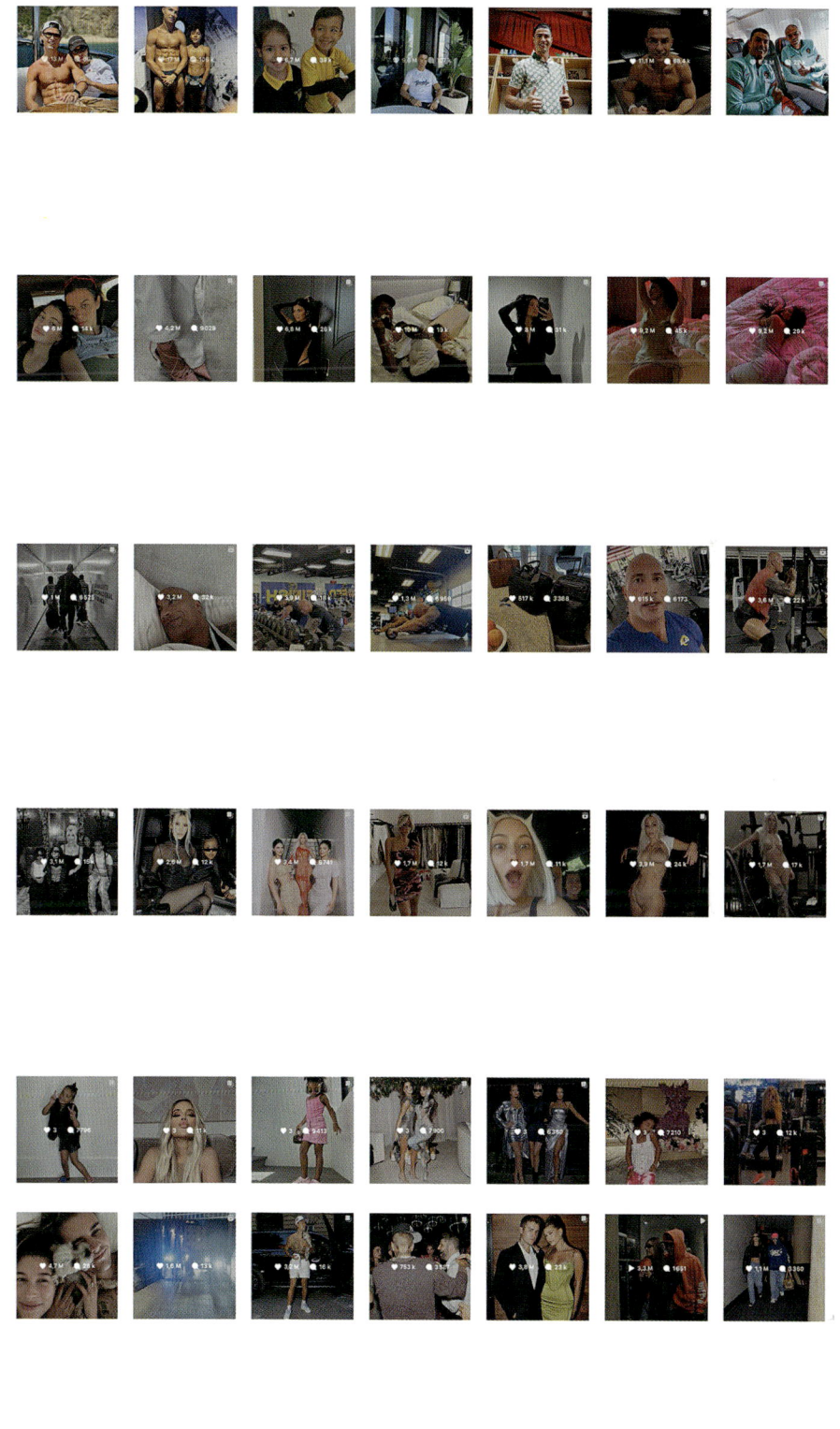

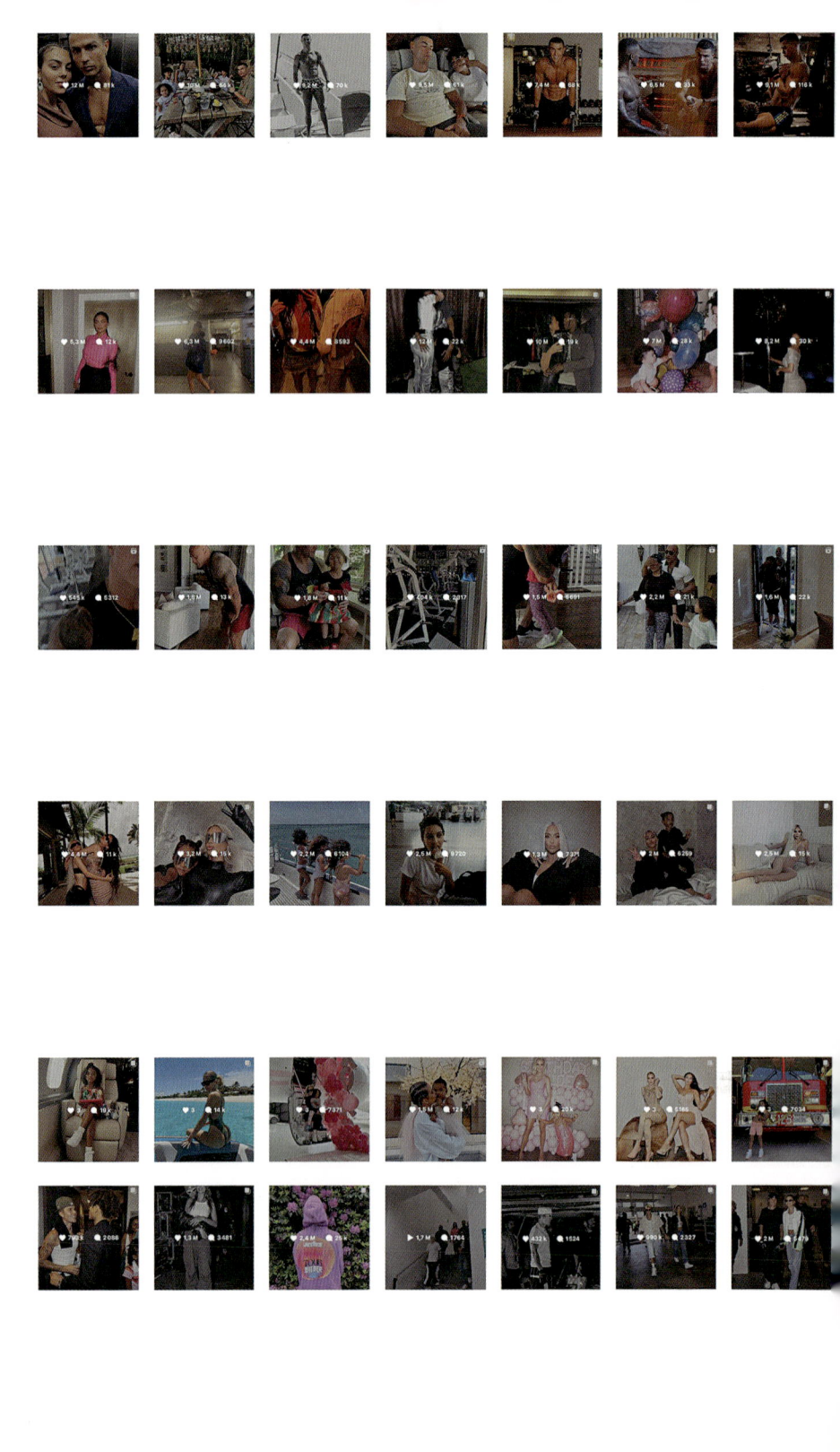

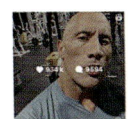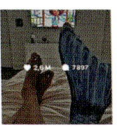

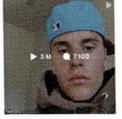

   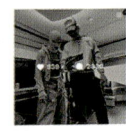  

Argan, Aldo Rossi, and Alan Colquhoun in the 20th century, the understanding of type and typology in architecture has undergone significant changes in the last two centuries. Additionally, the emergence of social media platforms in the 21st century has created new spaces of an ephemeral, performative, and commercial nature, further bolstered by the user's identity and ability to perform within the platform's algorithmic structures. This chapter examines the new architectural types mediated by social networks, with a special emphasis on Instagram as one of the dominant applications shaping contemporary architectural episteme through the production, editing, and massive circulation of images and videos. As of 2024, Instagram is one of the most popular platforms in the world, ranking third with 2 billion monthly active users, behind only Facebook and YouTube.[2]

Analyzing the top eleven Instagram accounts worldwide in 2022, the research questions the role that social media play in the contemporary redefinition of our domestic realm and its blurred boundaries—namely, how their representation directly impacts the material environment. Four of the most-followed accounts belong to members of the Kardashian-Jenner family, who have become famous by staging their daily lives since 2007 on the American television show *Keeping Up with the Kardashians*. Most of their posts on Instagram take place within their homes, presenting scenarios of domesticity and mediated interiors. In addition to Kim and Khloé Kardashian and Kylie Jenner, the usual scope of the top ten is expanded to eleven to include Kendall Jenner, an essential member of the family for understanding their home-staging strategy, and indeed the only one in the ranking who aims to be perceived as an interior designer. The other accounts belong to famous soccer players, singers, and actors, such as Cristiano Ronaldo, Leo Messi, Beyoncé, Selena Gomez, Ariana Grande, Justin Bieber, and The Rock.[3]

Operating within a framework of production/consumption, Instagram establishes hierarchies based on the success of content, and therefore defines both the most valued body types and their *topos*, presented for public consumption. These results reflect an immaterial market of online social networks permeating homes worldwide. The most-followed accounts predominantly feature heterosexual American celebrities, reinforcing norms and stereotypes that are framed and circulated within interior architecture. From an iconographic perspective, we can define specific spatial figures that can be classified into architectural types—

categories of sale of this immaterial market. The sofa, the bedroom, the bathroom, the dressing room, the gym, the elevator, private transportation (car, plane, or limousine), the backstage of an event, and the VIP area of a nightclub are all types of spaces—with their own architectural language— that we will find in the majority of the most-followed accounts of 2022.

Mediated Domesticity: The Staged Everyday

The analysis examines posts published in 2022 by the top eleven Instagram accounts worldwide, excluding those with an explicit commercial purpose. It focuses on the representation of the "staged everyday" or the supposed "behind-the-scenes" of their professional lives portrayed in interior spaces.[4] Instagram's media features suggest that all information communicated on the platform is taken on the go from the celebrity's own phone, and shared personally by the account owner. The entire process of photo production and editing is integrated into the app, allowing work on a single device: the smartphone.[5] Users are sold the idea of democratic access to the initiation, production, and appreciation of these media cultures without any distinction. This has radically transformed social and urban experiences of photography and audiovisual production, eliminating the need for photo studios, printing rooms, gallery displays, magazines, and books as necessary spaces or devices for the existence of these activities. However, this supposedly inclusive immateriality has made online networks a powerful capitalist center over the years—one that has developed its own processes of social distinction. Instagram generates different hierarchies based on the most successful content (such as the number of likes and follower count), the most valued body types (which remain predominantly heterosexual, American, white, and hypersexualized), and its material environment as exposed to public consumption.[6] All of these are products of this immaterial market, infiltrated into households worldwide.

The change in media culture generated by social networks has produced its own spatial and aesthetic references and its own background scenographic trends for the bodies of the accounts analyzed here, in which domestic spaces play a fundamental role. Domestic spaces are not only where social media celebrities live their private lives but the core of

Figure 1.2 The private gym: Posts published in 2022 by the most-followed Instagram accounts worldwide. From top to bottom: Cristiano Ronaldo, Leo Messi, The Rock, Ariana Grande, Kim Kardashian, Khloé Kardashian

their public existence. In a post, Kendall Jenner appears on the cover of *AD* in her home, in front of a work of art by James Turrell. Her sister, Kim Kardashian, is well known for the beige, light-pink, and muted-tone color palette of her interiors, with no distinction between her home, her office, or the interior of her car or private plane. Cristiano Ronaldo, whose Instagram account has the highest number of followers, shares his routine outside of work, whether in the living room of his house with his wife and children, or inside his gym. The homes of these celebrities—extensively documented architectural products in their own right—are equipped with weight rooms, gyms, dressing rooms, stages, and photo studios. On the one hand, once the delimited area of the house is defined, it allows both public and productive activities to enter, transforming it into a production center equipped with all the necessary technical devices to create a domestic interior where a routine is performed, represented, and recorded. On the other hand, the documentation of the everyday life of these famous people has exported these domestic activities outside the home. Their cars, private planes, or friends' houses are external domestic units that act as performative and expanded wrappers of their bodies, just like their homes.

The Body: The First Architectural Type of Social Media

Our material environment is directly affected by the evolution of technologies, as well as by the rhythms and processes used to represent it. In the book *Pornotopia*,[7] Paul Preciado showcased the radical change that *Playboy* magazine brought about in domestic spaces and interiors in the mid-20th century through simple yet infinitely reproducible images of female bodies in the Playboy Mansion. Through the mediation of sexualized bodies staged in architectural spaces, Hugh Hefner managed to physically impact American homes, profoundly transforming them by generating a new masculine ideal based on interior spaces. In the 21st century, Instagram has further expanded this access to staged intimacy and bodily representations, accelerating the pace of their distribution in the media. The affects produced are no longer the result of a unidirectional interaction between a published magazine and the domestic space of isolated readers. Physical and emotional affects now arise through interactions—deceptively equivalent—between celebrities' smartphones staging their bodies in their everyday spatial context, and the devices of multiple viewers who can directly react to this content.

The eleven accounts analyzed here present mediated bodies as the main object of their messages. Their representations are amplified, completed, modeled, and staged through a series of material devices that contribute to spreading an expanded definition of their executed bodily identity. Cosmetics, surgical implants, clothing, body prosthetics, gym machines, furniture, and interior spaces are the complements of this theatrical everyday life, and the eleven most-followed individuals each possess at least one commercial brand in these fields. They

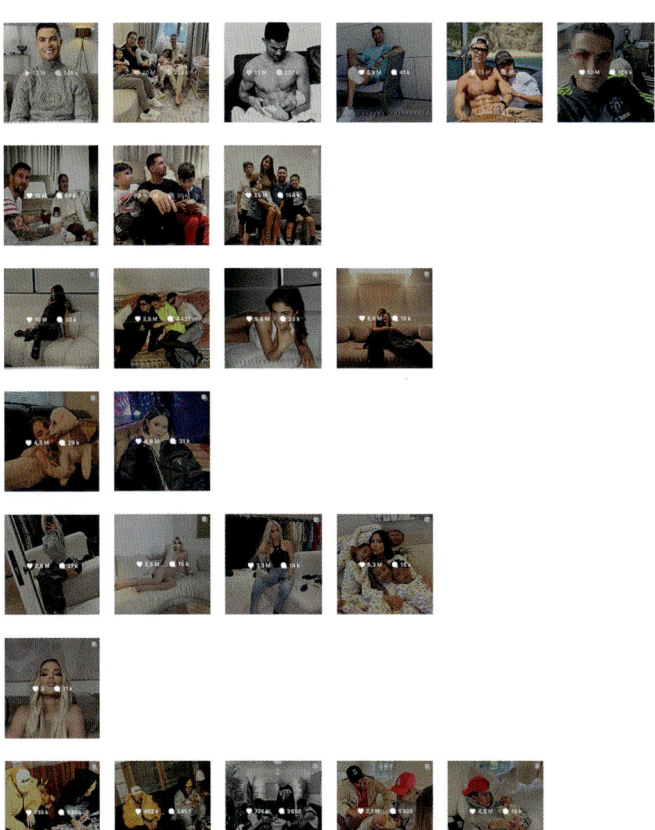

Figure 1.3 The sofa: Posts published in 2022 by the most-followed Instagram accounts worldwide. From top to bottom: Cristiano Ronaldo, Leo Messi, Kylie Jenner, Selena Gomez, Kim Kardashian, Khloé Kardashian, Justin Bieber

understand that, in order to construct their own public persona, it is apparently necessary to develop the spatial conditions of this narrated identity. To do this, they design their own bodies as the primary material object, the primordial space from which this identity is emitted. Utilizing Michel Foucault's notion of utopian corporality, the material equipment they use "makes of this body a fragment of imaginary space,"[8] a place where utopias crystallize, materialized in their flesh, with their own codes, hierarchies, and idealized models. Through their representation on social networks, bodies like those of the celebrities behind the top eleven Instagram accounts become utopian, infinite spaces, distanced from their aged, rough, and imperfect liveliness, which can be analyzed as a unique architectural type of social media: an immaterial space that supports the construction of the public visual identity of its owners.

Utopian Intimacy, Space, and Gender

In this context, one could speak of an expanded domesticity, where celebrities increasingly use domestic-like spaces on social media platforms to showcase their supposedly private lives through the staging of their bodies. The expression of this intimacy is depicted in a series of isolated spaces, a territory of domestic islands. Extracted from the archetypes of Western bourgeois homes of the 20th century, the living room, the sofa, or the bedroom are devices that display a normative and ideal conception of the house, a lasting utopia of late modernity.[9] In staged scenes of comfort and relaxation, celebrities like Kylie Jenner and the Kardashian sisters, for example, use their sofas to display their designer homes, luxurious lifestyles, and closeness to their children. Similarly, both Cristiano Ronaldo and Leo Messi use their sofas to showcase their heteronormative family lives and their connections with their wives and children.

To quote Gillian Rose, family photographs become "objects participating in an elaborate, multifaceted practice and through that participation, producing a specific and sometimes intense set of meanings, feelings and positions";[10] they corroborate the normative social definition of family and are composed or staged based on specific spatial characteristics. The sofa is the material element that represents and stages the living room of the traditional heterosexual and bourgeois Western home. It is portrayed as a place of gathering and performative family love. If Rose has noted that family photographs were traditionally exhibited by women, Instagram now points to another spatial gender differentiation. While sofas in photographs of women from the top eleven accounts function as public stages for the bonds of love the subjects maintain with their children, these women are almost never accompanied by a man. They construct their image as strong, self-sufficient, heterosexual, wealthy, cisgender women, independent of the

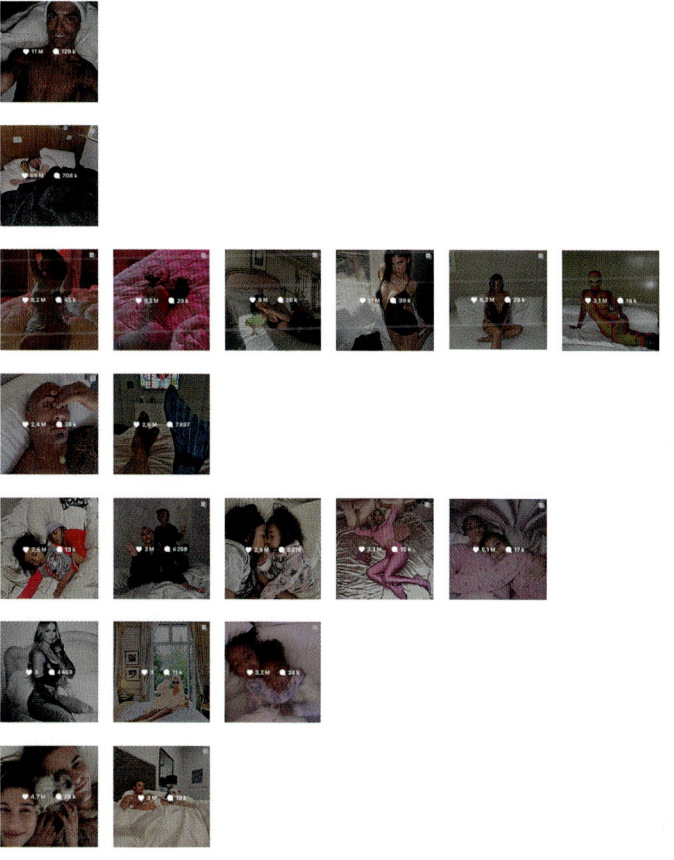

Figure 1.4 The bed: Posts published in 2022 by the most-followed Instagram accounts worldwide. From top to bottom: Cristiano Ronaldo, Leo Messi, Kylie Jenner, The Rock, Kim Kardashian, Khloé Kardashian, Justin Bieber

family nucleus. Without questioning the capitalist ideal and the masculine idea of success, they highlight their autonomy to achieve it by themselves. On the other hand, the men behind the most-followed accounts—Cristiano Ronaldo and Leo Messi—use their sofas to exhibit their nuclear family: a public guarantee of their heteronormative private life. Amid a feed full of images from the entirely male professional world in which they operate (which is also heavily homophobic),[11] the sofa is depicted as a performative space of their heteronormative masculinity.

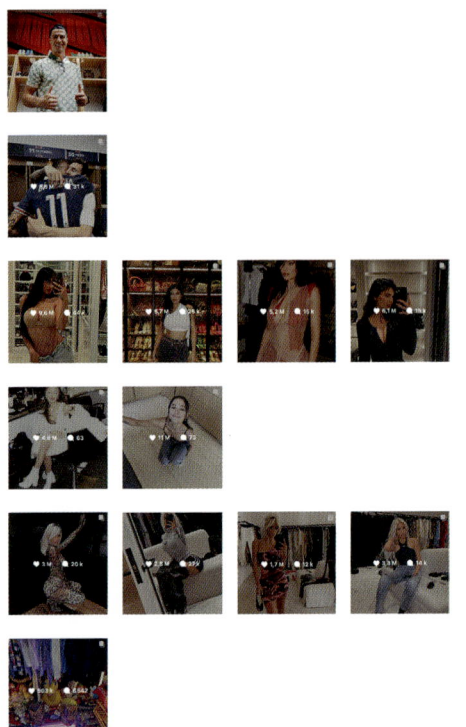

Figure 1.5 The dressing room: Posts published in 2022 by the most-followed Instagram accounts worldwide. From top to bottom: Cristiano Ronaldo, Leo Messi, Kylie Jenner, Ariana Grande, Kim Kardashian, Justin Bieber

The bed, on the other hand, appears in the most-visited Instagram accounts as a place of individual and intimate privacy. Its recurrent representation underscores the ambiguity between the bed as a place of rest, tranquility, sleep, and vulnerability, and one of hedonism, action, sexual activity, and power. It is the preferred place for the Kardashian–Jenner family to showcase their private life. It also appears in the accounts of Cristiano Ronaldo, Leo Messi, and Justin Bieber, providing a significant boost in the number of likes. Its representation, stemming from the smartphones of famous owners, allows viewers to peek into the most private sphere of celebrity life through their own Instagram accounts, creating an illusion of closeness and intimacy with these celebrities. In the

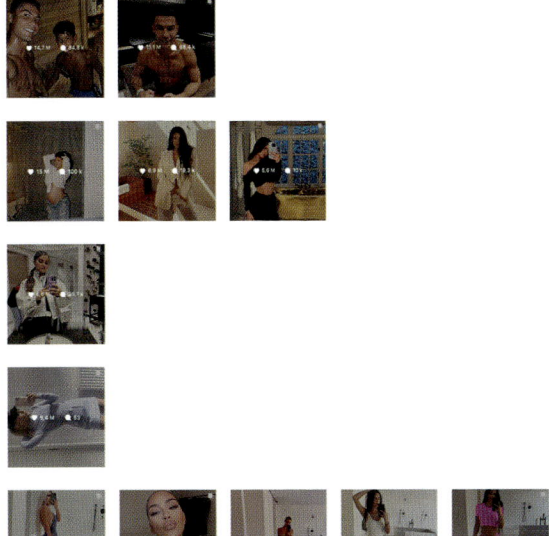

Figure 1.6 The bathroom: Posts published in 2022 by the most-followed Instagram accounts worldwide. From top to bottom: Cristiano Ronaldo, Kylie Jenner, Selena Gomez, Ariana Grande, Kim Kardashian

photographs, we can see that space and clothing directly dialogue with the body. The atmosphere of the bed (through the lighting, and the color and texture of the sheets, pillows, and mattress) both defines and is defined by the visual characteristics of the body. If its lighting is dim, the bed may be white to highlight it by contrast; if the clothing is of a strong pink tone, the sheets will be light beige to accentuate the body shape. Before social media, these domestic types were understood and conceptualized as places where private life was lived, behind the facade of buildings, where the most valued activities of normative Western domesticity took place within the room as an intimate space. Through social media, they have become places of individuality and privacy executed publicly. Although still separated from the physical public sphere by walls and doors, their delimited interiority is redefined thanks to their wide public dissemination. The bed and the sofa have become two architectural types of public domesticity, conceptualized as accessories for the hypersexualized heteronormative body.

Network Typology: Inhabiting the Global *Poché*

As we immerse ourselves in the architectural interiors of Instagram, it becomes clear that domestic spaces have undergone a fundamental transformation over the past decade—a shift that challenges the common conception of the hierarchical relationships between them. Spaces that in the 20th century were identified in architectural theory as servants are now venues for public performances. Places of domestic vulnerability once shielded from public view, places attentive to multiple and imperfect corporalities, are now publicly exhibited and represented. Building on the specificities of their architectural program, the accounts analyzed here publicly explore intimate vulnerability through the representation of these spaces. For example, Kylie Jenner often uses her bathroom to showcase her beauty routine and makeup products—which she also sells—dressed in her bathrobe, and looking in the mirror. Selena Gomez, on the other hand, posts videos in the bathroom, in which she discusses her mental health issues. Spaces that were once considered service spaces, unworthy of public attention, now become the theater of spatial performance on social media, staging bodily vulnerabilities.

Speculating on Jacques Lucan's concepts regarding the work of Venturi and Scott Brown and Colin Rowe,[12] the ideas of closed *poché* (residual enclosed spaces created when the exterior form does not match the interior form) and open/urban *poché* (functional interior spaces, often hatched when drawn in relation to their context, spanning multiple scales from technical servant rooms within a building to the urban fabric structured between private and public realms) could now be digitally extended to the spaces of online social networks to define a "global *poché*." Although it lies outside the scope of this chapter, it is worth recalling the famous bathroom selfie at the 2017 Met Gala, taken by Kylie Jenner, in the presence of Kim Kardashian and Kendall Jenner among a crowd of celebrities. Far from the frenzy of the most famous but invisible (or unphotographed) party of the year, the bathroom—once a place for the isolated transformation of the body in preparation for public appearance—becomes here, above all, a place of public visibility. As noted by *The Guardian*, "the photo is very much a family affair."[13] What most people experience daily and materially as servant spaces are instead displayed as served spaces for a select few. This careful inversion generates repetitive and non-contextual domestic islands floating within an unlimited and undefined networked territory. In this sense, the Kardashian–Jenners, as well as Ariana Grande, also use their dressing rooms to showcase both exclusive clothing and the transformation processes through which they become their public selves. They offer the public a glimpse of their seemingly unofficial appearance and private lives behind the doors of their non-situated private spheres.

In a progressive shift outside the home, circulation spaces have also come to dominate Instagram's interior spaces. The hotel hallway and elevator convey transition and movement, serving as a backdrop for quick exchanges with Instagram communities, between places and events in the busy, luxurious, and international public lives of the people behind the top eleven accounts. For example, Beyoncé repeatedly uses elevators in her Instagram posts to showcase her lifestyle. The Rock also regularly inserts himself in elevators, displaying his muscular body and fitness regimen. Selena Gomez and Ariana Grande use hotel hallways to showcase their behind-the-scenes moments, often exploring them as a backdrop for their elegant dresses before they enter events. In the city, the space of private transportation—a car, a plane, or a limousine—generates an inverted sense of empathy through luxury and exclusivity. Celebrities like Justin Bieber and The Rock often use their private transportation to show a moment of solitude and introspection. Similarly, in their posts, the Kardashians reflect on their life and career while traveling, offering privileged access to this private and seemingly spontaneous part of their existence. All the spaces behind the walls of the posted places, and behind the cameras that capture them, are the invisible and contemporary servant spaces of Instagram, in which the owners are producing voids to be publicly inhabited.

Social media culture has blurred the boundaries between the public and the private, the domestic and the professional, the everyday environment and staged advertising. It has generated its own interiorities, its own language, and its own architectural rules. "The bad news is that Playboy's pornotopia is dying. The good news is that we are all necrophiliacs,"[14] declared Paul Preciado in the conclusion of *Pornotopia*, emphasizing how recent radical changes in Western societies have transformed our media culture, turning us into horizontal workers staged in our own *topos*. Through repeated representations of these

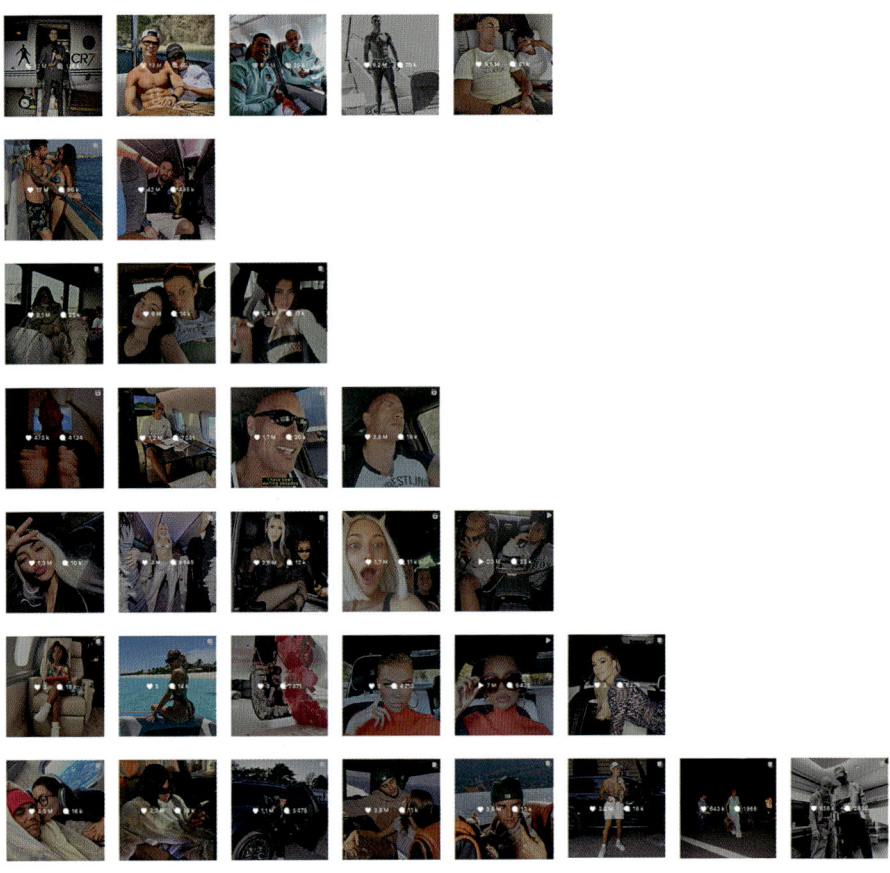

Figure 1.7 Private transport: Posts published in 2022 by the most-followed Instagram accounts worldwide. From top to bottom: Cristiano Ronaldo, Leo Messi, Kylie Jenner, The Rock, Kim Kardashian, Khloé Kardashian, Justin Bieber

spaces, the owners of the eleven Instagram accounts analyzed here are encoding contemporary domesticity as a networked territory, made up of fragments of interior typologies, infinitely reproducible and ready to be consumed like the performative spaces of their utopian bodies. This text emphasizes the transformations that this shift in media culture is producing and questions how an unlimited domestic territory is represented by and about the bodies of its inhabitants. To address these interiorities through a typological classification is to recognize the fact that they are producing space and architecture through online categories, and therefore spatial behaviors and norms. The ultimate goal is not only to understand these domestic spaces but also to conceptualize them—and, in doing so, to thwart, through architectural action, the power relations they perpetuate.

This chapter was previously published in: *Burning Farm*, no. 14 (November 2024) / *PLOT*, no. 72 (February 2024): 174–183.

Notes

1 Rafael Moneo, "On Typology," *Oppositions*, no. 13 (1978), 23–45.

2 *Statista*, "Most popular social networks worldwide as of January 2024, by number of monthly active users" (accessed January 7, 2024), https://www.statista.com/statistics/272014/global-social-networks-ranked-by-number-of-uɛorɛ/

3 The top eleven at the time in descending order were: @cristiano, @leomessi, @kyliejenner, @selenagomez, @therock, @arianagrande, @kimkardashian, @beyonce, @khloekardashian, @justinbieber, @kendalljenner.

4 In this study, "interior space" is understood as a place with the following qualities: its material boundaries are visible in the image (walls, ceilings, vegetation, etc.); the perspective of the photograph and its central subject (the body itself) are within these boundaries; and the interior is not freely accessible owing to physical, economic, or social constraints.

5 Lev Manovich, "Instagram and Contemporary Image, Part 1" (2015) (accessed January 7, 2024), https://manovich.net/index.php/projects/instagram-and-contemporary-image, 11.

6 The majority of the most-liked content posted in 2022 by the eleven accounts analyzed here shows heteronormative patterns. A notable exception is the presence of Caitlyn Marie Jenner, the transgender mother of Kendall and Kylie Jenner, in her daughters' posts. While qualitatively significant, her presence is quantitatively minimal in terms of the total number of posts from her daughters in 2022 and, above all, in terms of likes, pointing to a certain form of sociological behavior that prioritizes heteronormativity. Likewise, out of the 47 posts in total on Ariana Grande's account in 2022, the one that received the most likes featured a photo with her boyfriend, while the one that generated the fewest likes included the phrase "protect & defend trans youth fund."

7 See: Paul Preciado, *Pornotopia: An Essay on Playboy's Architecture and Biopolitics* (New York: Zone Books, 2019). First published in Spanish as *Pornotopía: Arquitectura y sexualidad en "Playboy" durante la Guerra Fría* (Barcelona: Anagrama, 2010).

8 Michel Foucault, *The Utopian Body* (*Le corps utopique*, radio lecture delivered on December 7, 1966, on France Culture), in Caroline A. Jones (ed.), *Sensorium: Embodied Experience, Technology, and Contemporary Art* (Cambridge, MA: MIT Press, 2006), 229–234.

9 Hartmut Rosa, *Alienation and Acceleration: Towards a Critical Theory of Late-Modern Temporality* (Copenhagen: NSU Press, 2020), 10. First published in 2010.

10 Gillian Rose, *Doing Family Photography: The Domestic, the Public and the Politics of Sentiment* (Farnham: Ashgate, 2010), 17.

11 Alexander Herbinet, "Homophobie: Pourquoi le sport a un problème à régler," *RMC Sport*, September 16, 2019 (accessed January 7, 2024), https://rmcsport.bfmtv.com/football/homophobie-pourquoi-le-sport-a-un-probleme-a-regler_AV-201909160376.html

12 Jacques Lucan, "Généalogie du poché—de l'espace au vide." *Matière*, no. 7 (2004), 41–54.

13 Jess Cartner-Morley, "Kylie Jenner's bathroom selfie and Diddy's stairway nap: power moves at the Met Gala 2017," *The Guardian*, May 2, 2017 (accessed January 7, 2024), https://www.theguardian.com/fashion/2017/may/02/kylie-diddy-power-moves-met-gala-2017

14 Paul Preciado, *Pornotopia: An Essay on Playboy's Architecture and Biopolitics*, 215.

2

SCREENS WITHIN SCREENS: THE INTERIORS OF TWITCH

Javier Fernández Contreras

I am broadcasting live video of my life 24/7 to the internet. I started Justin.tv because I thought it would be awesome for people to see what it was like to be Justin. I convinced three of my friends (Emmett, Michael, and Kyle) to join me out in San Francisco. Now, we're starting a company to make broadcasting live video on the web easy. Thanks for watching Justin.tv. Let me know what you like and don't like about the show; I hope to hear from you soon![1]

JUSTIN.TV. Lifecast, May 22, 2007, 12:09:01 a.m. (PST).

Justin Kan's bio

The relationship between architecture, online interaction, and mediated empathy defines the history of Twitch. Since its origins, the platform has explored the tension between livestreaming and the archiving of multimedia content, whether edited, shortened, or removed from public access. Originally Justin.tv, a live-broadcasting website founded in 2007 by Justin Kan, Emmett Shear, Michael Seiber, and Kyle Vogt, the social network soon focused on video game streaming and was rebranded as Twitch in 2011. It quickly became the go-to destination for gamers to livestream their gameplay and, by 2013, the platform had more than 45 million unique viewers.[2] In 2023, that number increased to

Figure 2.1 Justin.tv. Lifecast. May 22, 2007, 12:09:01 a.m. (PST). Courtesy of Justin Kan

140 million, with an average of 103,000 streamers live at any moment,[3] mostly broadcasting from within interior spaces.

Twitch streamers often use their homes (or studios with aesthetics reminiscent of teenage bedrooms) as backdrops, giving viewers an intimate glimpse into new forms of mediated domesticity. In this digital landscape, involvement with the external world is constructed through calculated interactions. Streamers curate their online personas and maintain a degree of privacy while simultaneously engaging with a global audience, broadcasting from within the confines of their rooms. Twitch belongs to the tradition of empathy within multimedia—the *mise en abyme* of TV programs where spectators see screens within screens and people inserted in them. These programs originated in the 20th century, widely circulating the architecture of domestic interiors to their audiences.

However, Twitch embodies a fundamental shift. As a platform for producing and distributing content—streamed from within a variety of fragmented domesticities—it serves as a case study for understanding contemporary interiors as places where the entanglements between live broadcasts, digital interactions, and archival content occur simultaneously. The platform has progressively diversified its offerings. Today, content varies from eSports to gaming, music to IRL (in real life), and live sports to a plethora of other popular cultural activities. Twitch simultaneously merges architecture, livestreams, gaming, community interaction, and content production through its distribution system, ultimately exploring the specificities of the medium as a territory where the politics of domestic spaces are played out.

This chapter explores the role Twitch plays in the construction of contemporary interiors as networked domains, contextualizing it within a broader history of image production and TV shows. It also discusses the multiplication of spatial representations, as seen with online influencers and their everyday lives. Methodologically, the chapter analyzes the ten most-followed accounts worldwide and the thirty most-watched videos per account from 2022. Together, these videos provide a one-year snapshot: an architectural cross-section within a larger whole. As the analysis illustrates, some Twitch streamers, such as xQc and Auronplay, delete all videos after the stream while others, like Ninja and Tfue, edit and archive all their material online. Some broadcast regularly for three or four hours at a time, whereas others go up to ten or fifteen hours. Outside the top ten, Emilycc has been streaming non-stop for more than 700 days as part of a *subathon*, a format in which the influencer goes live for a minimum duration, which is extended each time a new follower subscribes. These livestreams can therefore last for days, weeks, months, or even years, as the definitive triumph of a Warholian mediatized existence. Among the ten most-followed accounts there is only one woman, Pokimane, who also tested her persona as an avatar in 2020, following a common trend of virtualization during the quarantine. They all stream from interior spaces and, in most cases, appear disconnected from any circadian rhythm, regularly cut off from natural light. Welcome to the interiors of Twitch, a new architectural geography.

Mediated Empathy: The Archaeology of Twitch

Few viewing devices have played such an important role in the representation of interior spaces as the frame. For Johannes Vermeer, framing was a way of seeing through interior spaces, and, as David Hockney points out, in Vermeer's paintings "we see the most vivid use of optics,"[4] referring to the use of lenses to depict domesticity in a photographic way. During the late 19th and early 20th centuries, the arrival of photography and cinema institutionalized the relationship between visual material and rectangular border, formalized as a primitive screen, forever transforming the art of the image. The paintings of Vilhelm Hammershøi, the photographs of Roger Fenton, and the films of Yasujiro Ozu all employ frame-within-frame composition techniques, using architectural elements such as doorways and windows as thresholds within their images to show depth and perspective, as well as to create a sense of introspection and voyeurism.

These mediums present content that was composed, painted, photographed, filmed, and edited before its distribution. Parallel to these experiments, 20th-century TV culture produced one of the most consequential transformations in the way people experience interiors: the screen broadcast within a room, a radical format in which viewers watch people looking at, reacting to, and commenting on audiovisual content. One notable case is *Mystery Science Theater 3000* (1988–1999),[5] which featured characters providing humorous commentary on science fiction B-movies. The show created a screen within a screen. Filmed from the perspective of a moviegoer, it used the theater's interior as a framing device. Through this lens, the TV audience at home watched the main characters watching the movie from within a film theater decor. Similarly, *Beavis and Butt-Head* (1993–2011)[6] was an animated series that followed two teenage boys as they viewed and commented on music videos and TV shows. *Gogglebox* (2013–present), a British reality show that films families and friends reacting to

Figure 2.2 *Mystery Science Theater 3000*. Episode 12: "Fugitive Alien." February 5, 1989

various TV programs, is the most recent successful program of this type. These examples demonstrate the enduring appeal of watching others watch TV. Going further, however, they also illustrate the ways in which this type of programming can create a sense of shared experience and mediated empathy among viewers. Unlike painting and photography, this ephemeral empathy has historically held excitement in its transience, as a moment of shared exhilaration, laughter, or instant connection.

Twitch is the 21st-century heir to these practices, embodying the contemporary transition of mediated images to multimedia empathy, from an individual regard to a collective interaction. Its ubiquity has led to significant changes in its interface, starting from its predecessor, Justin.tv. Launched in 2007, Justin.tv was originally a single-channel platform featuring founder Justin Kan, who broadcast his life 24/7, popularizing the term "lifecasting"—the practice of continually livestreaming events in a person's life through digital media. Soon, the project developed into a network with thousands of channels, allowing streamers to freely broadcast to unlimited viewers.[7] In 2010, live interaction with online communities convinced the founders of Justin.tv that videogaming was the most sought-after content. In 2011, the platform transformed into Twitch, whose new interface featured a simple layout with a chat window and video player. Since then, the medium of streaming has continued to expand and grow in popularity, with Twitch incorporating additional sections such as a directory of channels, recommended streams, and featured content.

Owing to its gaming DNA, Twitch has always prioritized community interaction, introducing features such as subscriptions, chat emotes, and badges early on. The latest interface, introduced in 2015 to enhance user engagement, places the livestream at the center, the chat on the right, and the menu and live channels on the left. Twitch allows streamers to utilize various types of interfaces for livestreaming, including full-screen self-streaming, insertion into the live screen of the video game, use of avatars, or virtual co-streaming with different avatars while being physically remote. Followers have the option to choose between live and archived content, watching livestreams as they happen or accessing past broadcasts, highlights, or clips. As a developed form of hybrid media, Twitch merges the audiovisual stream with the online archive, bringing individual contemplation and collective interaction together via an endless accumulation of screens.

Ten Twitch Streamers in 2022: The Non-Circadian Interior

> Without an on-off button, there would be no hacking machine, no nearly unlimited programming on the console, no *Spacewar!* The symbiotic hacker-machine ecosystem was in place, thanks to three components: bright students eager to program, professors like Jack Dennis and Marvin Minsky, the co-director of the new artificial intelligence laboratory, who understood that it was better to let hackers practice instead of restricting access, and finally a computer, the PDP-1, around which a nocturnal lifestyle would be organized, in small groups, facing the console.[8]
>
> MATHIEU TRICLOT, *Philosophie des jeux vidéo*, 2011

The spatialization of the video game—that is, its ability to create spatial configurations both within the screen and in the physical environment—

has interested historians and theorists of the medium since its origins. In his book *Philosophie des jeux vidéo*, Mathieu Triclot studies the historical evolution and cognitive implications of video games, also analyzing the spatial ecosystems in which this occurs, from American university laboratories in the 1960s to the first home video game consoles and commercial arcades in the 1970s. Although he does not conduct a detailed study of the subject, Triclot does not overlook the nocturnality present in the DNA of gaming. He emphasizes the nocturnal hacker system that facilitated the creation of *Spacewar!*, one of the most important foundational video games in history, at the Massachusetts Institute of Technology in 1962. After detailing the limited temporal access to the PDP-1 computer, and especially to the TX-0, which meant that students had to organize themselves in nocturnal shifts to be able to use them and program quickly, he adds, "during a weekend, six hackers working continuously, without sleep, devouring their usual meal of Chinese noodles and Coca-Cola, completed the work in a true programming orgy."[9]

This nocturnal dimension, or more specifically, the ability of video games to disrupt the circadian rhythm, runs through the history of the medium to the present day. Twitch has integrated complete streaming and video production processes, allowing everything to be done on the computer. This integration continues to be influenced both by the origins of the platform and by gaming culture, which favors the landscape format for video games. The shift in design culture brought about by social media has led to its own spatial and aesthetic references, creating a screen-based temporality that influences both the rooms and the online identity of the ten Twitch streamers analyzed here.[10]

Ninja is a 32-year-old American streamer with 18.4 million followers on the platform. He mainly plays *Fortnite* and streams for an average of four hours, regularly avoiding full-screen presence. His studio setup creates a blue atmosphere with a digital aesthetic. Auronplay, a 33-year-old Spanish streamer with nearly 15 million followers, creates diverse content spanning multiple games and organizes events such as *Squid Craft Games*, a collaboration with other Spanish-speaking online influencers, as an adaptation in *Minecraft* of the popular Korean series *Squid Game*. His videos last around three hours, during which he

Figure 2.3 The ten most-followed streamers on Twitch in 2022, from left to right. Top row: Ninja, Auronplay, El Rubius, Ibai, xQc; bottom row: Tfue, TheGrefg, Shroud, JuanSGuarnizo, Pokimane.

engages in lively conversations with other players. El Rubius, a 33-year-old Spanish streamer, has 13.7 million subscribers. He livestreams for an average of six hours and creates content with popular games such as *Fortnite* and *Minecraft*, often accompanied by others. Ibai is a 27-year-old Spanish influencer with 12.7 million followers. He produces varied content, including eSports and soccer programs. His livestreams last an average of three hours, and he often hosts live match broadcasts. xQc is a 27-year-old Canadian streamer with 11.6 million followers. Widely recognized as a professional *Overwatch* player, he livestreams for long periods, from ten to seventeen hours, and engages in conversations during gameplay. Tfue, a 25-year-old American who primarily plays *Fortnite* and *Call of Duty*, has 11.3 million subscribers. His videos end with a farewell message, and he is usually in a relatively empty room. TheGrefg, a 25-year-old Spanish streamer with over 11 million subscribers, mainly plays *Fortnite* and *Minecraft*. Details about his videos are limited, as only one video from 2022 is available online. Shroud, a 28-year-old American streamer, has 10.4 million subscribers and shares diverse content. He regularly appears inserted over the gameplay and streams from a living room with light and beige tones. JuanSGuarnizo, a 26-year-old Colombian/Mexican streamer with 10.1 million followers, produces varied content, but no videos from 2022 are available on Twitch. Pokimane, the only woman among the top ten, is 28 years old and has 9.3 million subscribers. She began streaming in 2013 after reaching Platinum rank in *League of Legends*. She works from a bedroom turned into a studio, often accompanied by plush toys

and her cat in vlog-style segments, while her background is illuminated with violet and blue LED lights.

The way content is displayed varies from one streamer to another, generating a specific architecture within the screen. Most appear in a medium close-up within their spaces, especially at the beginning of their broadcasts. They then overlay this window onto the video game or event being streamed, simultaneously incorporating oral and chat conversations with the audience. The viewpoint differs from a classic cinematic shot, as Twitch largely inherits the tradition of placing webcams on top of PC monitors, resulting in distorted diagonal views where the streamers' faces appear exaggerated. Tfue reveals more space than others, with his body diminished, while Shroud frequently avoids showing himself in full screen. Pokimane positions herself on the symmetry axis and incorporates her room's background into the frame frontally. Also worthy of note is the cluttered decoration of the adolescent rooms of Auronplay, El Rubius, TheGrefg, and JuanSGuarnizo, who appear surrounded by objects and posters of animated series and digital culture.

Most streamers regularly appear in "non-circadian" interiors, that is, artificially illuminated spaces with color palettes that bring about physiological changes regarding the 24-hour solar cycle. As an exception, Shroud is the only one who incorporates a window (architectural) with natural light directly visible in the frame into his broadcasts. Daylight occasionally enters xQc's, Auronplay's, and Pokimane's rooms through openings behind the monitors to avoid

Figure 2.4 Ninja. Streaming room in 2022. Courtesy of Richard Tyler Blevins (Ninja)

backlighting effects, but electric illumination predominates in the image. In the rooms and studios of the other streamers analyzed here, the lighting is exclusively artificial. The range of lights used in most of these interiors, dominated by blue and violet tones, is a visually appealing choice that increases viewers' attention (and attraction). From a scientific point of view, it is known that the human retina's non-visual photoreceptors show little or no sensitivity to longer wavelengths of light, such as yellow, orange, and red,[11] while exposure to blue or violet light activates these photoreceptors, suppressing melatonin secretion and disrupting the need for sleep.[12] Therefore, some Twitch rooms influence human physiology by using colors that modify the sunlight spectrum and disrupt the circadian rhythm, which naturally shifts toward reddish tones at dawn and dusk.

In *subathons*, the format that can last several months or years, streamers like Emilycc can exhibit temporary biological needs such as sleeping—processes that are socially and economically validated by viewers following a logic of "more subscriptions > longer stream > greater circadian disruption." In short livestreams, influencers can choose to appear on camera or show themselves as avatars moving in sync with their bodily kinetics, disguising their possible fatigue as an extension of their working time. These avatars, known as V-Tubers, allow them to jointly conduct live broadcasts, even if they are not in the same place—something that became a common practice during the 2020 lockdown. Conversely, in the Twitch-con format, streamers gather in physical venues where they play and are watched by their followers, marking the possible expansion from multiple ubiquitous screens to territorializations located in the physical world.

Digital Archives: The Topos of the Screen

Since anyone can stream from anywhere at any time, Twitch promotes the perception of equal access to the creation and consumption of media, eliminating barriers and reducing the need for traditional production spaces such as studios or editing rooms. While this digital inclusivity often differs from the lived realities of individuals—both content creators and consumers—and their physical environments, domestic interiors play a role in mediating this tension. They serve to mask, reveal, or camouflage the disparity between an apparently equitable virtual territory and an unequal material world, both among the most-followed streamers (mostly male, white, and broadcasting in English or Spanish) and among amateur users.

However, digital hierarchy and segmentation of ranking, roles, and views operate on both sides of the screen, affecting both viewers and streamers. From the audience's perspective, on Twitch, specific channels can be followed for free, although subscriptions are available for additional benefits, including acquiring emblems, accessing ad-free videos and exclusive emoticons, and enjoying privileged interaction with content creators. From the influencers' perspective, architectural interiors structure the hierarchy and community dynamics, including progressively professionalized studios that showcase their status. Likewise, archiving practices display a wide variety of approaches, influenced by factors such

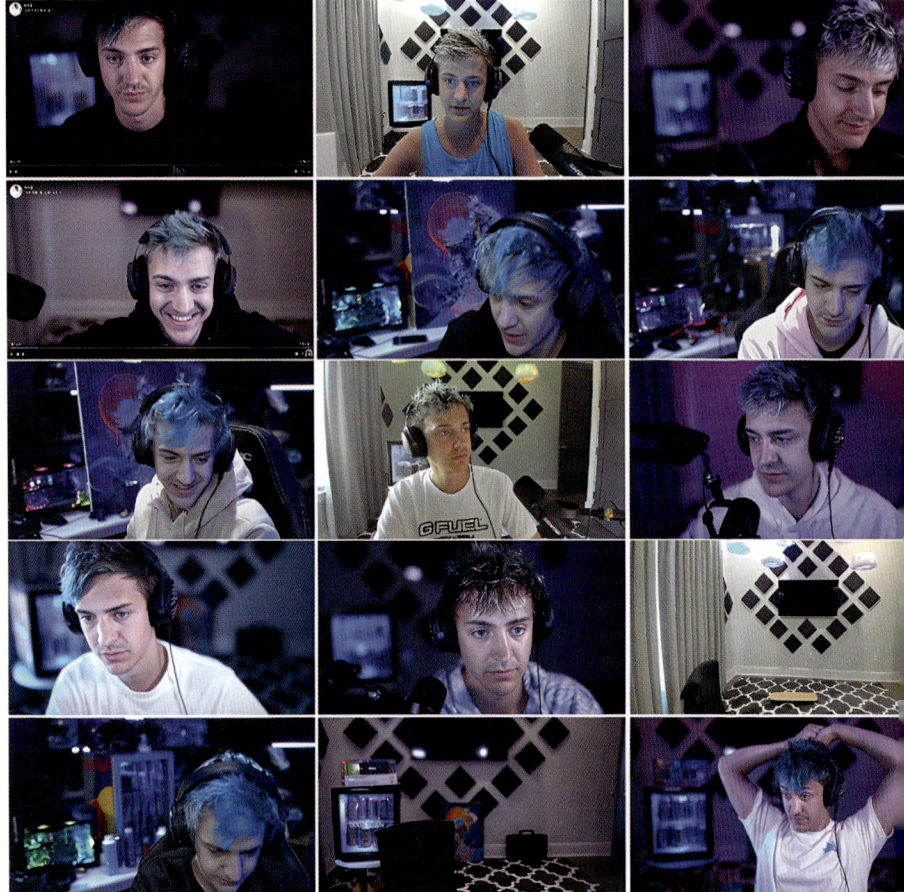

Figure 2.5 Ninja's room during the thirty most-watched streams of 2022

as copyright regulations and content guidelines. At the time of the writing of this essay, all streams from 2022 by Ninja, Tfue, Shroud, and Pokimane were available online, while Auronplay, El Rubius, and TheGrefg showed only one video from that year, and JuanSGuarnizo and xQc did not disclose any. Some creators prefer not to make their livestreams available for replay to avoid copyright issues, especially with background music, owing to the difficulty of anticipating and avoiding infringements during live broadcasts. For example, in 2020, xQc received a Digital Millennium Copyright Act (DMCA) claim to avoid potential rights issues for the content posted on his Twitter account, which was blocked.[13]

Streamers have autonomy to decide whether they want to store their videos on Twitch, without necessarily making them publicly accessible.

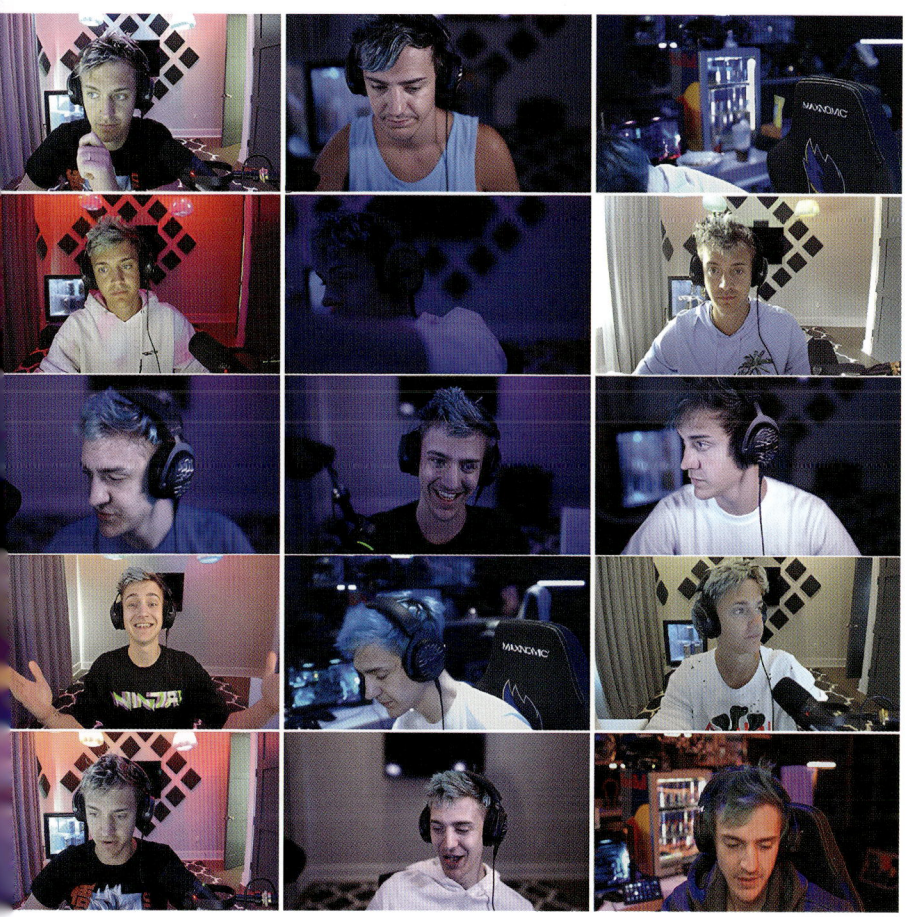

They have control over their archived content, such as the ability to modify titles, thumbnails, and categories. Many users also download their videos locally to share them on other platforms such as TikTok or YouTube, where viewers can find compilations of highlights from their long broadcasts. Archived material allows for the decentralized traceability of the evolution of interior spaces and, above all, facilitates the final disconnection from the diurnal episteme of architecture. Although most Twitch livestreams do not indicate the time, nor do they show windows or daylight, their "live" status situates their temporal ethos regardless of the viewer's geographic location. However, the archived material of non-circadian interiors ultimately disconnects them from any solar/lunar relationship, creating a flat

Figure 2.6 Pokimane's room during the thirty most-watched streams of 2022

time zone alongside architectural materials whose chromaticism and luminescence operate within and through the digital topos of the screen.

The dematerialization of tectonics in architectural interiors is evident in how streamers navigate the ephemeral nature of their content. They employ visualization and spatial design within the screen as strategies to track and simultaneously edit, preserve, or delete their digital creations amid the constantly evolving landscape of internet culture. In

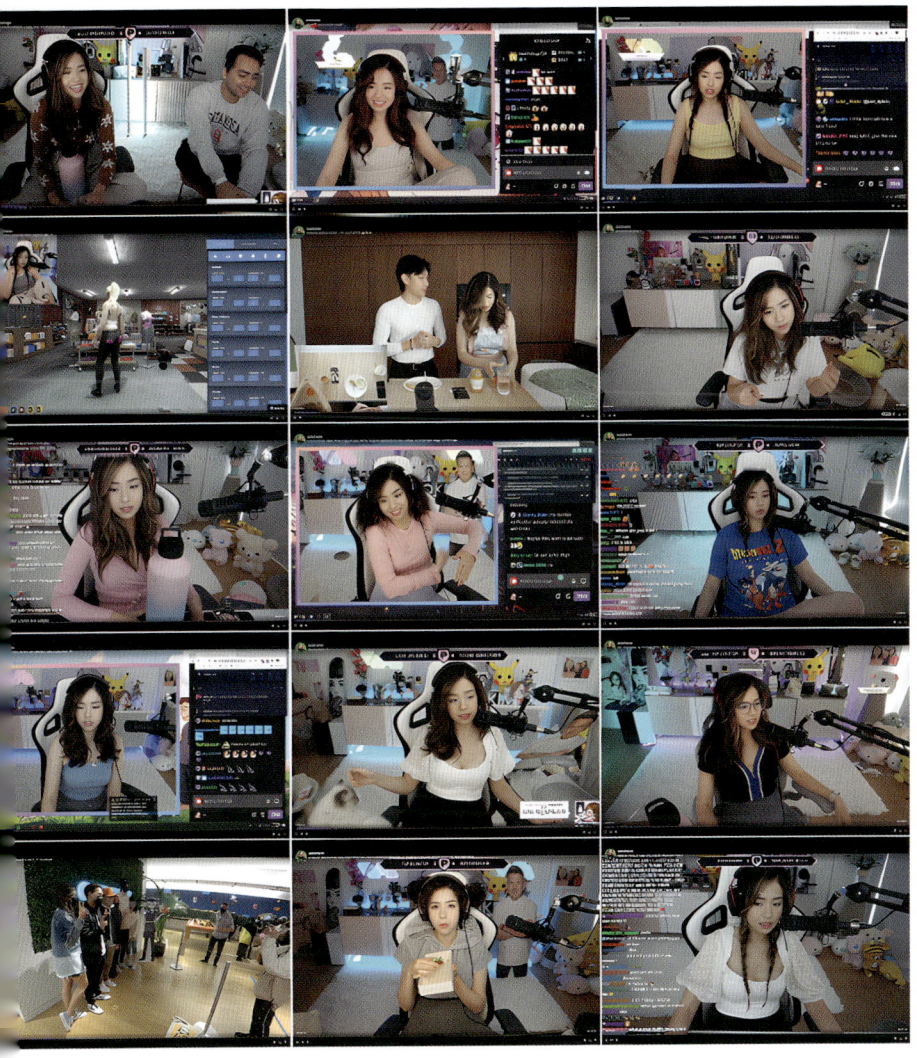

2022, the top ten Twitch streamers mostly broadcasted while seated in a gaming chair with headphones and a microphone in front of their computer. The background was mainly static: typically a space designed for the apparent production of domestic videos. Traditional axioms, such as architecture's dependence on daylight or the tectonic threshold as a mediator between interior and exterior, are challenged and often replaced by simple screens that serve as surfaces of connection with the outside world.

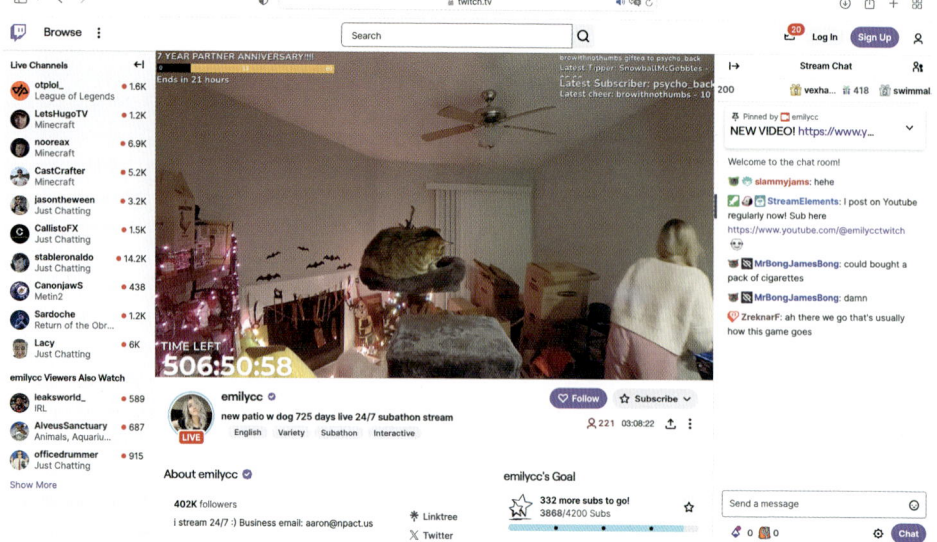

Figure 2.7 Emilycc's subathon on Twitch, November 2, 2023. Reads: 725 days live 24/7; Time left: 506:50:58; Latest subscriber: psycho_back

From Virtual to Physical: The Era of Mirrored Rooms

There are 2.5 billion gamers around the world, a diverse group united by their love of e-sports and gaming—and by being an overlooked group from a life-at-home perspective. But that is about to change: the new gaming range developed by IKEA in collaboration with Republic of Gamers (ROG) was launched at IKEA China on January 29, 2021 [. . .] From May 2021 it will be available at IKEA Japan, and globally from October 2021.[14]

IKEA, "Furniture that puts gaming first," 2021

Approximately 4.42 billion individuals utilize mobile devices to access the internet globally, many using their smartphones to watch videos. The latest available estimate in 2023, however, suggests that only about 35 percent of Twitch views originate from mobile devices.[15] Twitch followers consume content online, within interior spaces and on desktop computers—as opposed to other forms of social media, which are mostly consumed on mobile phones. This spatial distinction produces a mirror of rooms: the room of the Twitch streamer and that of the viewer, normally physically isolated yet constantly interacting with other users online. As Hito Steyerl proposed in 2013, when analyzing the impact of the internet on the physical world, "if images start pouring across screens and invading subject and object matter, the major and quite overlooked consequence is that reality now widely consists of images; or rather, of things, constellations, and processes formerly evident as images." She added: "Reality itself is post-produced and scripted, affect rendered as after-effect."[16]

The reference to affect is particularly relevant. In this sense, Twitch transforms video games into a domestic show, infusing a new dimension by introducing a window showcasing the person playing, framed within space. This dual-screen overlay adds depth and a more empathetic, or affective, experience than just watching the gameplay, with implications also for contemporary domesticity. In 2021, IKEA launched its catalog of interiors for gamers together with Republic of Gamers (ROG), a brand specialized in laptops for gaming. According to the press release by IKEA, "the collaboration aimed to democratize the gaming experience, by creating relevant, functional, beautiful and affordable products and complete gaming solutions to make it easier for everyone to create the setup and the home they want."[17] Notably, the IKEA and ROG collection was launched in January 2021, almost a year into the pandemic. The year 2020 marked a significant period for the streaming world, as enforced stay-at-home measures led to an exponential surge in live content consumption, including hours spent in front of the desktop computer.

In the context of the ten most-followed Twitch accounts analyzed in this chapter, the interiors where the streamers operate serve as the backdrop for their streaming activities, playing a significant role in shaping their online presence. The specific design and arrangement of these spaces are curated to align with the streamers' personal brands, effectively making them their workplace. The streamers, like traditional TV presenters, assume a commentator's role when engaging with their viewers, but they do so in a live and interactive manner. They frame their content within the boundaries of the setup visible on screens, creating a controlled interaction with the outside world through streaming within the confines of a seemingly domestic setting.

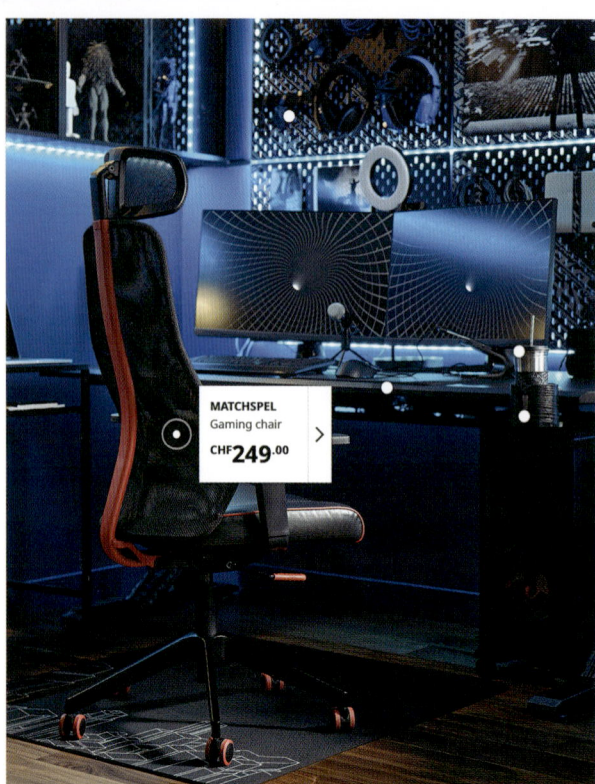

Figure 2.8 IKEA. Matchspel, gaming chair, 2023. Courtesy of IKEA

This visual identity underscores the importance of these interiors in creating an attractive and addictive environment in their disruption of the circadian rhythm. Notably, the photographs in the catalog for the IKEA gaming furniture display intense LED lighting and blue gradients that move away from the company's characteristic color palette and are more similar to the hues and tones associated with videogaming. From an architectural perspective, this highlights the influence of digitally consumed interiors on the other side of the screen—those of anonymous users. The streamers, as technologically enabled actors, display their streaming environments, fulfilling their role as both content creators and space designers. To that extent, the institutionalization of social media has led to a proliferation of these digitally influenced physical spaces, where architecture is atomized and shared through a network of rooms or a cloud of data.

In the frame-within-frame compositions of Vermeer, Hammershøi, and Ozu referred to at the beginning of this chapter, the perspective or camera was always pointing in one direction, rendering invisible what lies behind the looking eye. However, if users' screens look equally at them and their rooms, rendering the directionality of the camera twofold, then millions of domestic interiors are back in circulation online. This circulation redefines the domestic sphere as a performative interface, where rooms are continuously aestheticized, curated, and monetized through their digital visibility. In this sense, the home becomes both a site of production and projection, revealing a paradigmatic shift in architectural authorship toward collective and algorithmically mediated spatial practices, shaped by what is streamed, edited, and mirrored on both sides of the screen.

This chapter was previously published in: *Burning Farm*, no. 3 (December 2023) / *PLOT*, no. 72 (February 2024): 164–173.

Analysis conducted as part of the *Theory of Mediated Spaces* module HEAD – Genève (HES-SO). Spring Semester 2023
Professor: Javier Fernández Contreras
Data Analytics (BA students in Interior Architecture):
— Charlene Claveria, Lisa Divorne, and Noémie Castella

Notes

1 "Justin.TV Network Launches: More Shows to Come," *TechCrunch*, May 22, 2007 (accessed October 31, 2023), https://techcrunch.com/2007/05/22/justin-tv-network-launches-more-shows-to-come/

2 "Twitch (service)," *Wikipedia*, last edited on December 9, 2023, 22:33 (UTC), https://en.wikipedia.org/wiki/Twitch_(service)

3 Daniel Ruby, "Twitch Statistics 2023—(Users, Revenue & Insights)," *Demandsage*, August 2, 2023 (accessed October 31, 2023), https://www.demandsage.com/twitch-users/

4 *David Hockney: Secret Knowledge* [TV program] directed by Randall Wright (BBC, 2001), 20:19.

5 *Mystery Science Theater 3000* originally ran for ten seasons from 1988 to 1999. It was revived in 2017 on Netflix (for two seasons), and then a new revival season (season 13) was distributed in 2022 via the Gizmoplex platform.

6 *Beavis and Butt-Head* ran for seven seasons from 1993 to 1997. It was revived with an eighth season that aired on MTV in 2011.

7 "Justin.tv," *Wikipedia*, last edited on September 23, 2023, 12:30 (UTC), https://en.wikipedia.org/wiki/Justin.tv

8 Mathieu Triclot, *Philosophie des jeux vidéo* (Paris: La Découverte, 2017) (author's translation), 126. First published: Paris: Zones, 2011.

9 Ibid., 127.

10 Age and follower count of each Twitch streamer as of March 2023.

11 George Brainard, John Hanifin, Jeffrey Greeson, Brenda Byrne, Gena Glickman, Edward Gerner, Mark Rollag, "Action Spectrum for Melatonin Regulation in Humans: Evidence for a Novel Circadian Photoreceptor," *Journal of Neuroscience*, no. 21 (16) (2001), 6405–6412.

12 "Blue light has a dark side," *Harvard Health Publishing*, July 7, 2020 (accessed October 31, 2023), https://www.health.harvard.edu/staying-healthy/blue-light-has-a-dark-side

13 Zackerie Fairfax, "Twitch Streamer Gets DMCA Strike on Twitter for His Own Year-Old Clip," *Screen Rant*, December 30, 2020 (accessed October 31, 2023), https://screenrant.com/twitch-streamer-xqc-dmca-copyright-strike-twitter-clip/

14 "Furniture that puts gaming first," *IKEA Newsroom*, February 2, 2021 (accessed October 31, 2023), https://www.ikea.com/global/en/newsroom/collaborations/furniture-that-puts-gaming-first-210202/

15 Daniel Ruby, "Twitch Statistics 2023."

16 Hito Steyerl, "Too Much World: Is the Internet Dead?", *e-flux Journal* #49 (November 2013) (accessed October 31, 2023), https://www.e-flux.com/journal/49/60004/too-much-world-is-the-internet-dead/

17 "Furniture that puts gaming first," *IKEA Newsroom*.

3

ROOMS, PINS, AND BOARDS: THE HYPER-INTERIORS OF PINTEREST

Javier Fernández Contreras and Michela Bassanelli

"Take your desires for reality!" can be understood as the ultimate slogan of power since in a nonreferential world, even the confusion of the reality principle and the principle of desire is less dangerous than contagious hyperreality.[1]

JEAN BAUDRILLARD, *Simulacra and Simulation*, 1981

Gen Z-ers are making aspirational boards about houses they want to live in, places they want to visit, and even people they want to date.[2]

SARA POLLACK, Pinterest's head of consumer marketing, 2023

The construction of aspirational realities through the assemblage of visual material traverses the history of Pinterest. Originally created in 2009 as *Tote*—an app envisioned as a virtual replacement for paper catalogs—its users embraced it for sharing favorite items on themes such as architecture, food, and fashion. This inspired its founders, Ben Silbermann, Paul Sciarra, and Evan Sharp, to launch Pinterest in 2010

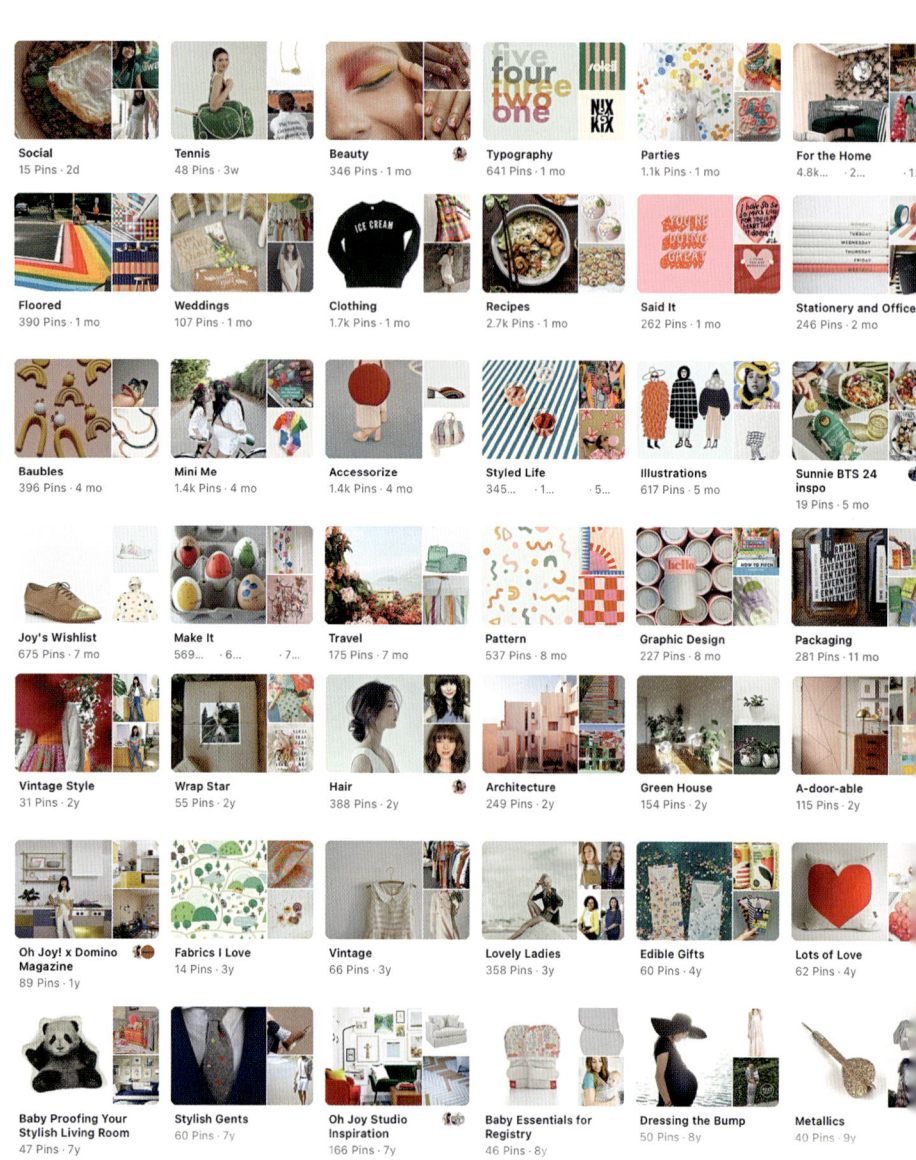

Figure 3.1 Oh Joy! Pinterest boards, April 2024. Architectural boards: "A-door-able," "Architecture," "Baby Proofing Your Home," "Dream Homes," "Floored," "For the Home," "Giftables," "Green House," "Japan," "Oh Baby," "Oh Joy for Target," "Oh Joy Studio Inspiration," "Oh Joy! x Domino Magazine," "Oh Joy! Builds a House," "Outdoor Living," "Pattern," "Prints I Love," "Retail Inspiration," "Stationery and Office," "Tabletop"

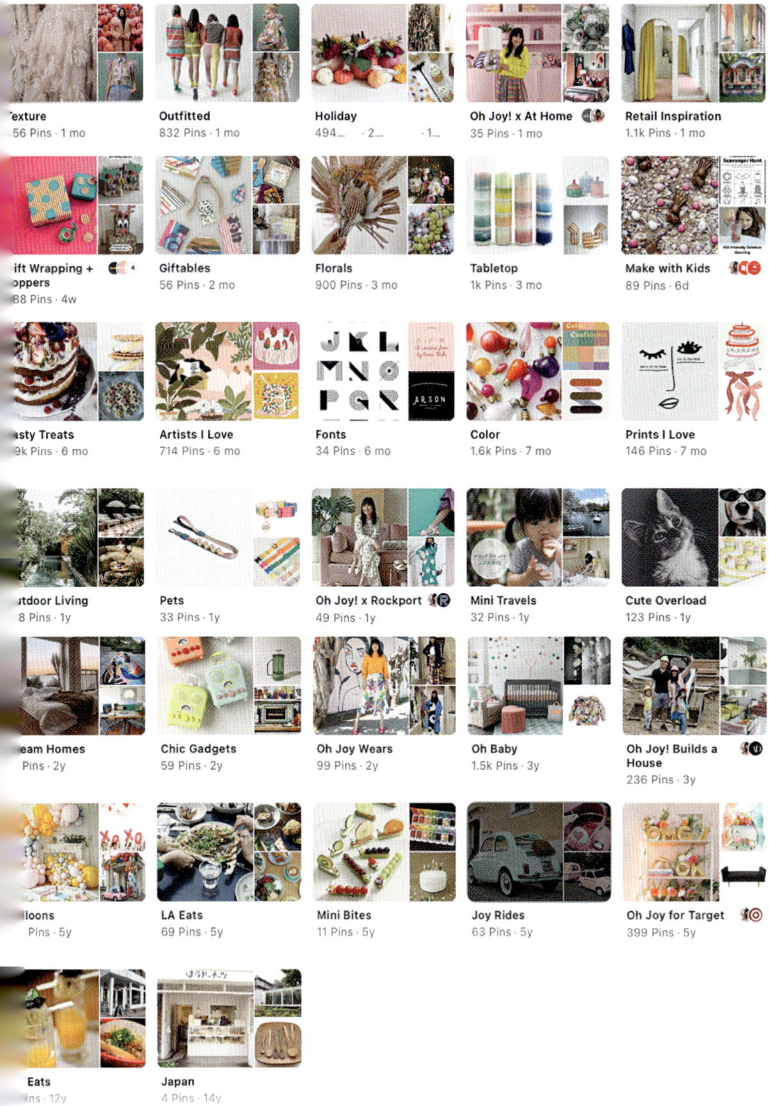

Texture
56 Pins · 1 mo

Outfitted
832 Pins · 1 mo

Holiday
494... · 2... · 1...

Oh Joy! x At Home
35 Pins · 1 mo

Retail Inspiration
1.1k Pins · 1 mo

Gift Wrapping + Toppers
88 Pins · 4w

Giftables
56 Pins · 2 mo

Florals
900 Pins · 3 mo

Tabletop
1k Pins · 3 mo

Make with Kids
89 Pins · 6d

Tasty Treats
9k Pins · 6 mo

Artists I Love
714 Pins · 6 mo

Fonts
34 Pins · 6 mo

Color
1.6k Pins · 7 mo

Prints I Love
146 Pins · 7 mo

Outdoor Living
8 Pins · 1y

Pets
33 Pins · 1y

Oh Joy! x Rockport
49 Pins · 1y

Mini Travels
32 Pins · 1y

Cute Overload
123 Pins · 1y

Dream Homes
Pins · 2y

Chic Gadgets
59 Pins · 2y

Oh Joy Wears
99 Pins · 2y

Oh Baby
1.5k Pins · 3y

Oh Joy! Builds a House
236 Pins · 3y

Balloons
Pins · 5y

LA Eats
69 Pins · 5y

Mini Bites
11 Pins · 5y

Joy Rides
63 Pins · 5y

Oh Joy for Target
399 Pins · 5y

Eats
ins · 12y

Japan
4 Pins · 14y

as a visual discovery platform where people could save and share "pins" onto categorized "boards."[3] A pin is an image (or, since 2016, also a video) either directly uploaded by the user or linked from a different website or social network. Boards are personalized collections where pins are categorized and organized thematically. Pins from one board can be saved to someone else's. This process, originally known as "Pin it" (now "Save"),[4] has made Pinterest one of the most nonlinear hypermedia platforms to navigate, since most pins simultaneously belong to multiple boards as a form of endless, ubiquitous locus. Unlike other social media sites, where most interactions are based on likes and follows, Pinterest is primarily used for curating images and videos by placing them next to other visual references, including architectural rooms, in endless collections of digitized spaces.

This chapter examines the architecture of the most-followed Pinterest accounts in 2024, focusing on those created by individual influencers rather than by companies.[5] By analyzing the most pinned and circulated spaces on the platform, it investigates the emergence of a new disciplinary territory: the "hyper-interior." Here, the prefix *hyper-*, borrowed from the tech world, indicates an expanded realm between physical and virtual spaces. While the term "hypertext" was coined by Ted Nelson in the 1960s to refer to text containing links to other textual references—creating a nonlinear reading experience—"hyperreal" was coined by Jean Baudrillard in the 1980s to describe a phenomenon of nonreferential representation without any original source, literally "the generation by models of a real without origin or reality."[6] The use of this prefix has expanded in recent decades with the introduction of terms such as "hyperconnectivity" by Anabel Quan-Haase and Barry Wellman in the 2000s, which refers to the unprecedented level of communication between humans and digital devices in the computer age, and more recently, "hyper-personalization," which describes the use of real-time data, artificial intelligence (AI), and predictive analytics to create customer-specific, personalized online experiences and services.[7] The idea of hyper-interior spaces builds on these concepts, exploring how the intensified mediatization, connectivity, and experiential convergence of physical and virtual realms impact human perception and generate novel architectural constructs characterized by simultaneously networked and individualized rooms, detached from original references and endlessly re-sampled without temporal or spatial boundaries.

Over the years, Pinterest has moved beyond social networking, prioritizing visual search and e-commerce, to the point of becoming a search engine that is simultaneously textual and visual.[8] Likes were removed in 2017,[9] and pins are rarely commented upon. And yet, some Pinterest celebrities have more impact than others, with their boards being the most followed. This has an impact on the fabrication of architectural futures by anonymous users and professionals alike, since major visitors of the platform also include architects and interior designers who utilize it to search for inspiration in the initial design phase.[10] From Oh Joy!, the biggest celebrity on the platform with over 15 million followers, to Pejper, who has 7 million followers, the top profiles present specific boards on architecture, most of them centered on interior spaces. They are all curated by women, who display a clear preference for a spatiality with pastel and beige hues, devoid of human presence, and a diurnal ethos with the spaces rarely pictured at night. There are neither elders nor disabled individuals in the most followed, repinned, and shared hyper-interiors of Pinterest. In fact, humans appear in less than 15 percent of the pictures, while other animal species feature in less than 3 percent. Domesticity can be navigated visually from one room to another, by scrolling down, pinning, or clicking. Users also plan their spaces, whether homes or offices, restaurants, or gyms, on the platform. If aspirational futures are constructed from these hyperlinked rooms, taking desires for reality, this might suggest a flattened, lifeless spatiality in which pluralities are obliterated—one that deserves architectural attention.

From Spatialized to Digital Boards: An Architectural Genealogy

Pinterest belongs to the tradition of multiscreen mediated rooms. As forms of primitive interactive boards, these rooms originated in the 20th century, with American historical precedents. In the 1950s, Charles and Ray Eames pioneered a display system using diverse image connections

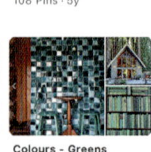

Figure 3.2 Poppy Talk. Pinterest boards, April 2024. Architectural boards: "Architecture," "At the Lake — Interiors," "Backyard Cottages and Sheds," "Bathrooms," "Cabins, Cottages + Summerhouses," "Camping," "Chairs," "Container Homes," "Cool Decorating Tricks," "Dining Rooms," "Entry + Hallways," "Flooring + Rugs," "Gardening," "Holiday Decor," "Home Office," "Hotel Style," "IKEA Hacks," "Kids Rooms," "Kitchens," "Laundry Room," "Library + Shelving," "Light," "Living Rooms," "Patio + Deck," "Pre-Fab Homes," "Room with a View," "Special Places," "Stairways," "The Art of the Display," "Wallpaper + Walls," "What Home Means To Me"

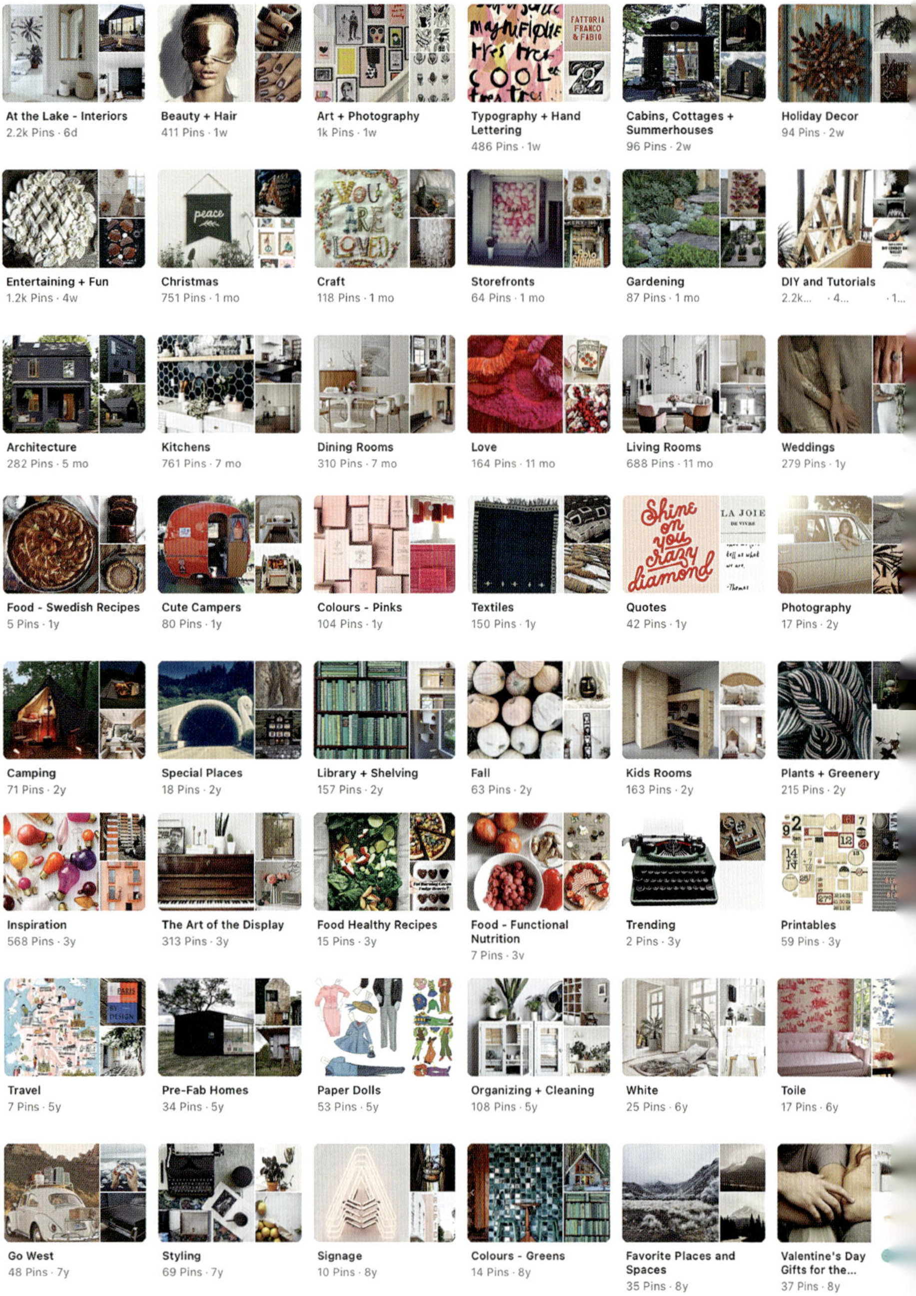

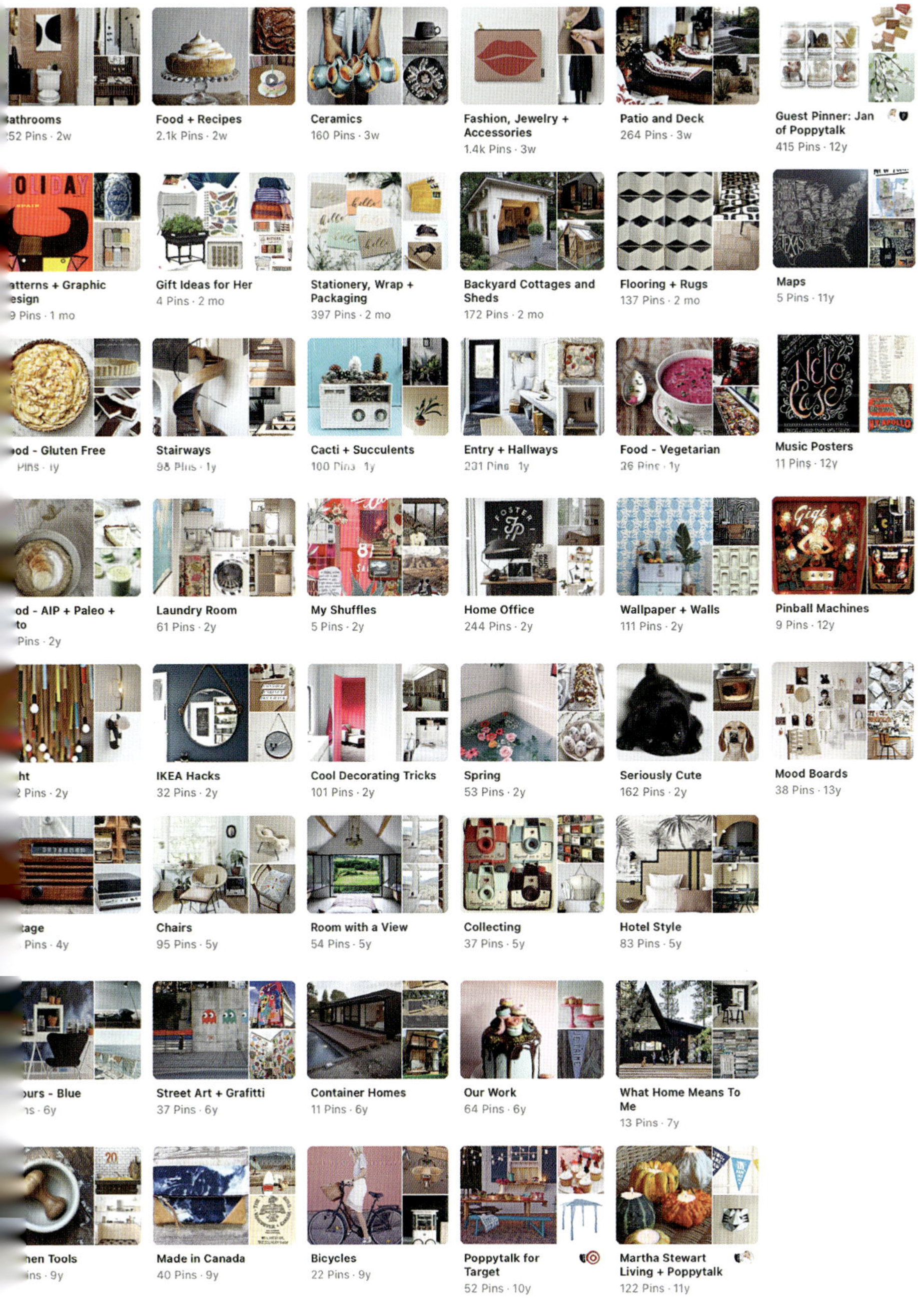

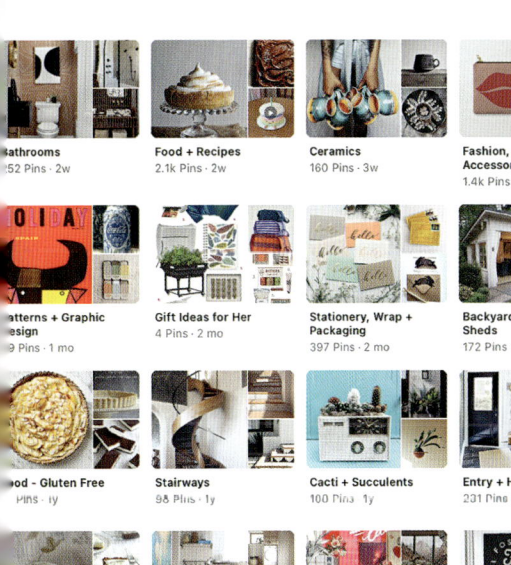
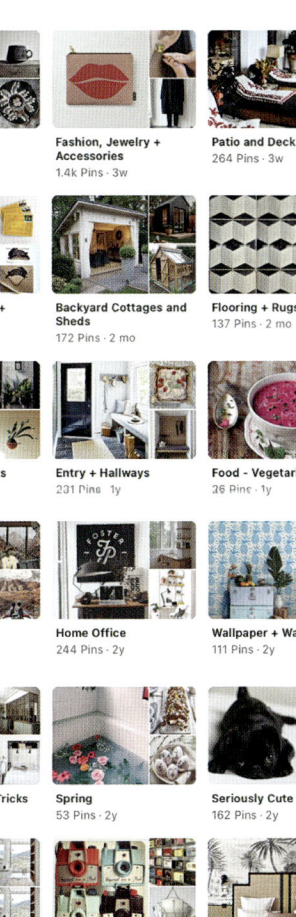
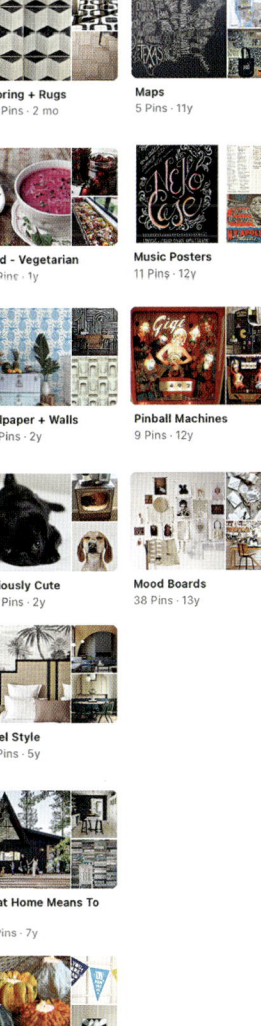

Bathrooms
252 Pins · 2w

Food + Recipes
2.1k Pins · 2w

Ceramics
160 Pins · 3w

Fashion, Jewelry + Accessories
1.4k Pins · 3w

Patio and Deck
264 Pins · 3w

Guest Pinner: Jan of Poppytalk
415 Pins · 12y

Patterns + Graphic Design
9 Pins · 1 mo

Gift Ideas for Her
4 Pins · 2 mo

Stationery, Wrap + Packaging
397 Pins · 2 mo

Backyard Cottages and Sheds
172 Pins · 2 mo

Flooring + Rugs
137 Pins · 2 mo

Maps
5 Pins · 11y

Food - Gluten Free
Pins · 1y

Stairways
98 Plns · 1y

Cacti + Succulents
100 Pins · 1y

Entry + Hallways
231 Pins · 1y

Food - Vegetarian
26 Pins · 1y

Music Posters
11 Pins · 12y

Food - AIP + Paleo + Keto
Pins · 2y

Laundry Room
61 Pins · 2y

My Shuffles
5 Pins · 2y

Home Office
244 Pins · 2y

Wallpaper + Walls
111 Pins · 2y

Pinball Machines
9 Pins · 12y

Light
2 Pins · 2y

IKEA Hacks
32 Pins · 2y

Cool Decorating Tricks
101 Pins · 2y

Spring
53 Pins · 2y

Seriously Cute
162 Pins · 2y

Mood Boards
38 Pins · 13y

Vintage
Pins · 4y

Chairs
95 Pins · 5y

Room with a View
54 Pins · 5y

Collecting
37 Pins · 5y

Hotel Style
83 Pins · 5y

Colours - Blue
ns · 6y

Street Art + Grafitti
37 Pins · 6y

Container Homes
11 Pins · 6y

Our Work
64 Pins · 6y

What Home Means To Me
13 Pins · 7y

Kitchen Tools
ns · 9y

Made in Canada
40 Pins · 9y

Bicycles
22 Pins · 9y

Poppytalk for Target
52 Pins · 10y

Martha Stewart Living + Poppytalk
122 Pins · 11y

and employed the multiscreen method to showcase their film *Glimpses of the USA* at the 1959 American National Exhibition in Moscow. Seven screens, arranged in two rows within Buckminster Fuller's dome, depicted typical American workdays and weekend lifestyles. As Beatriz Colomina argues, the installation of this projection created a form of multimedia architecture with an immersion into the private facets of people's lives.[11] Similarly, the multiscreen film *Think*, shown at the IBM Ovoid theater for the 1964 World's Fair in New York, aimed to connect problem-solving concepts with everyday routines through twenty-two screens enveloping the viewer. During the same period, American designer Ken Isaacs, while teaching at the Illinois Institute of Technology, conceived the *Knowledge Box* with the aim of creating a new model for learning: "a cube of wood, masonite, and steel equipped with twenty-four slide projectors and audio-suppliers. Briefly, a pre-internet device to transmit narratives in a non-linear way, an immersive environment between artistic installation and interaction design which questioned the 'passive' models of transmission of information."[12] This learning machine used continuous images grouped by specific subjects—i.e., boards—to stimulate an active process by comparing disparate elements.

It is worth recalling the grouping of images described in these early experiences and the contemporary way of looking at social networks like Pinterest, which work on the continuous juxtaposition of pictures. However, the architecture that Pinterest took as a reference in its origins was not spatial but that of the printed page in commercial catalogs, transitioning it into digital boards. The difference is significant, for the immersion and collectivity that the projection theater produce are inverted on Pinterest, producing a mediated intimacy in which the eyes that individually look at the screen are continuously presented with personalized content, and tracked and analyzed in their behavior. If Tote, Pinterest's predecessor, failed owing to the limited mobile payment technology available at the time, it is no accident that the recent evolution of the platform has transformed it into both a virtual storefront and a visual encyclopedia. Businesses can utilize Pinterest as a platform to market and sell their products, many of them framed within spaces, much like in a physical store. Users can browse through disparate profiles and selected items, making purchases directly through the platform. Additionally, Pinterest serves as a visual encyclopedia owing to its diverse range of topics and the ability for users to organize boards in a personalized manner.

A careful look at the development of Pinterest reveals that the most radical changes have occurred not in the in-between space of images within boards (where each pin maintains the same width but varies in height), but within the images themselves, which have become data-based and fragmentable surfaces loaded with information and links.[13] As the platform has evolved, so has its user interface (UI). In 2012, Pinterest launched business accounts, with web analytics added one year later. In 2013, it began displaying advertisements in the form of "Promoted Pins." Critically, that same year, it introduced a new tool called "Rich Pins," which allows additional information (e.g., product details) to be displayed directly within pins and linked to external sources. This feature is fundamental to the relational, hypermedia nature of the platform, as linked content is automatically synced when updated. This databasing has been paired with the searchable nature of images. In 2015, Pinterest introduced the "Visual Search" tool, allowing users to search for elements in images as isolated fragments that link to similar elements, and unveiled "Buyable Pins" (renamed "Product Pins" in 2018) in partnership with Shopify. Significantly, in 2017, Pinterest launched "Lens," allowing users to take or upload photos to find related pins, and "Shop the Look," now called "Shop Similar Items," which superimposes circle buttons on individual items that, when tapped, open related pins. For design and architecture, this means that when users click on objects like lamps, chairs, or tables within an image, Pinterest displays an array of similar objects next to it, implying a preference for images with identifiable, individualizable objects in terms of morphology and color scheme, as opposed to spaces characterized by clutter, disorder, or ambiguity. While the spaces within the Eames' screens demanded site-specific, time-situated immersion, holistic in both experience and perception, the hyper-interiors of Pinterest are still lives whose elements can be individualized, clicked, linked, highlighted, synced, purchased, and consumed at any time.

Pinterest: Diurnal, Domestic, Bodyless Interiors

The most-followed accounts on Pinterest in 2024 present models of spatial representation that display architecture—especially interior spaces—that can be read photographically as autonomous installments.

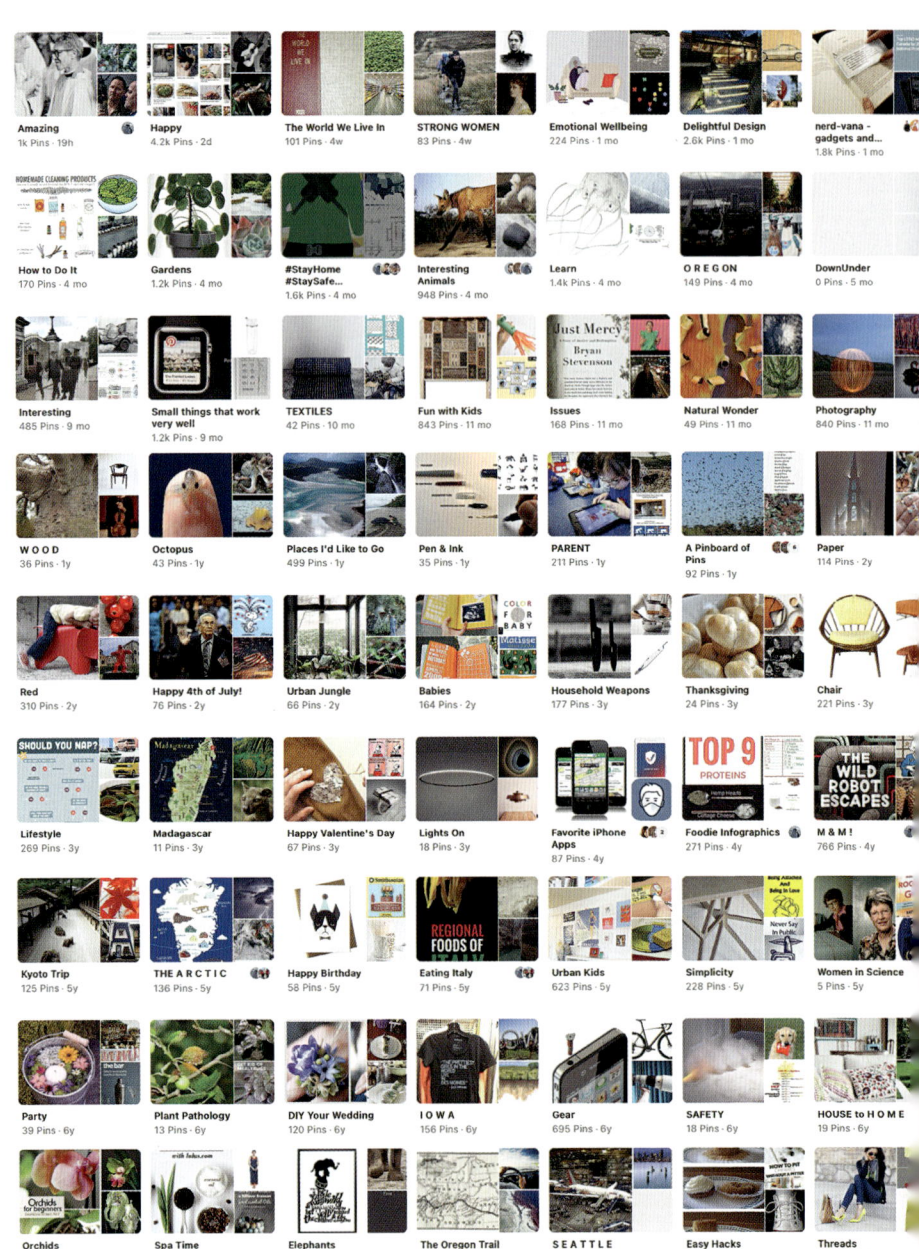

Figure 3.3 Jane Wang. Pinterest boards, April 2024. Architectural boards: "Delightful Design," "House to Home," "India," "Japan," "Kyoto Trip," "Natural Wonder," "Oregon," "Patterns and Proportion," "Places I'd Like to Go," "Simplicity," "The World We Live In," "Urban Jungle," "Urban Kids," "Wood"

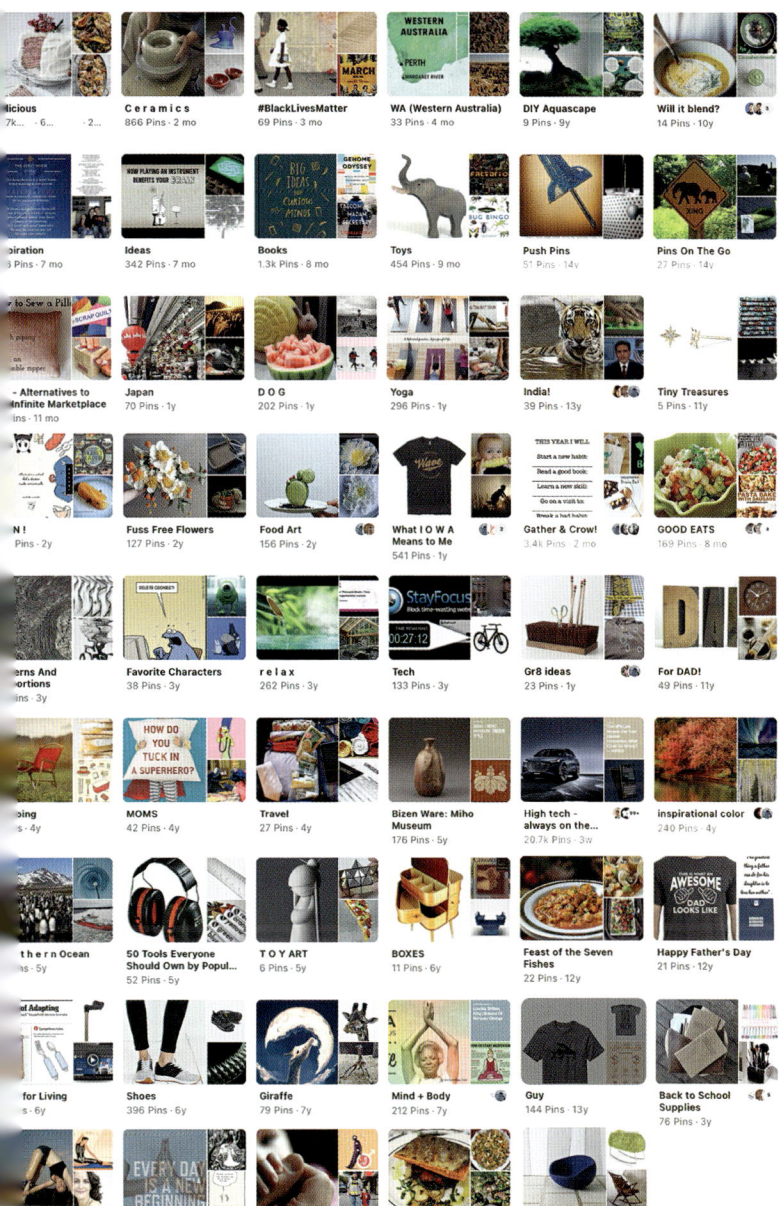

licious 7k... · 6... · 2...	C e r a m i c s 866 Pins · 2 mo	#BlackLivesMatter 69 Pins · 3 mo	WA (Western Australia) 33 Pins · 4 mo	DIY Aquascape 9 Pins · 9y	Will it blend? 14 Pins · 10y
piration Pins · 7 mo	Ideas 342 Pins · 7 mo	Books 1.3k Pins · 8 mo	Toys 454 Pins · 9 mo	Push Pins 51 Pins · 14y	Pins On The Go 27 Pins · 14y
- Alternatives to Infinite Marketplace Pins · 11 mo	Japan 70 Pins · 1y	D O G 202 Pins · 1y	Yoga 296 Pins · 1y	India! 39 Pins · 13y	Tiny Treasures 5 Pins · 11y
N ! Pins · 2y	Fuss Free Flowers 127 Pins · 2y	Food Art 156 Pins · 2y	What I O W A Means to Me 541 Pins · 1y	Gather & Crow! 3.4k Pins · 2 mo	GOOD EATS 169 Pins · 8 mo
erns And ortions Pins · 3y	Favorite Characters 38 Pins · 3y	r e l a x 262 Pins · 3y	Tech 133 Pins · 3y	Gr8 ideas 23 Pins · 1y	For DAD! 49 Pins · 11y
ng s · 4y	MOMS 42 Pins · 4y	Travel 27 Pins · 4y	Bizen Ware: Miho Museum 176 Pins · 5y	High tech - always on the... 20.7k Pins · 3w	inspirational color 240 Pins · 6y
thern Ocean s · 5y	50 Tools Everyone Should Own by Popul... 52 Pins · 5y	T O Y ART 6 Pins · 5y	BOXES 11 Pins · 6y	Feast of the Seven Fishes 22 Pins · 12y	Happy Father's Day 21 Pins · 12y
for Living s · 6y	Shoes 396 Pins · 6y	Giraffe 79 Pins · 7y	Mind + Body 212 Pins · 7y	Guy 144 Pins · 13y	Back to School Supplies 76 Pins · 3y
n the ines ns · 1y	Inspired 240 Pins · 1y	COOL DADS 41 Pins · 9y	Family Favorite Recipes 69 Pins · 4y	Rocking Chairs 67 Pins · 14y	

All these profiles feature boards related to furnishing rooms such as bedrooms, kitchens, bathrooms, and dressing rooms. They range from generic cross-categories like "Architecture" to highly specialized ones like "DIY Upholstery," as well as individual components such as "Doors," "Windows," "Floors," "Lighting," and "Fireplaces." It is not only objects and furniture that are classified within specific categories. So, too, are living beings such as "Babies," "Pets," and "Plants," which regularly feature on dedicated boards, becoming both the subject and the target of marketable consumer goods. A common aspect—and a form of post-COVID networked domesticity—is the presence of boards dedicated to creating workspaces within the home, indicating a growing interest in the programmatic performativity of domestic interiors. Outdoor spaces, meanwhile, regularly feature greenery and gardening activities. Ancillary rooms, traditionally obliterated in architectural media, take a significant role on the platform, with dedicated boards such as "Laundry Rooms" or "Closets," which regularly feature in the most-followed accounts. The founders of these accounts range from influencers to professionals specializing in specific fields such as interior design, communication, art direction, or photography. They are all women and address a young audience, that of Pinterest, where 70 percent of users are female.[14] They regularly mix architecture with fashion, travel, food, health, and family-oriented lifestyle boards, while showing a scarcity of sports activities and a complete absence of night photography.

The most-followed account worldwide, Oh Joy!, founded by Thai–American designer and blogger Joy Cho, shows content related to home decoration, fashion, travel, and lifestyle. A significant share of her more than seventy boards is dedicated to architecture and interior design, with specific boards such as "For the Home," "Retail Inspiration," and even a reality-show-like board titled "Oh Joy! Builds a House," where the influencer shared the construction and decoration process of her own house in Los Angeles between 2019 and 2020, in collaboration with *Architectural Digest*. Among the content related to design and rooms, pink and beige color palettes dominate the designer's preferences, favoring images without people or animals, that are entirely diurnal, with a central perspective for space and a white background for objects and design. The second-most-followed account, Poppytalk, founded by Canadian communication specialist Jan Halvarson, expands the list of specific boards dedicated to individual spaces such as kitchens, bathrooms, staircases, entryways, and children's rooms. At the time of the analysis in April 2024, there were more than 21,000 pins in the "Saved" section and a total of 94 boards, which could be grouped into categories such as interior design, architecture, DIY crafts, food, fashion, beauty, arts, holidays, objects, plants, colors, and miscellanea. The predominant colors were white, brown, and gray, and the boards mainly featured daytime interior images that focused on both spaces and furnishings, with the visual representation alternating between frontal and diagonal views.

Maryann Rizzo, an American decoration blogger, and Cathie Hong, a Korean–American interior designer, are both profiles created by self-taught professionals who focus on space design and architecture. Maryann Rizzo's page is more related to generic inspirational material, combining eclectic styles, finishings, and furniture for both public and private interiors. In contrast, Cathie Hong takes a more curatorial approach with a precise and selective choice of images showcasing high-end residential design. Although almost all the images are saved from other platforms, Hong also features a specific board named "Cathie Hong Interiors," consisting solely of images of her studio projects. These images, taken during the daytime, reinforce a bright and uncluttered aesthetic that also appears in her other boards. The color palette is dominated by soft, warm tones with a prevalence of white surfaces and wood as a material. Similarly, Bonnie Tsang, a Chinese–American art director and photographer, maintains a notably meticulous profile, as reflected in the details and choices characterizing her twenty-six boards on decoration, art, and lifestyle. Half of the boards focus on architecture and design, while the rest are dedicated to graphic design, photography, fashion, and beauty. The "Living Spaces" board is the most followed, with 3.49 million subscribers. It features images taken from other websites, which account for 97 percent of the content. The images are predominantly captured during the daytime (94 percent) and indoors (96 percent), and they are devoid of any human or animal presence. The "Workspaces" board, with 3.47 million subscribers, is the second most followed and has a repost rate of nearly 90 percent. It is characterized by images featuring soft materials and colors, creating a work environment that promotes concentration.

Finally, the HonestlyWTF, Pejper, and Jane Wang accounts complete the variety of the most-followed profiles on Pinterest. Founded by

Figure 3.4 Maryann Rizzo. "Laundry Rooms" board, April 2024. 247 pins: 100% saved from a different platform; 99% interior spaces; 97% diurnal; 98% bodyless; 40% frontal view

Asian–American Erica Chan Coffman, HonestlyWTF is a lifestyle blog curating stories covering fashion, art, travel, interior design, and DIY, whose content is also shared on other social media platforms. Following a classic pattern on Pinterest, boards on interior design, which number more than thirty, are mostly organized according to themes such as "Bathrooms," "Dining Rooms," "Kitchens," elements like "Doors," "Walls," and "Furniture," and boards with a personal touch such as "Inspiration" and "Home Sweet Home." On a different note, Pejper, directed by Swedish web designer Anna Karin, focuses on interiors, plants, and greenery. Of the seventy boards, 65 percent are dedicated to space design, while the rest consist of a miscellany of categories comprising fashion, nature, typography, humans, animals, textures, food, and music. Favoring Scandinavian design and aesthetics with white color palettes and wooden finishes, many images prominently feature green elements, showcased in dedicated boards such as "Green Interior," "Green Living—Green House," and "Kitchen Garden." As an exception to the accounts discussed previously, Jane Wang, an American influencer with 115 boards and over 19,600 pins, has been active exclusively on Pinterest since the platform's creation in 2010 and is the mother of the platform's co-founder Ben Silbermann. A practicing ophthalmologist in Iowa, she uses Pinterest mainly as a hobby without monetizing her online activity. Her profile, which lacks a specific strategy, covers a broad range of topics such as travel, animals, art, design, food, and technology. Although she does not have boards exclusively dedicated to interior design, some, such as "Delightful Design" and "House to Home," include interiors, while travel boards such as "Kyoto trip" and "India" also feature diverse spaces and landscapes.

The architectural spaces of these Pinterest accounts are intertwined with the identity of their creators, who are mainly women under 50, often based in America and of Asian descent. Some influencers, such as Jane Wang and Maryann Rizzo, are secretive about their private lives,[15] while others, like Oh Joy! and Bonnie Tsang, regularly share details about their personal lives as part of their work as online lifestyle curators.[16] Within the diversity of these profiles, different patterns can be traced regarding the representation of space and the construction of images. The angle, brightness, and colors vary from board to board, but the photos are predominantly taken during the daytime. With nocturnal photography accounting for less than 1 percent of the images, there is

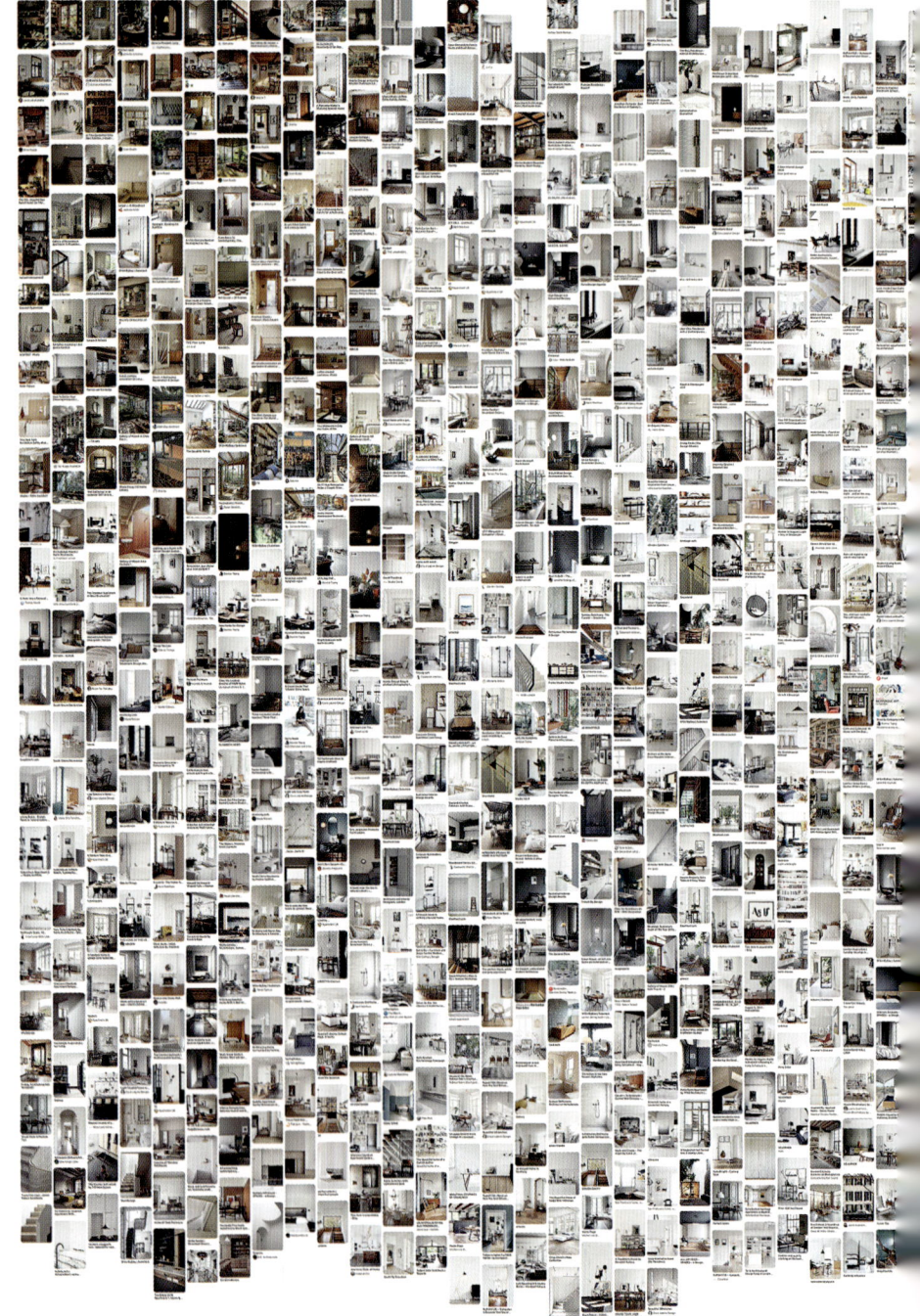

Figure 3.5 Bonnie Tsang. "Living Spaces" board, fragment, April 2024. 3,721 pins: 97% saved from a different platform; 96% interior spaces; 94% diurnal; 96% bodyless; 72% frontal view

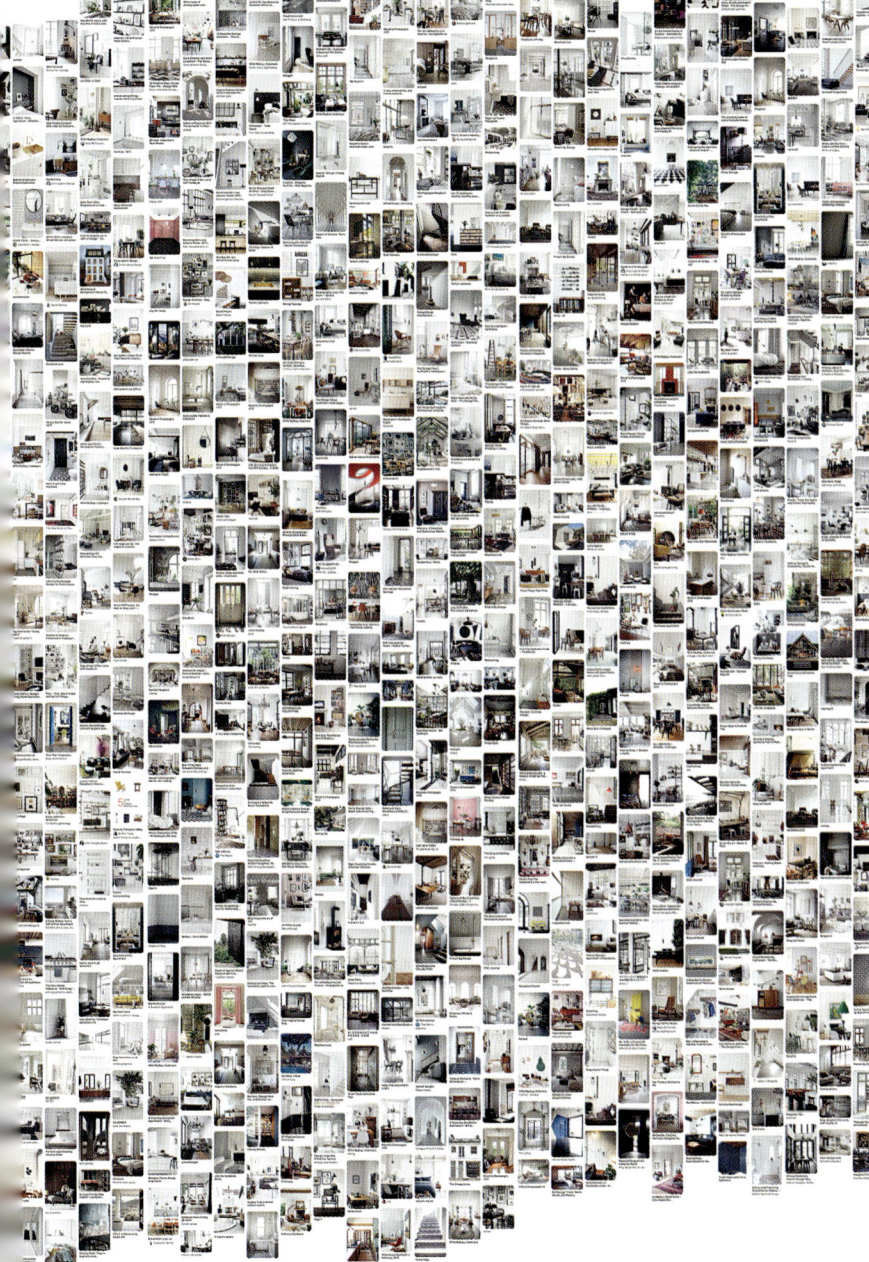

Figure 3.6 HonestlyWTF. "Doors" board, April 2024. 136 pins: 93% saved from a different platform; 13% interior spaces; 98% diurnal; 100% bodyless; 100% frontal view

no night in the architectural boards of the most-followed Pinterest accounts, and artificial light is mainly displayed in boards dedicated to objects such as lamps, mostly pictured over white backgrounds. This is consistent with the color palettes of these spaces, which display a clear preference for white, beige, and pastel tones for walls, and wood, tiles, and upholstery for finishings and furniture, awash in natural light. If night is suspicious, the diurnal imagery constructs an idea of health and healthy lifestyles (keywords regularly used on the platform), which is reinforced by the use of greenery and plants as props for a supposedly deeper connection with nature—that is, artificially controlled gardens within interior spaces, patios, and terraces. This trend mirrors the broader popularity of residential themes, which encompass houses and apartments and dominate the platform's indoor landscape. "Home," "homey," or "cozy" are repeated terms, and the house is the hub of broader activities that have reintegrated labor into the domestic sphere, including the office, and monetized leisure routines.

Interestingly, while many Pinterest influencers focus their content on fashion, beauty, food, and health, human bodies often disappear in boards dedicated to architecture and interior design. Users are rarely observed in their domestic interiors, suggesting a preference for staged interiors over those actively in use. To emphasize the space, these images are also devoid of animals, which are regularly confined to

Figure 3.7 Pejper. "Green Interior" board, April 2024. 28 pins: 100% saved from a different platform; 100% interior spaces; 100% diurnal; 100% bodyless; 80% frontal view

boards specifically dedicated to pets. A telling example from outside the individual accounts analyzed so far is the account of Mamas Uncut, "a parenting site focused on mom Q&A, parenting news and trends as well as home hacks,"[17] which ranks eighth worldwide on Pinterest with 8.5 million followers and, as of July 2024, presents twenty-nine boards covering a variety of topics such as "Wedding," "Pregnancy," "Little Ones," and "Pet Stuffs." These boards display bodies of different species, ages, and races. The featured humans are mostly under 40 and are depicted as living heteronormative lifestyles. Yet, in the specialized board "Home Hacks and Decor Ideas," itself subdivided into "Dining Room Ideas," "Bedroom Ideas," "Indoor Plants," "casa—ny apartment," and "casa—Diger," bodies completely disappear, the only living beings being plants reified as images of their online selves. The interiors of Pinterest are bodyless. This is consistent with the absence of workout routines, gaming, and sports in most of the platform's domestic images, with these activities sometimes having their own specific, independent boards. The digital navigation of domesticity, facilitated through scrolling, pinning, and clicking, enables Pinterest users to meticulously plan and personalize spaces that are nonetheless flattened and highly repetitive because they are regularly similar to each other. Bodies are reserved for fashion, family, and pet-oriented boards, but they disappear in those addressing spaces and architecture, as if the ethos of the hyper-interior were supposed to be incorporeal, composed of objects staged for photography but not meant to be used, their emptiness meant to be looked at, linked, and used by any potential, indeterminate, invisible, online, anonymous user.

Potrero Hill House & Studio

23 Pins

Belmont Glass House

18 Pins

campbell modern home

20 Pins

palo alto multi-generational home

24 Pins

Los Gatos Bathrooms

2 Pins

Figure 3.8 Cathie Hong. "Cathie Hong Interiors" board, April 2024. 139 pins: 100% own image 100% interior spaces; 100% diurnal; 100% bodyless; 82% frontal view. Sub-boards: "Potrero House & Studio," "Belmont Glass House," "scandinavian modern home," "Hide & Seek House "campbell modern home," "palo alto multi-generational home," "san diego kitchen and office "eichler kitchen renovation," "Los Gatos Bathrooms"

scandinavian modern home
17 Pins

Hide & Seek House
12 Pins

san diego kitchen and office
15 Pins

eichler kitchen renovation
8 Pins

Scrolling, Saving, Consuming Futures: Interior Spaces in the Age of Social Media

The diffuse house relies on immaterial economies. The diffuse house is post-Fordist. The diffuse house constitutes the germ of the "Grand Interior," the continuous spatial core of late capitalism.[18]

MAIO, "The Diffuse House," January 2021

498 million people use Pinterest every month to find new ideas and plan their next purchase. They're here to visualize and act on their future. And they're eager to hear from brands like yours.[19]

PINTEREST BUSINESS, May 2024

Dining Room Ideas
25 Pins

Bedroom Ideas
25 Pins

Indoor Plants
25 Pins

Figure 3.9 Mamas Uncut. "Home Hacks and Decor Ideas" board, April 2024. Sub-boards: "Dining Room Ideas," "Bedroom Ideas," "Indoor Plants," "casa—ny apartment," "casa—Diğer"

The idea of the infinite interior traverses decades of architectural visions, imaginaries, and debates. Between 1956 and 1974, Constant Nieuwenhuys's *New Babylon* envisioned a nomadic future city with interconnected, adaptable spaces. In 1969, the Italian group Archizoom introduced *No-Stop City*, conceptualizing an endless interior with a repetitive grid and continuous structure, while Superstudio's *Continuous Monument* critiqued modernism with its vast, unbroken global structure. In 1972, Rem Koolhaas's *Exodus, or the Voluntary Prisoners of Architecture* offered a vision of a secluded London with an infinite architectural strip. More recently, the societal and economic implications of controlled, endless spaces were analyzed by Peter Sloterdijk in 2013 in "The Grand Interior."[20] Taking Crystal Palace as the epitome of an era, it parallels globalization and capitalism with the establishment and expansion of a world interior whose boundaries are invisible. In 2021, aligned with Sloterdijk's concepts, the architecture office MAIO proposed an interpretation of contemporary domesticity as the "diffuse house"— an endless landscape composed of technologies, objects, and spaces. Emphasizing the post-era (post-Fordist, post-national), the proposal envisions that the home, in today's globalized world and gig-economy

casa - ny apartment
71 Pins

casa – Diğer
562 Pins

society, finds its definitive gizmo in the Roomba, which has been Wi-Fi-enabled since 2015 and is therefore capable of producing maps of interiors worldwide while their owners work in fragmented, deterritorialized economies. "Maybe, for the first time, 'thanks' to Roomba and its data mapping, we can potentially imagine, as in a Borges tale, the possibility of creating a virtual map of the interiors of the whole world. Just imagine an endless negative of Giambattista Nolli's *Plan of Rome*; a plan that could be extended to the whole surface of the earth."[21] Embedding work, rest, and leisure, 21st-century homes are part of this "diffuse house," a completely horizontal structure that combines production and consumption.

In the face of Nolli maps, No-Stop cities, and Roomba geographies, the hyper-interiors of Pinterest seem to propose an alternative, complementary model: that of the saved image. This is an endless collection of hyperlinked rooms, without clear origin or end, neither spatial nor temporal, navigated through photographic views. There are no floor plans of the hyper-interiors of Pinterest, nor do users care about their cohesive existence. On the architecture-related boards of Oh Joy!, most images are saved from elsewhere. Who? Where? When? The origins of images can be individually traced, but it is their ubiquitous, flat coexistence on the board, on the digital screen, that matters. The Pinterest influencer curated them, put them together, and they are ready to be scrolled, saved, and consumed, no matter their original reference, if any. As of July 2024, of the more than 4,700 pins on Oh Joy!'s "For the Room" board, 92 percent were saved from other sources. On boards like "Architecture," "Dream Homes," or "Floored," the ratio of own images was even more unbalanced. Only on the "Oh Joy! Builds a House" board, and on those featuring collaborations with brands such as Target and *domino* magazine, do original images account for a representative share of the total. Oh Joy!'s profile and services are equally accessible on her professional website, blog, academy, and other social media platforms. This is a relational, omnichannel business strategy that aims to seamlessly navigate across mediums, including regular collaborations with magazines and brands.

Other Pinterest celebrities follow similar strategies, always capitalizing on the relational, hyperlinked, and networked nature of the platform. Eighty percent of Bonnie Tsang's total pins are external, 85 percent in the case of Cathie Hong, 90 percent in Poppytalk's, 98 percent for Pejper, 100 percent for Maryann Rizzo, and so on. This asymmetry might be based on the fact that Bonnie Tsang and Cathie Hong are, respectively, a professional photographer and an interior designer, and might want to claim a share of origin and "tangible" reality in their profiles, as opposed to other influencers whose creative DNA is purely based on curating (or sampling) and repinning. They mostly communicate interior spaces that are endlessly hyperlinked, even within the surface of each individual image. Objects can be individualized and purchased from within most images. The platform's structure also enables indirect promotions. When their designs incorporate products, users are seamlessly directed to explore analogous offerings from other suppliers, inadvertently amplifying various profiles and businesses. This is consistent with Pinterest's strategy of becoming a de facto online storefront for brands, maximizing the pixels that can be monetized. If users enter Pinterest to visualize and act on their future, it is a commercial one.

The interiors of Pinterest are hyper—not because they are digitally linked, but precisely because they cannot exist in a different condition. "Rich Pins" create spaces of metadata, as linked content is automatically synced when updated from external sources. Publicity is embedded in the scroll-down of images and videos, while the "Image Search" and "Shop Similar Items" functions allow for the precise fragmentation of content into monetized still lives. The platform itself has evolved to create more interactions in relation to the user's device. Initially launched as a desktop-focused site, Pinterest prioritized a grid-style layout with larger images, catering to users exploring and pinning inspiration. As mobile usage surged, Pinterest adapted by introducing a more streamlined, vertically oriented interface optimized for smaller screens, emphasizing ease of pinning and browsing on the go. By 2017, approximately 85 percent of Pinterest users were accessing the platform via mobile devices, which is also why the company placed the search bar on the main home tab of its app.[22] "I think it's a really important signifier that Pinterest is a search company,"[23] declared Pinterest co-founder Evan Sharp at the time, highlighting the platform's successful transition to a mobile-first experience. This shift also indicates a transition to searchable futures, a merge between consumption and futuring that has driven the company's recent evolution.

Pinterest exemplifies a space where the architecture of desires unfolds through an intricate web of shared imagery and collective sampling. Users creates links and boards between images that, through their similarity, repeat, replicate, and perpetuate diurnal, bodyless spaces and tendencies. In this case, the influence on architecture is direct, not only because this platform is used as a design tool by professionals in the creative phase, but also because it produces an infinite series of links based on the machine's ability to search for similar interiors. The interior space loses its value as a three-dimensional tactile volume and becomes a collection of dimensionalities of contingent physical translation. This phenomenon, rooted in the interconnectedness of images and ideas across multiple boards, mirrors broader trends in hyperconnectivity and hyper-personalization, redefining how individuals perceive and interact with environments both tangible and digital. Pinterest's spaces are not hyper-personal, but rather generic and flattened. Devoid of bodies, nights, and cluttered imperfections, as the boundaries between real and simulated experiences blur within these hyper-interiors, they construct not only aesthetic inspiration but also political emotions, thoughts, and behaviors, shaping aspirational realities through the amalgamation of visual narratives meant to be purchased. In a telling metaphor of contemporaneity, there are progressively fewer pixels for non-marketable objects in Pinterest's hyper-interiors. The mobile phone carries a second home, a network of contingent futures in a transportable window where humans are linked with spaces virtually consumed, eternally diurnal, bodyless, buyable, and generic.

Analysis conducted as part of the *Theory of Mediated Spaces* module
HEAD – Genève (HES-SO). Spring Semester 2024
Professor: Javier Fernández Contreras
Data Analytics (BA students in Interior Architecture):
  —Oh Joy!: Benjamin Dohollou, Tiago Dos Santos Pinto, and Carla Ferey
  —Poppytalk: Bryan Jefferson Reyes, Anna Smiian, and Kateryna Sushynska
  —Maryann Rizzo: Norah Pittet, Zoé Mettraux, and Luca Negro
  —Cathie Hong: Cléa Bertossa, Aurore Biache, and Alexia Dahman
  —Jane Wang: Missilia Mendy, Elise Mathis, and Marie Mamou Blanché
  —HonestlyWTF: Mireille Gidi, Hippolyte Giraud, and Ambre Gravina
  —Bonnie Tsang: Martin Annen, Nassim Baron, and Giona Leo Baumann
  —Pejper: Alexis Lang, Manon Lebon, and Maelle Mabru
  —Mamas Uncut: Jiwon Juk, Yan Vasquez, and Nina Wallimann

Notes

1 Jean Baudrillard, *Simulacra and Simulation*, trans. Sheila Faria Glaser (Ann Arbor: The University of Michigan Press, 1994), 17. First published in French as *Simulacres et Simulation* (Paris: Éditions Galilée, 1981).

2 Amanda Hoover, "Pinterest Is Having a Moment: Millennials May Have Popularized Pinterest, but Gen Z Is Pushing the Platform to New Heights," *Wired*, December 14, 2023 (accessed July 28, 2024), https://www.wired.com/story/pinterest-gen-z-future/

3 "Pinterest," *Wikipedia*, last edited on July 19, 2024, 18:40 (UTC), https://en.wikipedia.org/wiki/Pinterest

4 In 2016, the "Pin it" button but was renamed "Save" owing to international expansion, making the site more intuitive to new users.

5 As of July 2024, the most-followed Pinterest accounts were: Wattpad: 32.5 million followers; Oh Joy!: 15.1 million followers; Poppytalk: 10 million followers; Tasty: 10.3 million followers; Etsy: 9.7 million followers; Maryann Rizzo: 9 million followers; Behance: 8.7 million followers; Mamas Uncut: 8.5 million followers; Cathie Hong: 7.9 million followers; Jane Wang: 7.7 million followers; Shein: 7.6 million followers; HonestlyWTF: 7.2 million followers; Bonnie Tsang: 7 million followers; Evelyn: 6.8 million followers; and Pejper: 6.7 million followers. This chapter focuses on accounts originally created by individual influencers rather than by companies or enterprises.

6 Jean Baudrillard, *Simulacra and Simulation*, 3.

7 Since 2018, *Forbes* has regularly published essays on the economics of hyper-personalization. See, for instance: Tomoko Yokoi, "Getting Started in Hyper-Personalization," *Forbes*, March 2, 2021 (accessed July 28, 2024), https://www.forbes.com/sites/tomokoyokoi/2021/03/02/getting-started-in-hyper-personalization/

8 "The app also brings a more visual alternative to traditional search. Some Gen Z-ers are ditching Google, substituting the search engine by browsing on TikTok, Instagram, and now Pinterest." Amanda Hoover, "Pinterest Is Having a Moment."

9 In 2017, Pinterest removed the post "liking" feature as it seemed redundant to "boards." Users' existing indexes of liked posts were converted into a collection ("board") named as such.

10 Shirin Izadpanah, "Evaluating the Role of Pinterest in Education and the Profession of Interior Architecture," *Idil Journal of Art and Language*, no. 10 (87) (2021), 1559–1572, https://doi.org/10.7816/idil-10-87-01

11 Beatriz Colomina, "Enclosed by Images: The Eames' Multimedia Architecture," *Grey Room*, no. 2 (2001), 5–29.

12 Mariabruna Fabrizi, "The Knowledge Box by Ken Isaacs (1962)," *Socks*, May 2, 2016 (accessed July 28, 2024), https://socks-studio. com/2016/05/02/the-knowledge-box-by-ken-isaacs-1962/

13 "Timeline of Pinterest," *Wikipedia*, last edited on July 4, 2023, 10:00 (UTC), https://en.wikipedia.org/wiki/Timeline_of_Pinterest

14 "Gen Z is our fastest growing audience, making up 42% of our global user base. (…) Audience composition: 70% females 18+; 28% males 18+." Pinterest Business, "Your audience is here. And they're ready to shop" (accessed July 28, 2024), https://business.pinterest.com/en-gb/audience/

15 Bianca Bosker, "How People You've Never Heard of Got to Be the Most Powerful Users on Pinterest," *Wired*, December 19, 2014 (accessed July 28, 2024), https://www.wired.com/2014/12/how-people-youve-never-heard-of-got-to-be-the-most-powerful-users-on-pinterest/

16 Many Pinterest celebrities, like Oh Joy! and Bonnie Tsang, regularly update details of their personal lives on their dedicated websites and blogs. This integration of their private sphere into their public online personas also traverses the domestic, with their houses regularly at the center of their communication strategy.

17 Mamas Uncut. Description of the company on Pinterest, July 2024 (accessed July 28, 2024), https://www.pinterest.com/mamasuncutmain/

18 MAIO, "The Diffuse House," *e-flux Architecture*, January 2021 (accessed July 28, 2024), https://www.e-flux.com/architecture/confinement/373338/the-diffuse-house

19 Pinterest Business, "Your audience is here."

20 Peter Sloterdijk, *In the World Interior of Capital: Towards a Philosophical Theory of Globalization*, trans. Wieland Hoban (Malden, MA: Polity, 2013). First published in German as *Im Weltinnenraum des Kapitals. Für eine Philosophische Theorie der Globalisierung* (Frankfurt: Suhrkamp, 2005).

21 MAIO, "The Diffuse House".

22 Alex Heath, "Pinterest wants to be a search company, so it's putting search front and center," *Business Insider*, July 31, 2017 (accessed July 28, 2024), https://www.businessinsider.com/pinterest-wants-to-be-a-search-company-evan-sharp-2017-7

23 Ibid.

4
TIKTOK: VERTICAL EDITING

*Javier Fernández Contreras, Camille Bodin,
Annie Bornet, and Taiana Broillet*

The thirty most-watched videos posted by the ten most-followed
accounts worldwide in 2022

Note: Data as of April 2023

Khabane Lame
23 years old
Italian/Senegalese
Follower count: 155.5 million
Content type: Comical sketches
105 videos in 2022

Charli D'Amelio
18 years old
American
Follower count: 150.2 million
Content type: Dance
342 videos in 2022

Denarie Taylor/Bella Poarch
26 years old
American
Follower count: 92.9 million
Content type: Gaming, cosplay, synchronized facial expressions
121 videos in 2022

Addison Rae
22 years old
American
Follower count: 88.8 million
Content type: Dance
158 videos in 2022

Zachary Michael King
33 years old
American
Follower count: 74.1 million
Content type: Magic, illusion
47 videos in 2022

Kimberly Guadalupe Loaiza Martinez
25 years old
Mexican
Follower count: 73.5 million
Content type: Dance
657 videos in 2022

Dixie D'Amelio
21 years old
American
Follower count: 57.3 million
Content type: Dance
209 videos in 2022

Spencer Polanco Knight
31 years old
American
Follower count: 55.3 million
Content type: Beatboxing
41 videos in 2022

Loren Gray

20 years old
American
Follower count: 54.4 million
Content type: Dance
134 videos in 2022

Michael Le/Justmaiko

23 years old
American
Follower count: 52.1 million
Content type: Dance, challenges
80 videos in 2022

Total Statistics

(all videos)
84% indoors
74% domestic
79% daytime
69% one body
Average percentages for full video length

Analysis conducted as part of the *Theory of Mediated Spaces* module
HEAD – Genève (HES-SO). Spring Semester 2023
Professor: Javier Fernández Contreras
Data Analytics (BA students in Interior Architecture):
    —Camille Bodin, Annie Bornet, and Taiana Broillet

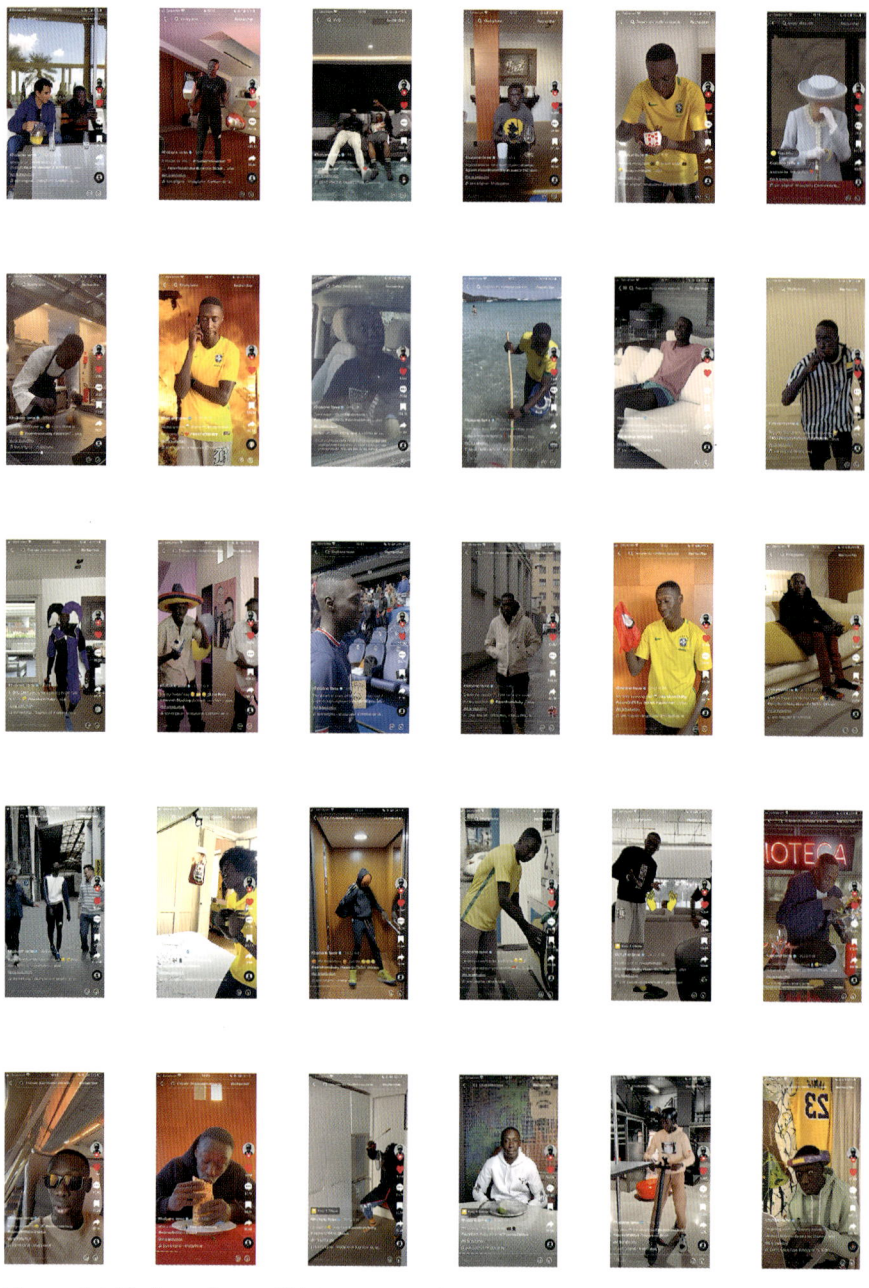

Figure 4.1 Khabane Lame. Thirty most-watched videos posted on his TikTok account in 2022: 63% indoors; 53% domestic; 73% daytime; 20% (exclusively) one body; for full video length

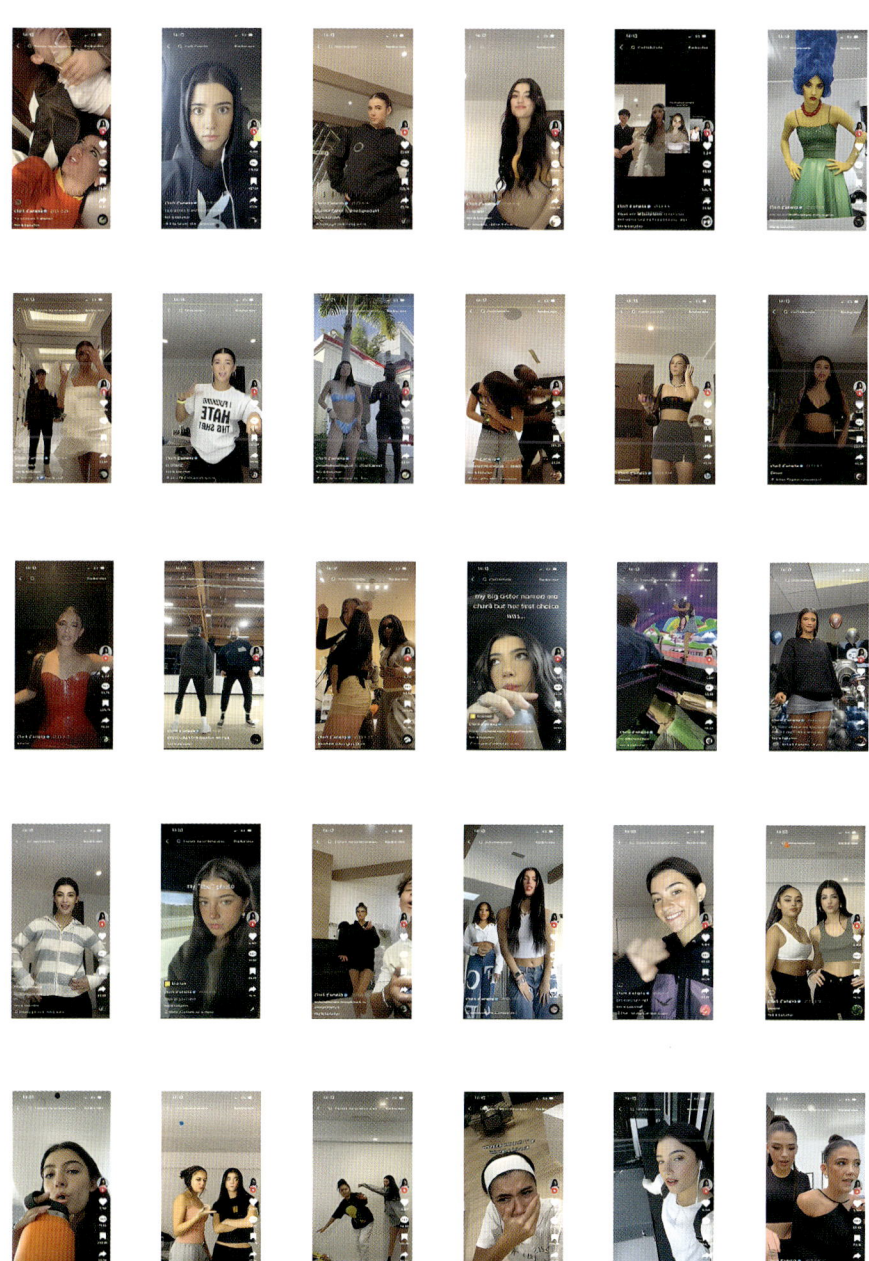

Figure 4.2 Charli D'Amelio. Thirty most-watched videos posted on her TikTok account in 2022: 94% indoors; 50% domestic; 47% daytime; 44% (exclusively) one body; for full video length

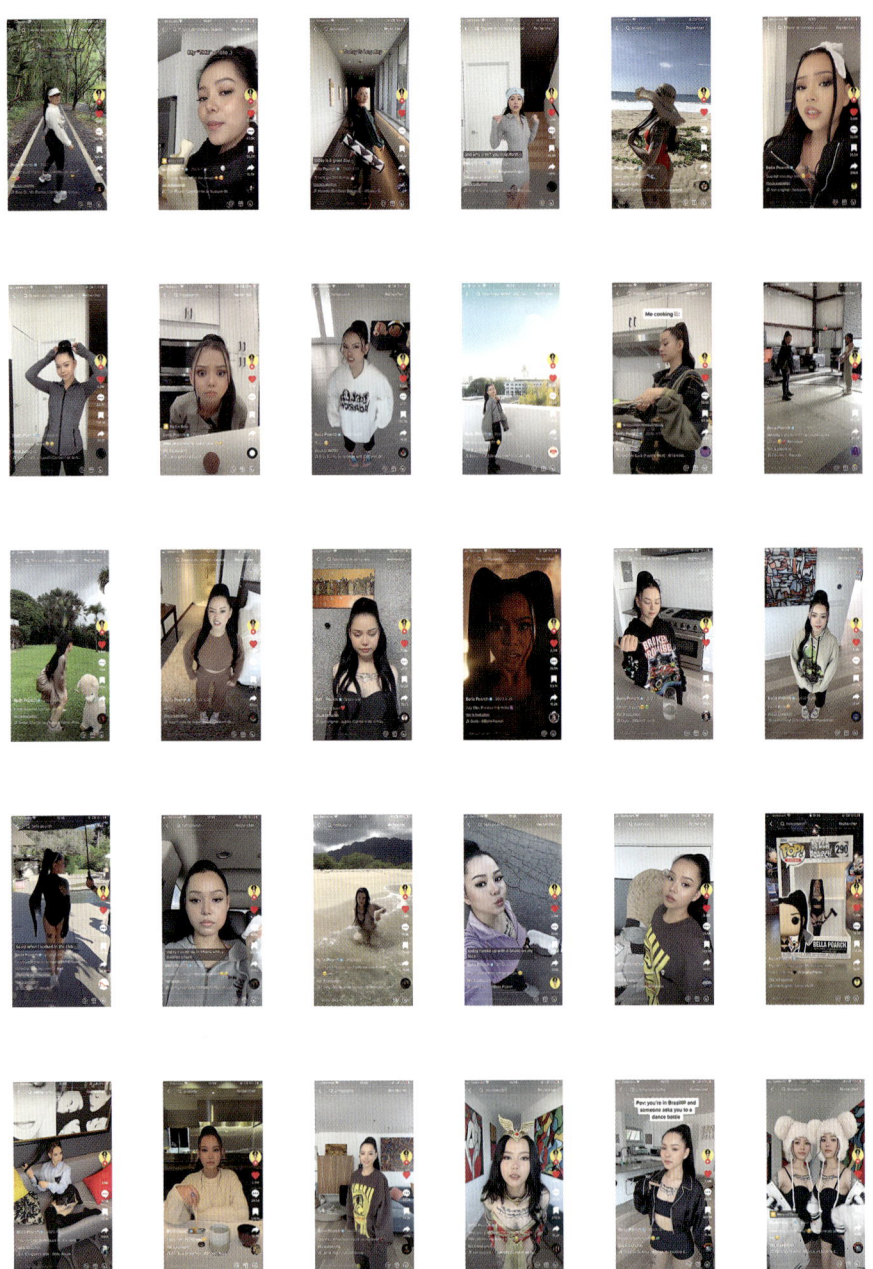

Figure 4.3 Denarie Taylor/Bella Poarch. Thirty most-watched videos posted on her TikTok account in 2022: 66% indoors; 56% domestic; 66% daytime; 73% (exclusively) one body; for full video length

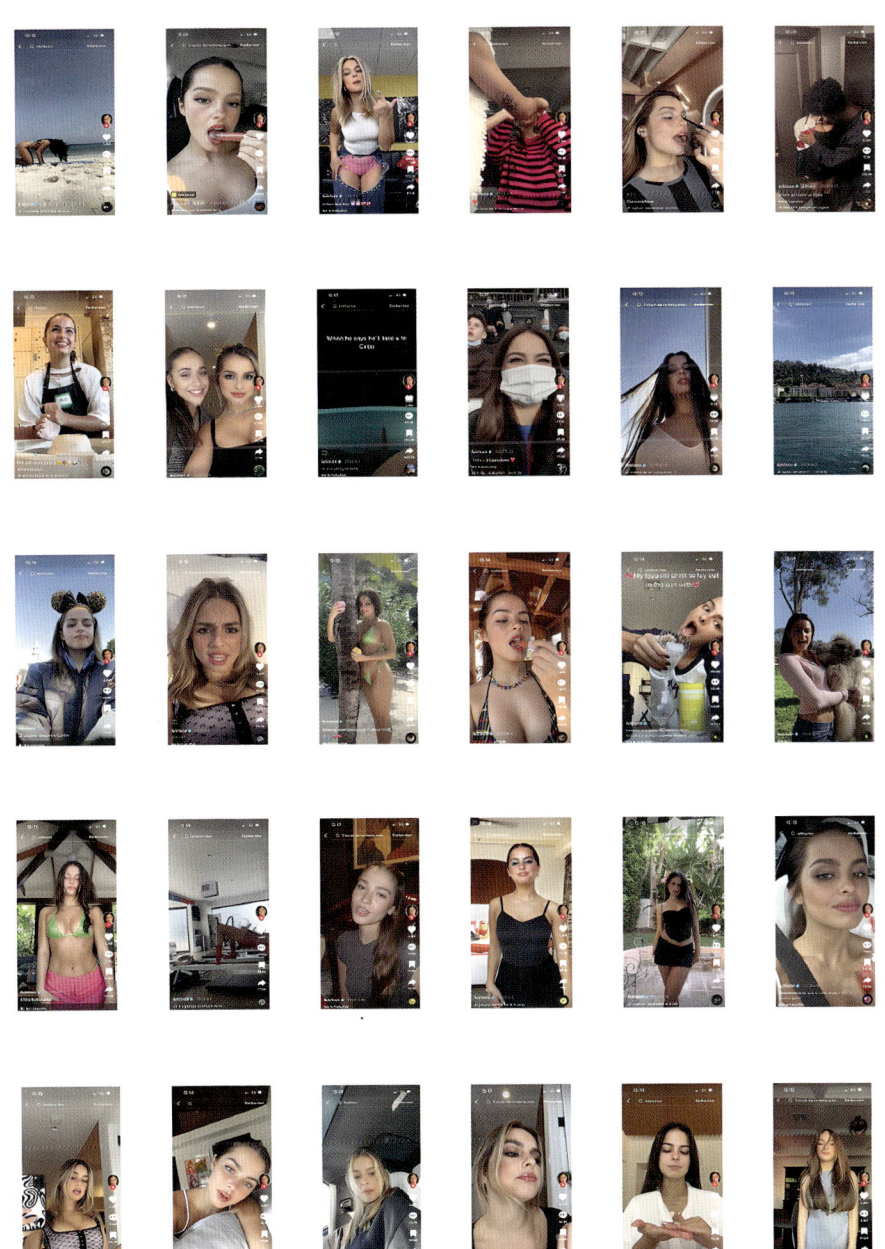

Figure 4.4 Addison Rae. Thirty most-watched videos posted on her TikTok account in 2022: 64% indoors; 24% domestic; 74% daytime; 77% (exclusively) one body; for full video length

Figure 4.5 Zachary Michael King. Thirty most-watched videos posted on his TikTok account in 2022: 40% indoors; 54% domestic; 76% daytime; 23% (exclusively) one body; for full video length

Figure 4.6 Kimberly Guadalupe Loaiza Martinez. Thirty most-watched videos posted on her TikTok account in 2022: 70% indoors: 100% domestic: 86% daytime: 50% (exclusively) one body; for full video length

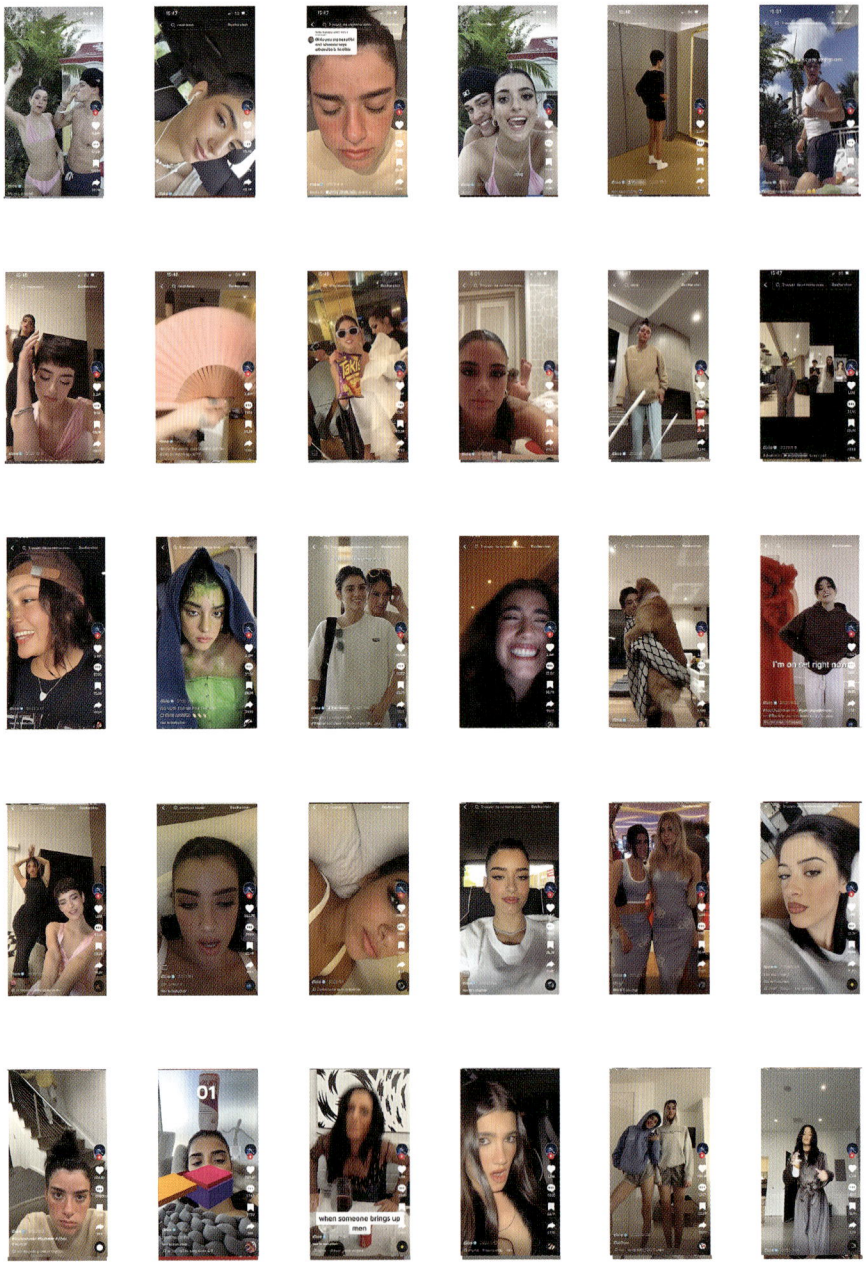

Figure 4.7 Dixie D'Amelio. Thirty most-watched videos posted on her TikTok account in 2022: 90% indoors; 50% domestic; 40% daytime; 40% (exclusively) one body; for full video length

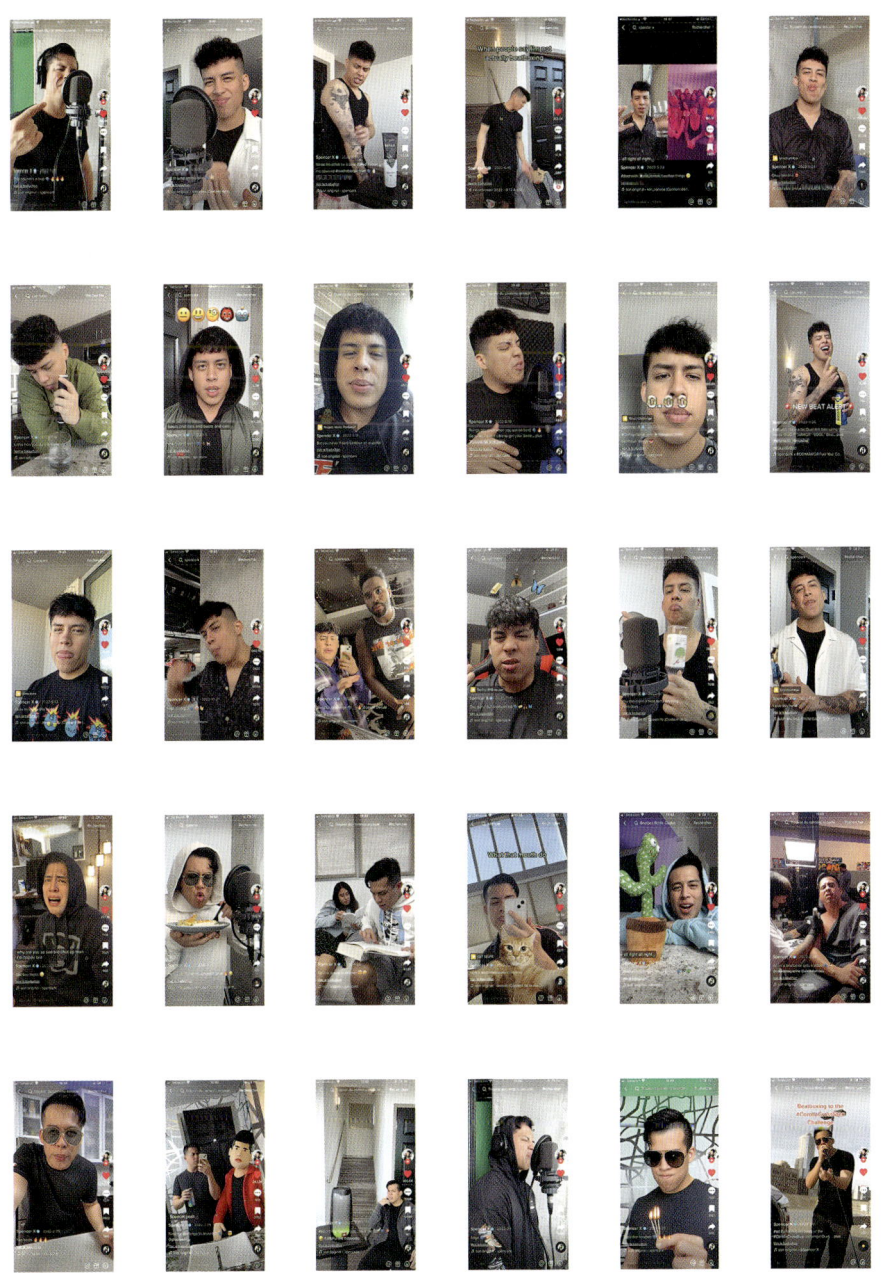

Figure 4.8 Spencer Polanco Knight. Thirty most-watched videos posted on his TikTok account in 2022: 96% indoors; 93% domestic; 83% daytime; 73% (exclusively) one body; for full video length

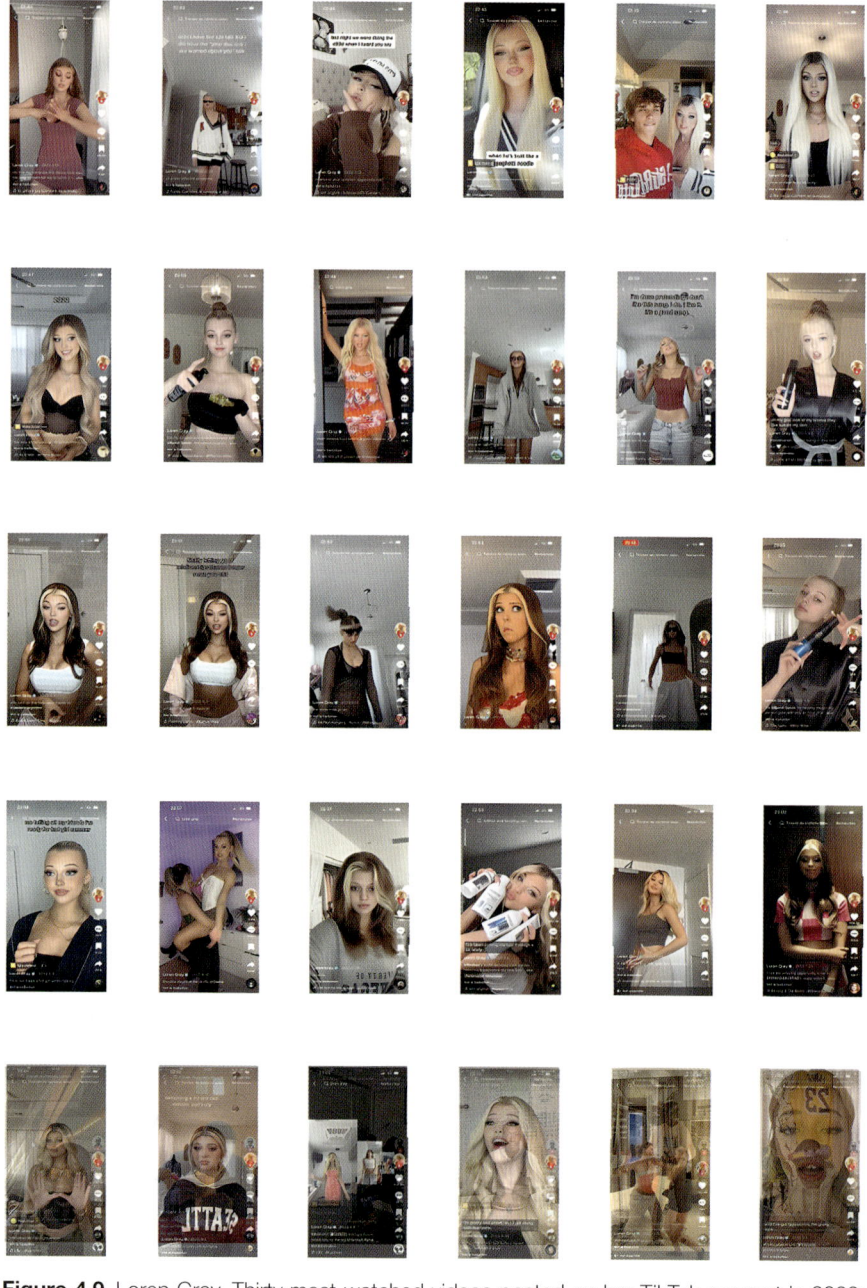

Figure 4.9 Loren Gray. Thirty most-watched videos posted on her TikTok account in 2022: 86% indoors; 90% domestic; 76% daytime; 73% (exclusively) one body; for full video length

Figure 4.10 Michael Le/Justmaiko. Thirty most-watched videos posted on his TikTok account in 2022: 90% indoors; 90% domestic; 63% daytime; 37% (exclusively) one body; for full video length

5
ARCHITECTURE, HUMANITARIANISM, AND SOCIAL MEDIA

*Javier Fernández Contreras and
Damien Greder*

In 1855, Roger Fenton, widely considered the first war photographer, covered the Crimean War for four months. Constrained by the technical limitations of the medium, his images were staged independently, with an exposure time of fifteen seconds each.[1] Today, civilians can livestream the daily impact of war, conflicts, and humanitarian crises. Pictures are created not only by external journalists but also directly by those involved. Equipped with a smartphone and internet access, victims also serve as *de facto* reporters. Social media is transforming the public's relationship with humanitarianism in two opposing but complementary ways. First, it is doing so through the standardization of global attention, as crises in local geographies are consumed globally through posts with similar imagery. Second, it is relocating architecture as a place of situated asymmetries, displaying spatial tectonics as props in constructing power, violence, resistance, or emancipation. In both cases, mobile phones foster mediated empathy by bringing viewers closer to the embodied experiences of victims. Unlike external reporters, civilians use smartphones to create real-time images and videos. This shift emphasizes bodies in space as expressions of suffering, relief, or resilience, where architecture is neither neutral nor uninvolved. At the same time, algorithms act as gatekeepers, often

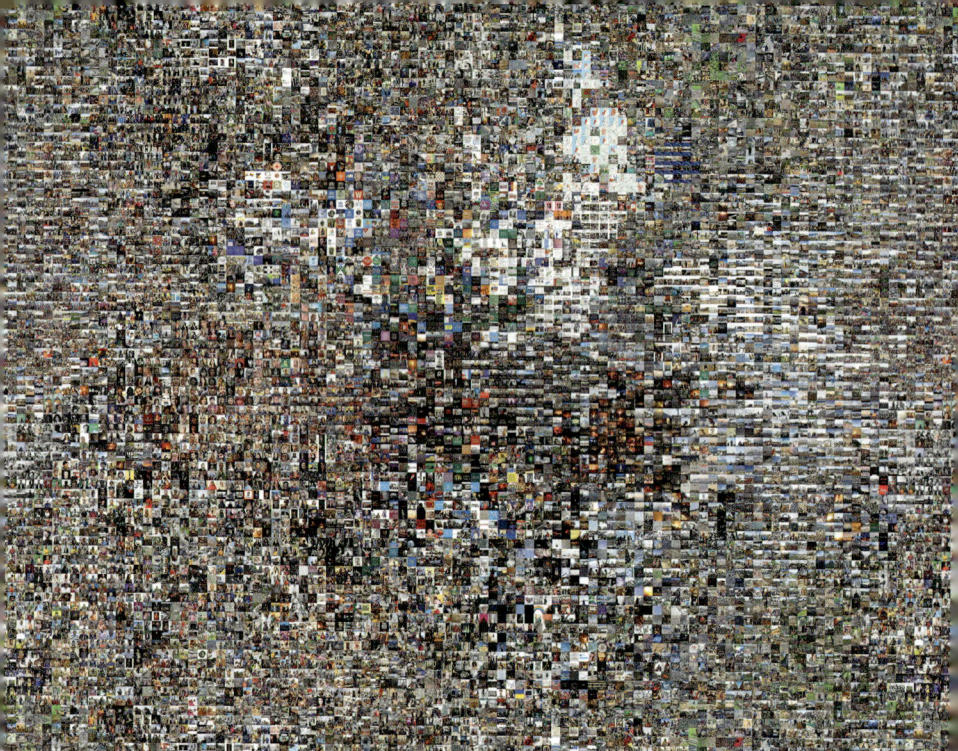

Figure 5.1 Self-organizing map based on the 7,559 images collected on social media platforms through October 2024. © Samuel Jaccard

operating as black boxes that can trigger new biases, such as the diffusion of a single, normalized version of conflicts.

The change brought about by digital imagery in the history of humanitarianism parallels previous paradigm shifts, from Robert Capa's frontline photography during the Spanish Civil War to American televised portrayals of the Vietnam War and, more recently, the use of social media in the 2023 Gaza War. As CNN reported in January 2024, "Palestinians are documenting the war for millions on social media. Their followers have come to see them as family."[2] If news feeds have recently seen a surge in conflict-related content, this crisis highlights the role of online social networks in shaping public perceptions of humanitarianism, which now appears alongside personal content—from friends' photos to influencers' posts. Examining less-publicized crises is therefore crucial to understanding new representations within the broader history of humanitarian imagery. Analyzing various sites of violence, conflict, and displacement—ranging from Ukraine and South

Figure 5.2 Global humanitarian images. Exterior spaces in 5,653 of the images collected from social media platforms through October 2024

Sudan to the Darién Gap and Bangladesh—and considering diverse perspectives, from international reporters and non-governmental organizations (NGOs) to local organizations and individuals (often victims), can reveal how social media is transforming contemporary perceptions of humanitarianism and architecture.

Genealogy of Humanitarian Imagery

The words "image," "imagination," and "imaginary" share an intricate genealogy, all deriving from the Latin *imago* (meaning picture, copy, likeness).[3] Historically, images have been produced and interpreted within specific social and geographic contexts. According to the philosopher Chiara Bottici, "[w]hereas the imagination tends to be conceived as a faculty that we possess as individuals, the concept of social imaginary is meant to encompass significations within which individuals are socialized and that thus precede the formation of individuals themselves."[4] In the context of humanitarianism, media scholar Lilie Chouliaraki coined the term "humanitarian imaginary" to refer to the "configuration of practices which use the communicative

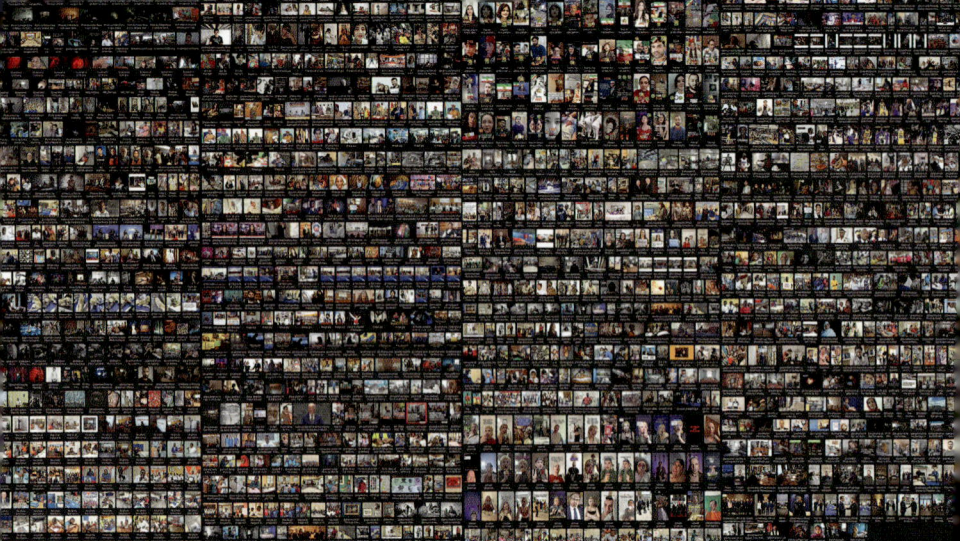

Figure 5.3 Global humanitarian images. Interior spaces in 1,446 of the images collected from social media platforms through October 2024

structure of the theatre in order to perform collective imaginations of vulnerable others in the West, with a view to cultivating a longer-term disposition to thinking, feeling, and acting towards these others."[5]

In other words, humanitarian images are constructed and evolve structurally according to the expectations and values within which they are intended to be interpreted. While Chouliaraki's concept refers to the cultural stages through which distant suffering is represented and made intelligible to Western audiences, the broader term "imagery" denotes the multiple representations used to evoke empathy and prompt action. This results in a corresponding political evolution of this gaze, alongside the historicity of image production, its techniques, and its modes of consumption, where any categorization is both ontological and chronological. Five evolutionary categories can be identified here: *narration*, *denunciation*, *activism*, *provocation,* and *participation*, suggesting that social media, as a form of online participation, has inaugurated a new iteration in recent decades. These categories are not strictly sequential but often overlap.

The genealogy of humanitarian imagery can first be traced back to its role in the narration of conflict. While Roger Fenton had to stage his photographs of the Crimean War (1853–1856) away from the battlefield, eighty years later, Robert Capa was able to capture the Spanish Civil War (1936–1939) with unprecedented immediacy and emotional depth from the frontline. This phase later evolved into what writer and critic Susan Sontag termed "tele-intimacy" during the Vietnam War (1955–1975), where the conflict penetrated viewers' daily lives through televised broadcasts.[6] The Gulf War (1990–1991) marked the culmination of this acceleration with CNN's live coverage, enabled by satellite transmission technology, itself becoming the object of journalistic debate.[7]

A second phase in the evolution of the humanitarian image unfolded through practices of denunciation. Works such as Jacob Riis's late-19th-century documentation of impoverished neighborhoods in New York (*How the Other Half Lives*, 1890), Walker Evans's focus on rural life during the Great Depression (e.g., *Let Us Now Praise Famous Men*, 1941), and Dorothea Lange's poignant portraits of migrants (e.g., *Migrant Mother*, 1936) sought to expose harsh realities and raise social awareness.

Third, from an activist perspective, the dissemination of pictures mobilized ideals of resistance. A major turning point in abolitionism, the political movement to end slavery and liberate enslaved individuals globally, came in the 1860s, when photographs such as *The Scourged Back* (1863)—depicting Gordon, an escaped slave from Louisiana, and taken by McPherson & Oliver—became powerful weapons in the visual arsenal of the movement. In the 20th century, Eglantyne Jebb's Save the Children campaign (founded in 1919) instrumentalized images of children to promote humanitarian objectives. The global utopia of collaboration reached its zenith with mass fundraising events like Live Aid (1985), which broadcast a problematic yet enduring narrative of suffering "through a technologized economy of pleasure."[8] Concurrently, individual action gained prominence, with Audrey Hepburn becoming the first UNICEF Goodwill Ambassador in 1988, embodying a personalized approach to humanitarian advocacy with celebrity status.

Conversely, humanitarian imagery also adopted critical standpoints in a fourth, provocative phase, directed both at its own principles and at a widespread social passivity. In this vein, the Colombian mockumentary *The Vampires of Poverty* (1977), by Luis Ospina and Carlos Mayolo, helped popularize the term "pornomiseria" (the practice of turning poverty into spectacle, indifferent to human suffering), by parodying misery shots alongside the "making of" of their staging. In a reverse register, transforming reality into advertising, photographer Oliviero Toscani's campaigns for Benetton in the 1990s were characterized by provocative and controversial images—drawing on themes such as

Figure 5.4 Global humanitarian images. Subject: group of people in 3,212 of the images collected from social media platforms through October 2024

AIDS, racism, war, and the death penalty—and aimed at questioning political issues and mobilizing broader communication channels. In the 21st century, Anne Poiret's documentary *Welcome to Refugeestan* (2017) adopted a confrontational standpoint by exposing the harsh reality of refugee camps as highly controlled, bureaucratic spaces resembling sprawling, prison-like zones, challenging viewers to confront the dehumanizing global refugee management system.

Finally, the proliferation of internet access and online platforms in recent decades has ushered in a participatory construction of humanitarian imagery. The coverage of Hurricane Katrina in 2005 marked a turning point as journalists, unable to report directly from the ground, relied heavily on weblogs, forums, and other tools to gather and share news.[9] This broad decentralization has become the norm today, at least in conflicts that attract global interest. Yet, a further evolution has recently emerged, with a computer-generated image, *All Eyes on Rafah* (2024), being re-shared more than 50 million times through social media. On the one hand, it amplified global attention on these narratives, drawing viewers closer to an anticipated escalation of the crisis. On the other hand, the visualization of a standardized and abstracted refugee camp obscured the impressive number of testimonies shared by Palestinians on the ground.[10]

Building on this apparent contradiction, the following section examines the most recent participatory phase of humanitarian imagery by exploring other conflicts that have yet to attract significant attention, aiming to assess the effects of globalized proximity enabled by social media.

Local Geographies, Global Posts

The humanitarian crises analyzed here were selected for their diversity in both geographic and societal terms, as well as for their entanglement with a range of political, economic, and ecological issues. These include natural disasters, such as the earthquakes in Haiti in 2010 and 2017; resistance movements against human rights violations, particularly those affecting women in Afghanistan and Iran; and armed conflicts, such as the war in Ukraine following the Russian invasion, and the development of the Israel–Lebanon conflict since October 2023. In addition, internal displacements in the Democratic Republic of the Congo (DRC) and Sudan are studied, along with transnational migrations spanning geographies as diverse as the West Sahel and the Darién Gap on the border between Colombia and Panama. The analysis also includes a comparative study of refugee camps with global significance, from Moria-Mavrovouni in Greece to Dadaab in Kenya and Kutupalong in Bangladesh, the largest refugee camp in the world.

From a methodological standpoint, the most active accounts producing humanitarian content were analyzed according to geographic area and platform. Most of the profiles studied come from Instagram, although in certain regions, other platforms such as Facebook, X, TikTok, and YouTube predominate, and these are also examined in detail. Using material available up to October 2024, all visual content related to humanitarianism was collected from each profile. In total, more than 7,000 images were gathered, corresponding to twelve different crises and originating from more than two hundred accounts ranging from large organizations and government entities to anonymous civilians or influencers dedicated to sharing humanitarian content. All this material was analyzed and classified according to criteria linked to media construction, including spatial dynamics (indoors/outdoors), subject representation (individual/group), point of view (aerial/eye-level), and circadian rhythm (day/night).

Figure 5.5 Global humanitarian images. Subject: individual subject in 1,691 of the images collected from social media platforms through October 2024

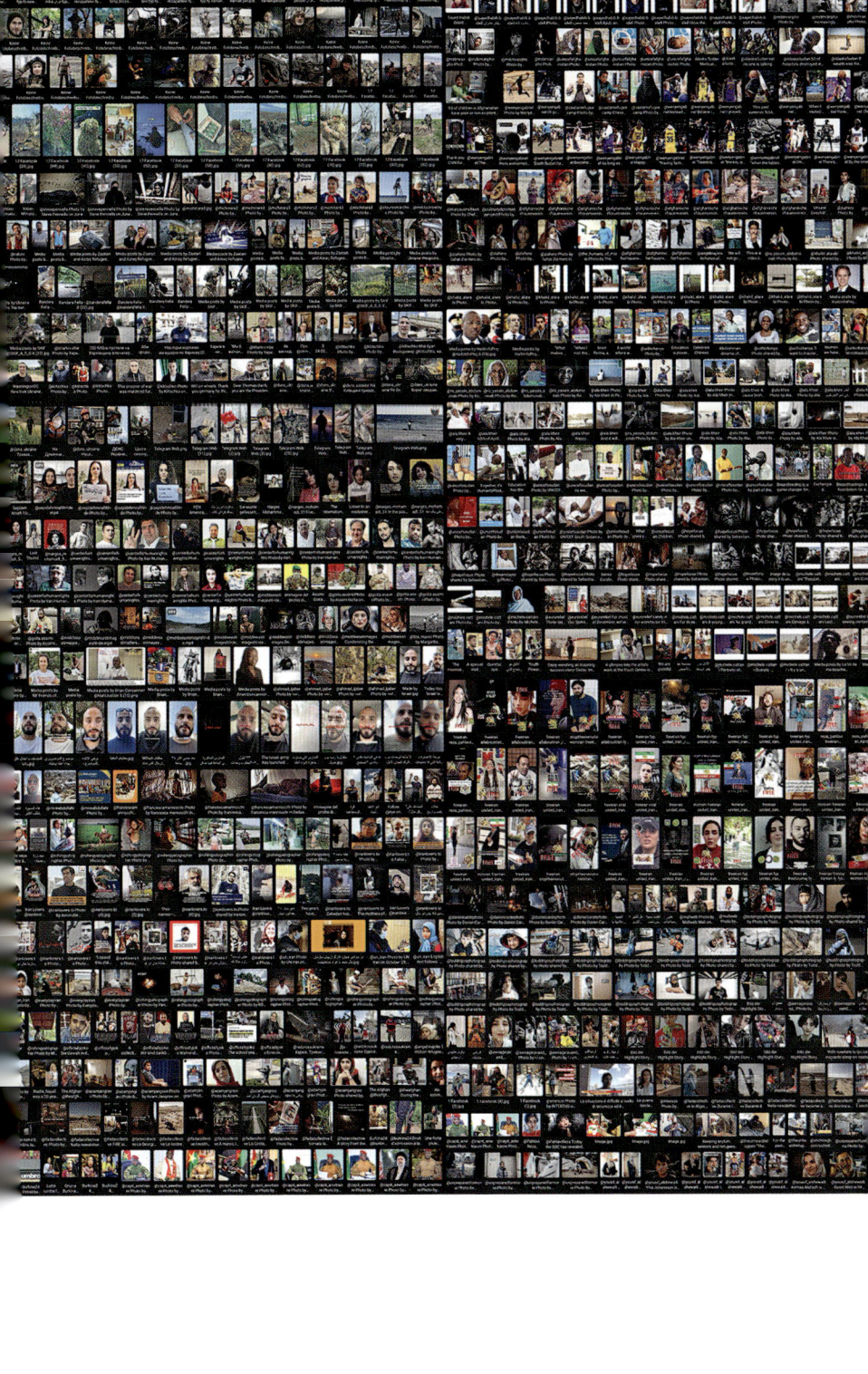

Figure 5.6 Global humanitarian images. Viewpoint: eye level in 5,470 of the images collected from social media platforms through October 2024

The accounts were also analyzed by comparing content per publisher type—posted by local organizations and users (often victims) vs. international institutions and individuals (often celebrities)—to understand the perspectives and situated knowledge shaping the production of discourses. This categorization explores whether global social media posts uniformize the perception of humanitarian emergencies by following the same codes dictated by organizations, or whether the content created by individuals results in a more local, nuanced, and sensitive portrayal of each situation. The initial quantitative analysis is subtle, showing a certain uniformization of the images published when considering most content. The subjectivities theoretically mobilized in social media are very much standardized. In other words, within each criterion, the tendencies in terms of majority lead toward a uniformization of the content.

An analysis of the images per publisher type—International Individual, International Organization, Local Individual, and Local Organization— reveals that the presence of the human body is the most unifying aspect of humanitarian images (individual: 22%; group: 43%; cumulative: 65%), with only 35 percent being bodyless—pictures that typically feature either architectural ruins or aerial views. Portraits—either locals reporting first-hand testimonies from specific sites or politicians speaking from international political arenas—are used as a mechanism for constructing mediated trust, whereas selfies often confront viewers with images of suffering, denunciation, or resilience where the human is depicted to

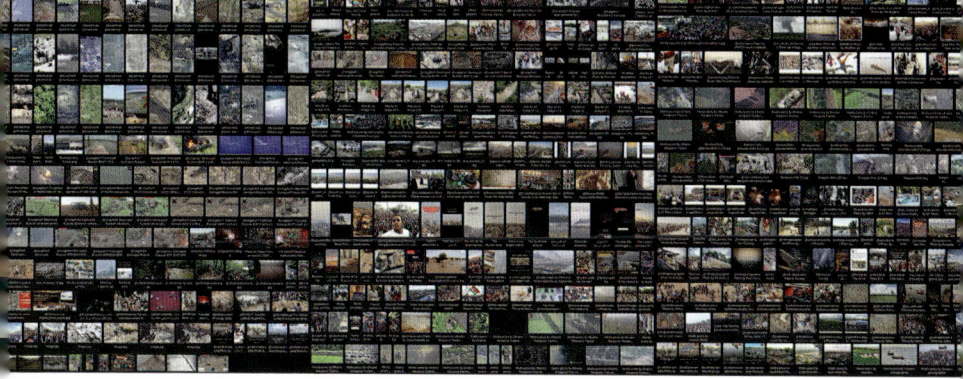

Figure 5.7 Global humanitarian images. Viewpoint: bird's-eye view in 595 of the images collected from social media platforms through October 2024

literally convey embodied messages. Meanwhile, group pictures regularly emphasize processes of displacement, construction, eating, or military resistance, in which the focus is on the action.

If we reconstruct the average humanitarian picture, it is in color (97%), taken from an eye-level point of view (83%), and shared by a local source (organization: 35%; individual: 33%; cumulative: 68%). This suggests that the images produced by witnesses are multiple and diverse, enacted en masse on-site by local entities, potentially opening up alternative narratives. Additionally, the typical humanitarian image features a group of people in an exterior space (67%) during daytime (93%).[11] However, such an exact "average" combination is rare, with only twenty pictures of the total sample precisely matching this set of criteria. Looking at a more granular level, it is possible to identify crises that diverge from the average image. Four are significant, for reasons that can be interpreted in relation with the particularity of each crisis: portraits within interiors in Iran; landscape views in the Darién Gap; bird's-eye views in Ukraine; and nocturnal images in Lebanon.

While humanitarian crises mostly attract attention with group pictures in external public spaces, Iran's case, on the contrary, mobilizes interior space as a setting where a single human body stands for resistance. What might typically occur outdoors—an environment neither inclusive nor safe enough for political action—moves into the ubiquitous private rooms of buildings, which are no longer mundane, anonymous spaces but instead become shelters for free speech.

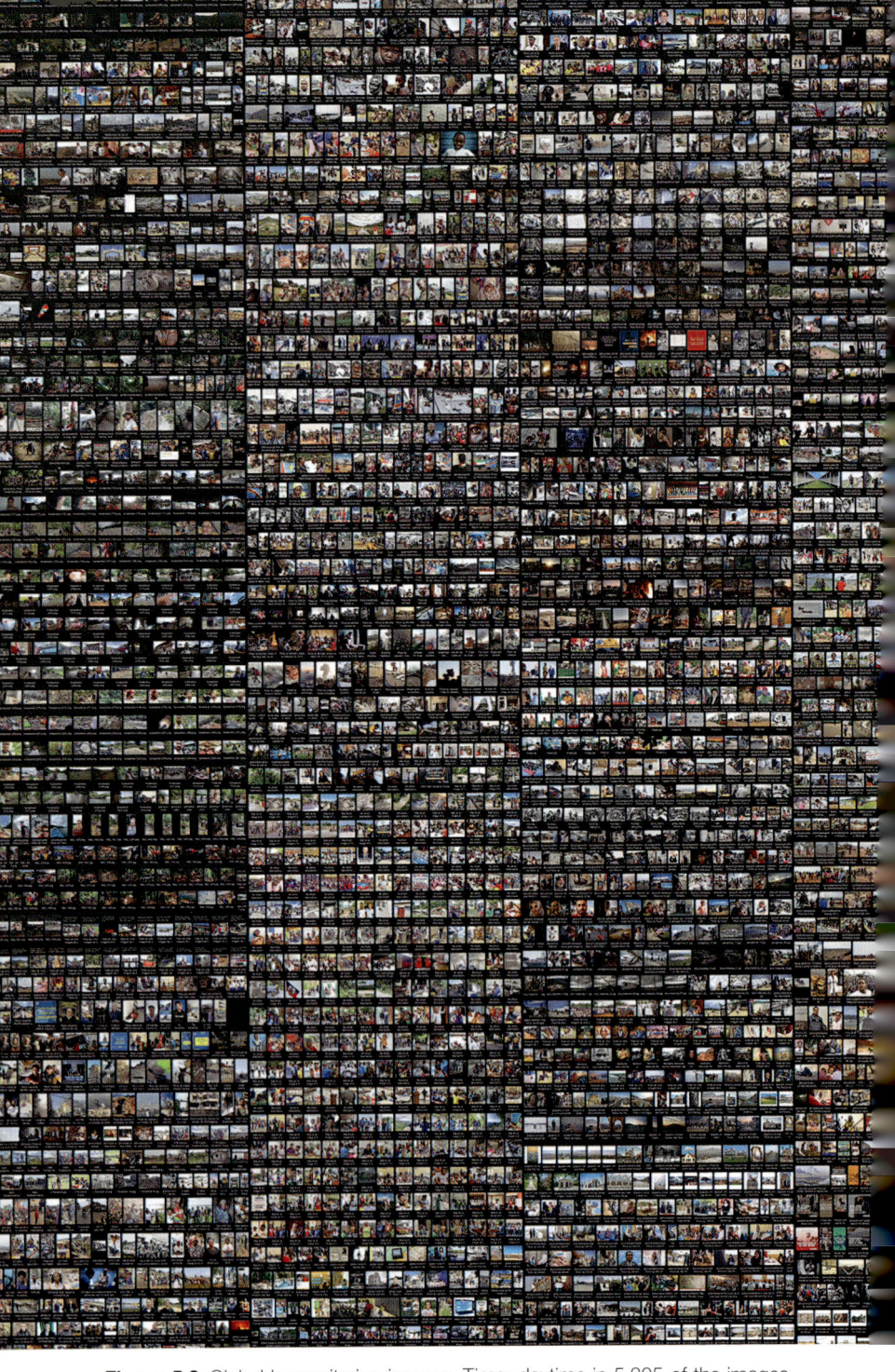

Figure 5.8 Global humanitarian images. Time: daytime in 5,305 of the images collected from social media platforms through October 2024

Figure 5.9 Global humanitarian images. Time: nighttime in 374 of the images collected from social media platforms through October 2024

While most images are divided between interior and exterior spaces, the jungle spanning the border between Colombia and Panama constitutes a different form of open-air interiority. Despite its recognized degree of peril, the Darién Gap has been crossed by over 700,000 people since early 2023.[12] This is reflected in image collections in two ways. First, pictures are mainly taken within a landscape context (49%). Second, a significant amount of data comes from international individuals—mostly YouTubers,[13] who document this problematic journey under questionable video titles such as "I Was Trafficked Through the World's Deadliest Jungle." This migration crisis was also the one most identified on YouTube, suggesting that the defined nature of the migrant's journey through the jungle is a good fit for the vlogging format.

Humanitarian narratives are mainly constructed from eye level, the most repeated viewpoint across all accounts, comprising 87 percent of all the images analyzed. This reinforces the sense of visual empathy, putting both communicators and viewers literally on the same level, with pictures often taken from smartphones. As an exception, in Ukraine, many posts on social media reflect the recent use of first-person view drones in warfare. Pictures captured with a bird's-eye perspective (21%) document Russia's numerous invasions in Ukraine and relate to the

Figure 5.10 Average humanitarian picture (diurnal, group-based, color photograph, eye-level perspective, shared by a local organization or individual) in twenty representative examples from the dataset of 7,559 images collected on social media platforms through October 2024

aesthetic of drone snapshots. In those cases, passive viewers scrolling through their device screens follow the active position of the drones on the battlefield.

Finally, the humanitarian image is mainly diurnal, with nocturnal shots accounting for less than 10 percent of images from most locations, except for Ukraine and Lebanon. This is related to the difficulty of accessing certain areas, such as refugee camps, at night, which might also create legal invisibilities. The absence of nocturnal representation in the humanitarian image is perpetuated or even reinforced on social media. As an exception, Israeli attacks over Lebanon are depicted in two unusual ways, primarily through ruins and explosions registered during nighttime (22%) and without human figures (69%). This could reflect not only the time of the bombings that the country faced, but also the urbicidal nature of the conflict. The shift from micro to macro scales

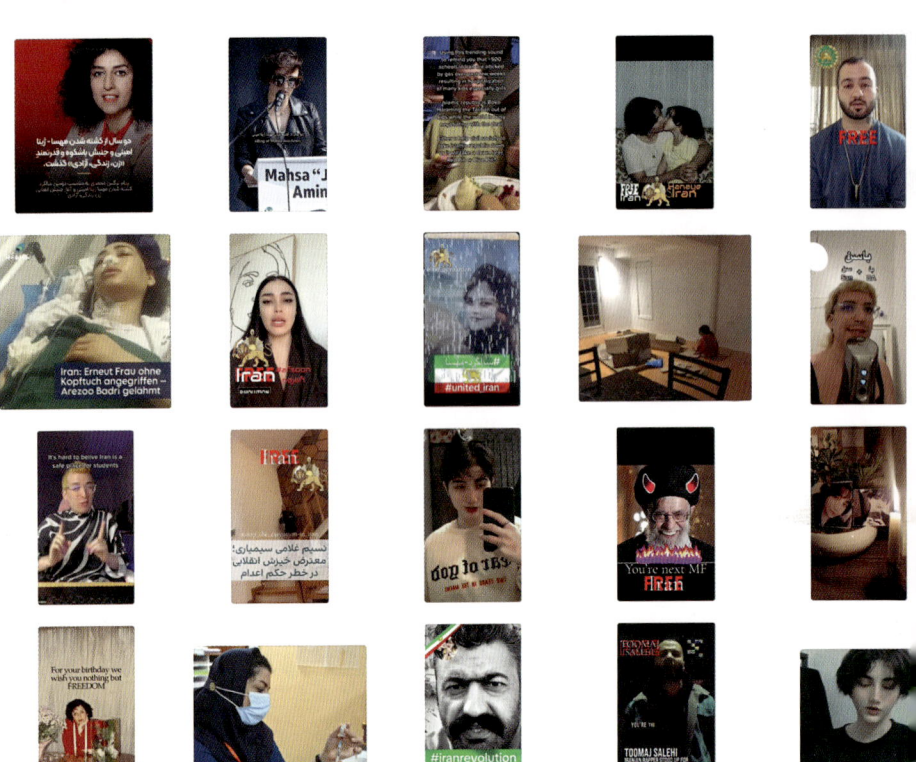

Figure 5.11 Iran. Portraits within interiors. Posts through October 2024

of destruction highlights a transition from personal to collective narratives, illustrating different levels of engagement with the war and making visible the night as a time of legal obscurity.

Mediated Constructions: Architecture as Situated Asymmetry

If social media can flatten the perception of humanitarian crises worldwide, architecture becomes a mediated territory that situates the asymmetries of space, its tectonics, and its politics. Across Afghanistan, Iran, the DRC, and the West Sahel, social media visualizes the gendered usage of space, exposing the deeply entrenched patriarchal norms within these humanitarian crises. Image analysis reveals how interior

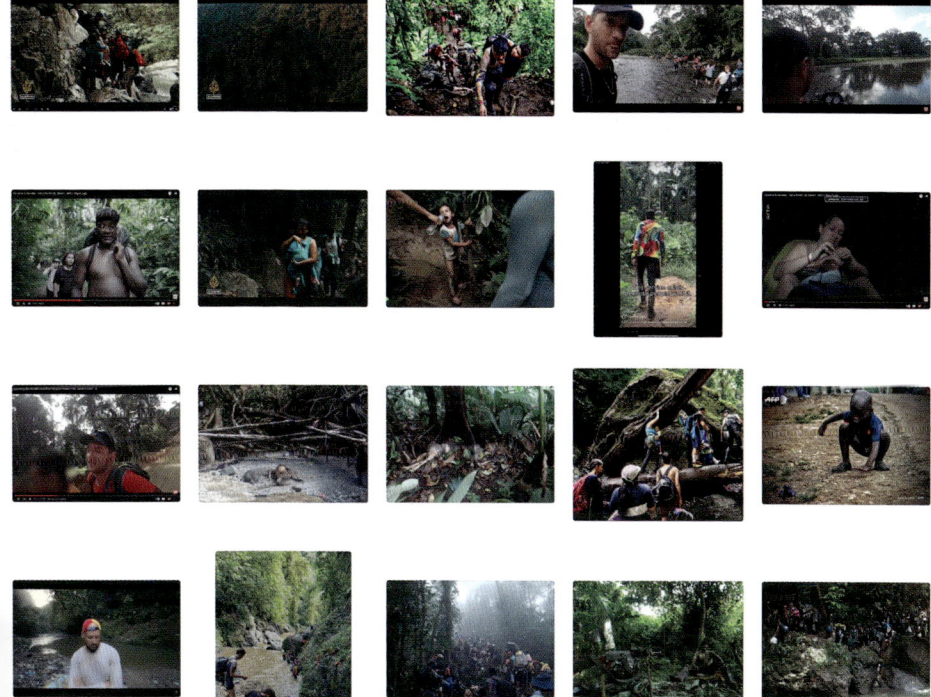

Figure 5.12 Darién Gap. Landscape views. Posts through October 2024

and exterior spaces are utilized to reinforce societal power structures and how visual representations of these spaces become political statements in themselves.

In Afghanistan, the divide between men's dominance of open, prestigious public spaces and women's confinement to interior settings like homes and hospitals highlights cultural and religious restrictions. Women's visibility is largely confined to domestic or controlled spaces, while men occupy scenes of authority in exteriors, such as conference rooms or sports fields, underscoring a social structure that prioritizes male freedom and female seclusion. This situated dynamic reflects how space reinforces authority, confining women's identities and movements under the strictures of Sharia law.

In Iran, similar gendered divisions manifest, especially through social media images from protests following Mahsa Amini's death in 2022, which saw women harness public spaces as sites of defiance. By

Figure 5.13 Ukraine. Bird's-eye views. Posts through October 2024

exposing their hair or using elevated urban props like cars and platforms, they transformed exterior spaces into powerful arenas of resistance against state-imposed morality laws, contrasting sharply with controlled indoor spaces used to display memorials or portraits of detained individuals. These visual expressions politicized exteriors as zones of collective defiance, while interiors reflect, still today, restrained forms of remembrance, directing attention toward global audiences as a more confined means of protest.

Alternatively, in the DRC and the West Sahel, architecture is gendered not only by the interior–exterior divide but also by the tectonics of public–private spaces, with public buildings typically constructed from solid materials like concrete and brick, and private, domestic settings often built from informal, tent-like materials whose physical lightness reflects the legal and material fragility of their inhabitants. In the DRC's Goma region, men are often depicted in concrete buildings associated with diplomacy or healthcare, while women and children appear in ephemeral,

Figure 5.14 Lebanon. Nocturnal images. Posts through October 2024

tent-like shelters, which underscores their precarious existence amid resource conflicts. Here, men's occupancy of stable structures reinforces perceptions of authority, whereas women are visualized in makeshift settings, symbolizing instability and ongoing struggles for basic security within the area's political and humanitarian crises.

In the West Sahel, the gendered use of space is visually marked by humanitarian imagery, where women are shown indoors with children, depicted through carefully styled representations of suffering and resilience. Men appear predominantly outdoors in scenes that convey action and authority, whether in roles of protection or combat, aligning with societal norms that position them as protectors and women as vulnerable. In the Sahel, interiors appear as spaces of emotional depth, where women are reduced to symbols of endurance amid displacement, while men's portrayal in outdoor settings suggests agency and control. Across these regions, the visual framing of architecture on social media perpetuates stereotyped gender roles, using interior and exterior spaces

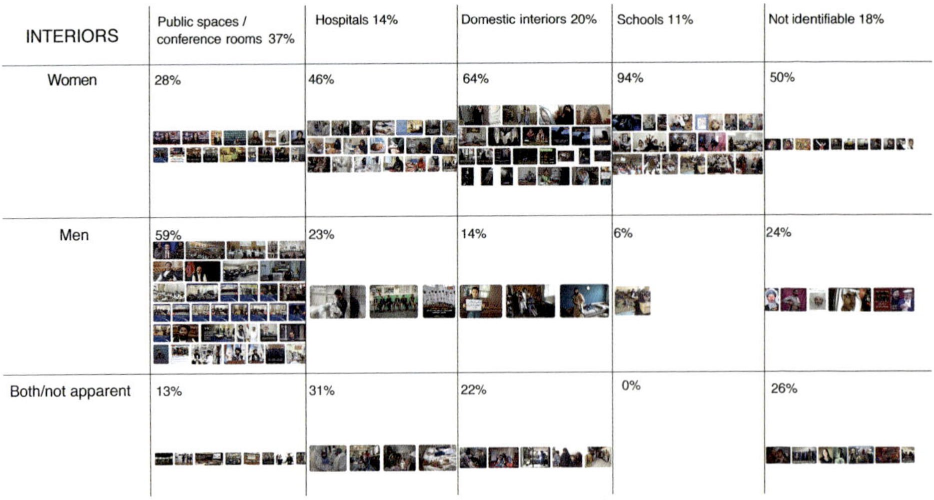

INTERIORS	Public spaces / conference rooms 37%	Hospitals 14%	Domestic interiors 20%	Schools 11%	Not identifiable 18%
Women	28%	46%	64%	94%	50%
Men	59%	23%	14%	6%	24%
Both/not apparent	13%	31%	22%	0%	26%

Figure 5.15 Afghanistan. Gendered interiors. Data visualization from social media posts through October 2024

to portray power, vulnerability, resistance, and restriction, ultimately either reinforcing societal norms or, occasionally, using these portrayals as a medium for political messaging.

In other locations, social media exposes the evolving nature of camps, transitioning from provisional to semi-permanent settlements that, paradoxically, become permanent places of transience. If, as suggested by architectural theorist Andrew Herscher, the "refugee camp is the normative form of humanitarian architecture,"[14] then it can be argued that social media platforms allow us to examine and question its constructed normalization, as both physical and temporal ethos. Online content reveals the temporary nature of spaces and the architectural constraints within the Dadaab refugee camp in Kenya, the Moria and Mavrovouni camps in Lesvos, Greece, and the Kutupalong camp in Bangladesh, as well as in the context of the Sudanese civil war. Images of the Dadaab camp found on Instagram—captured by international organizations, photographers, and journalists—document the overcrowded, structurally inadequate shelters initially built as temporary housing. Individuals' accounts reveal lightweight constructions like wood-frame and fabric tents, which persist as primary dwellings despite Dadaab's prolonged existence. Although some structures are built with brick and concrete, housing public facilities like

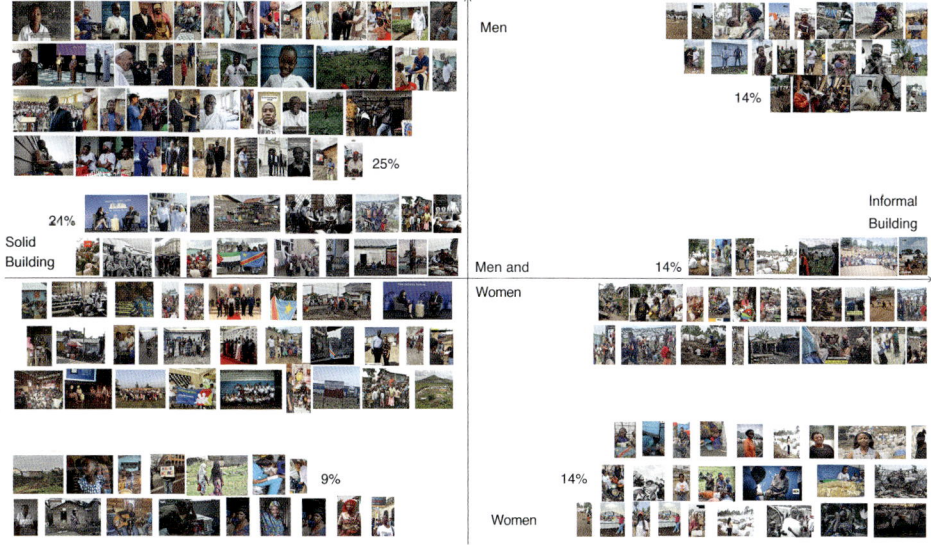

Men   14%

25%

24%

Solid Building

Informal Building

Men and Women   14%

9%   14%

Women

Figure 5.16 DRC. Gendered spaces. Data visualization from social media posts through October 2024

schools and administrative offices, such distinctions highlight the disparity in living conditions within the camp's physical hierarchy, underscoring the stark difference between refugee accommodations and institutional spaces.

On the Greek island of Lesvos, Instagram data reflects the precarious and transitory architecture of refugee camps. The documentation presents a sequence beginning with the Moria camp, destroyed by fire in September 2020 and permanently closed, and continuing with the forced relocation of the population to Mavrovouni, conceived as a temporary facility but remaining in operation. The images reveal a progression from improvised tents to more stable shelters with metal structures, simultaneously expressing both institutional efforts to stabilize conditions and the inherent temporariness of the camp's logic. The abundance of records in open spaces and the predominance of daytime shots emphasize the limited visibility of private and enclosed areas, underscoring both the exposure and vulnerability of residents and the infrastructural constraints.

Similarly, the humanitarian crises in the Rohingya camps in Bangladesh and in the Sudanese civil war shed light on the role of architecture in contexts of precarity and displacement. Analyzed content from Instagram, Facebook, YouTube, and X, relating to the Kutupalong

Figure 5.17 Dadaab camp, Kenya. Places of transience. Data visualization from social media posts through October 2024

camp, home to more than 600,000 Rohingya, predominantly features eye-level photographs, aiming to emphasize personal connections and the human experience of the camp. This perspective invites viewers to engage with narratives of resilience and adaptation, highlighting the multifunctionality of improvised structures and open-air environments, which often serve as spaces for education, cooking, and community hygiene. For instance, plastic coverings not only provide shelter but also function as surfaces for drying food (fish and vegetables), collecting rainwater for showers, and other uses, reflecting a fragile resilience.

In contrast, visual documentation of the Sudanese conflict—particularly on Instagram—presents a raw depiction of daily life amid turmoil. Outdoor environments illustrate the programmatic reality of conflict, with activities ranging from protest demonstrations to the search for and distribution of water. Displacement and flight from violence appear as recurring themes, and in moments of pause, trees emerge as a distinct local motif within the conflict. The practice of gathering under a tree—representing 10 percent of the total analyzed content—takes shape as a public space is transformed into a community

Figure 5.18 Moria–Mavrovouni camps, Greece. From left to right: Progression from improvised tents to stable shelters. Posts through October 2024

hub for rest and food preparation, as well as the setting for a political act of socialization, resistance, and online communication.

While camps and temporary settlements traverse contemporary humanitarian crises, a different, complementary narrative emerges in contexts where the city is transformed into a battlefield and its ruins are mediatized as stages of suffering and resistance. The difference between the portrayal of ruins in the Ukrainian war and the Israel–Hezbollah conflict in Lebanon illustrates the complex interplay between social media platforms and the narratives that emerge from warfare. In Ukraine, platforms such as Instagram, X, and Telegram facilitate a multifaceted portrayal of buildings. Categorizing architecture into three primary states—destroyed, ruined, and intact—provides insight into the functional status of architectural remnants. On social media, 35 percent of private buildings shown in Ukraine have been destroyed, while public

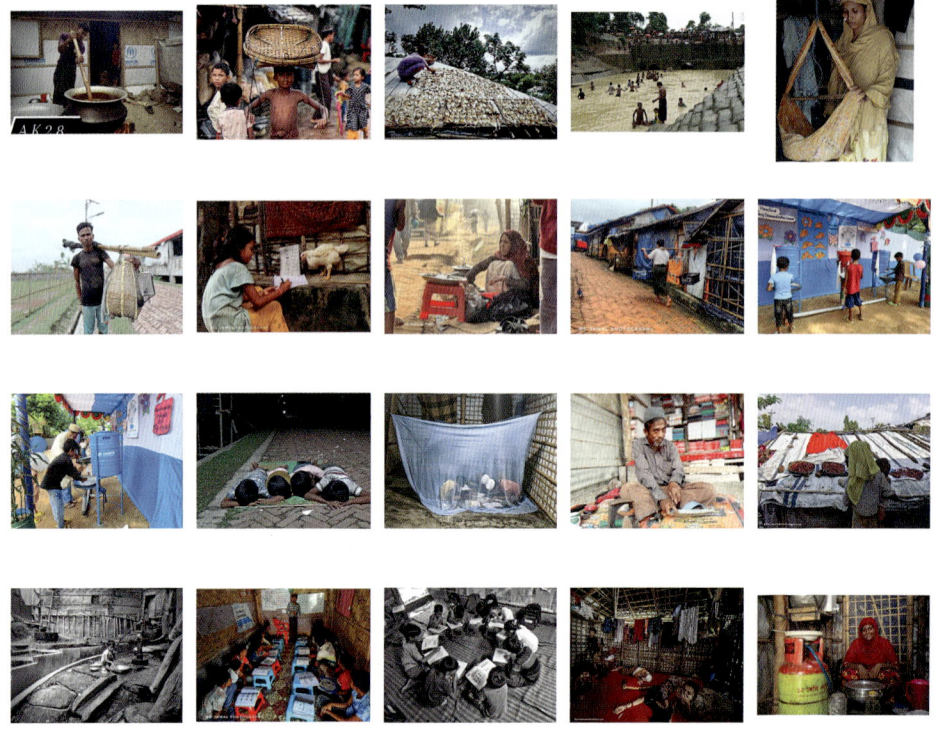

Figure 5.19 Kutupalong camp, Bangladesh. Narratives of resilience. Posts through October 2024

structures have suffered less, indicating a stark dichotomy in vulnerability based on ownership and usage. Most pictures focus on exteriors of both public and private buildings. Public interiors remain mostly intact, which might have to do with the fact that the majority of images taken in these settings depict meetings and greetings between the President and other important politicians. In contrast, pictures of private interiors account for less than 10 percent of the total—a fact that can be attributed to the extensive bombing of private buildings, rendering them too damaged to be photographed from the inside. This focus on exteriors reflects a narrative that prioritizes public resilience over the intimate suffering of individuals, thereby shaping public perception of the conflict.

In Lebanon, between September and mid-October 2024, Israel launched a massive offensive against Hezbollah—first with electronic explosions, then with large-scale bombings, and finally with a ground invasion. Here, the representation of the ruins was likewise mediated by social media platforms such as X, YouTube, and Twitch, which emphasized the architectural destruction through hashtags like #destroyed and #bombing. Approximately 60 percent of the analyzed images fall under these tags, revealing a fascination with spectacle and the dramatic effects of warfare. The analysis indicates a transition from macro narratives of urban destruction to micro representations of intimate, personal loss, with 80 percent of images devoid of human figures. This lack of human presence underscores a tendency to abstract the ruins from their socio-cultural contexts, producing a generalized image of devastation that prioritizes visibility over depth of understanding. Lebanon illustrates how, in some contexts, social media asymmetries reflect platform-specific focuses, audience dynamics, and technological affordances. In South Lebanon, distinct war narratives emerge across platforms. YouTube and Twitch, for instance, feature continuous landscape footage along the Lebanon–Israel border. By contrast, Instagram and X emphasize war-focused information-sharing, with local accounts editing content more heavily than broader, international ones.

Platform-specific narratives can also be observed in the context of the Haiti crisis. In the case of earthquakes, the dataset covers events from the first quake in 2010 up to the present, allowing for an analysis of how humanitarian crisis coverage has evolved over time. During this period, Facebook became established as a key platform for both local and international actors in disseminating humanitarian content, focusing on group-based humanitarian work in facilities such as community centers, schools, and hospitals. In contrast, Twitter/X offered a more institutional representation, focusing on political figures, news, and diplomatic meetings. Meanwhile, Instagram presented a more visually artistic lens, blending humanitarian content with creative expressions to offer a personalized and aestheticized portrayal of the crisis. These asymmetrical portrayals underscore the power of social media in shaping global crisis narratives, as they mediate visibility and emotional resonance, and ultimately influence international solidarity and response.

Finally, the Darién Gap stands out as a unique case of infrastructure, which has become a mediatized and commodified migration route. Migrants from South America, Europe, and Asia traverse this perilous

Displacement	Food / Water	Education
19%	23%	8%

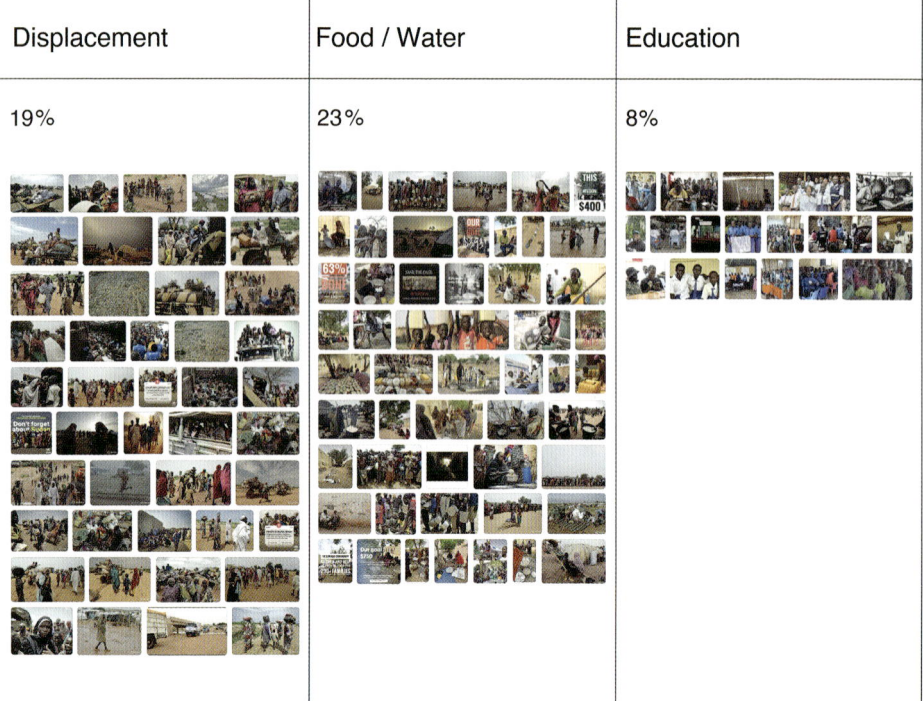

Figure 5.20 Sudan. Activities amid the crisis. Data visualization from social media posts through October 2024

jungle en route to the United States and Canada, often documenting their journeys on social media. This content exposes a growing economy surrounding the route, with influencers offering varied portrayals. An analysis of images across Instagram, Facebook, and YouTube categorized areas as commodified, decommodified, or infrastructure-absent. The emerging economy divides into formal infrastructures like monetized refuges and transportation services, and informal ones such as makeshift shelters and improvised paths. Informal structures highlight migrants' resilience in dangerous conditions. About 50 percent of the analyzed images show unstructured areas where migrants avoid authorities, while 31 percent depict decommodified resources like free shelters. Meanwhile, 19 percent feature commodified services, revealing a growing market for essential goods. These findings raise questions about how social media amplifies commodification and influences migrant experiences—simultaneously offering support and exposing them to exploitation.

Demonstration	Other activities
17%	33%

Humanitarian Images and Architectural Narratives: Future Directions

The visualization of distant suffering—analyzing how emotions such as empathy or spectators' consumption shape interaction on the other side of the screen—was described, long before its institutionalization on the internet, by intellectuals such as Susan Sontag and Luc Boltanski.[15] However, the critical re-evaluation of how crises are mediatized through architectural images on social media highlights the interrelationship between spatial representation, digital circulation, and the affective economies of distant suffering. This new scenario demands a deeper inquiry into how architectural structures—relentlessly circulating across online platforms—become visual indicators of resilience, vulnerability, or political neglect.

Figure 5.21 Haiti. Humanitarian images. Platform-specific focus: Facebook: group-based humanitarian work; X: institutional representation; Instagram: artistic storytelling, independent projects. Dat visualization from social media posts through October 2024

A comparative analysis of different geographic contexts shows that these representations are not neutral: they reaffirm gender asymmetries, make material inequalities visible, and consolidate hierarchies of power inscribed in spaces. Social media formulates a humanitarian cartography that moves between intimate suffering and macropolitical narratives: from the domestic interiors that circumscribe female presence in Afghanistan and Iran, and the ruins of Ukraine and Lebanon, turned into emblems of resilience or collective devastation, to the refugee camps of Dadaab and Kutupalong, which oscillate between transience and permanence. Architecture ceases to be a mere backdrop and becomes an active agent in the visual construction of contemporary humanitarianism, where the ethics of framing and the politics of space are inseparable.

The ceaseless proliferation of images generated by millions of users is producing a new pictorial and spatial topology that is iteratively

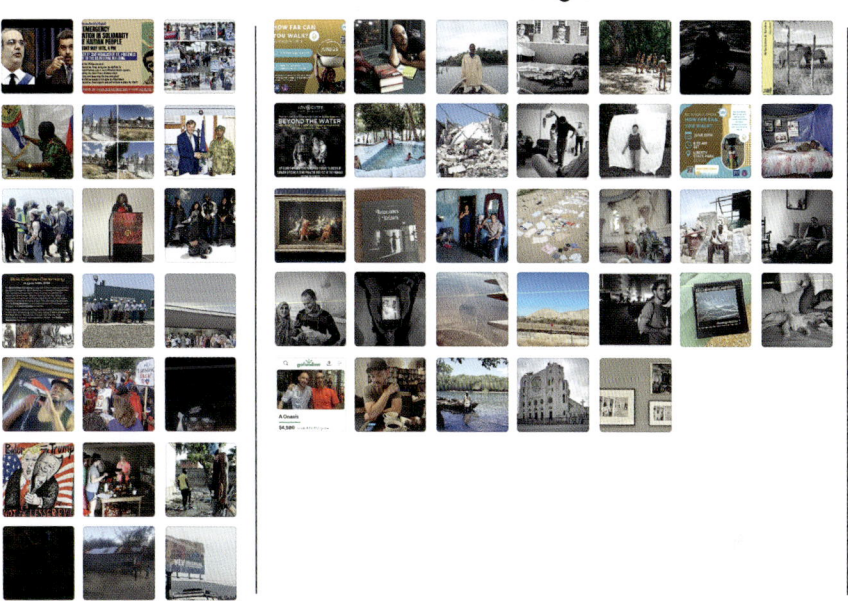

reconstituting the humanitarian imagery of crisis zones through networked acts of framing and filming. In this scenario, and in those to come, the performative labor that victims and survivors carry out to manage their suffering as digital content calls for urgent critique. It raises questions about the ethics of testimony, the instrumentalization of authenticity, and the extent to which architecture, as a mediated artifact, participates in negotiating recognition, aid, affective investment, and political legibility within the global humanitarian landscape.

Region	Account name	Description	Publisher type	Platform	Followers
Afghanistan	The Afghan	Activist	Local Individual	Instagram	294,000
Afghanistan	Sayed Habib Bidell	Photographer	Local Individual	Instagram	11,700
Afghanistan	Afghanischer Frauenverein e.V.	Nonprofit	International Organization	Instagram	17,200
Afghanistan	Angelina Jolie	Celebrity	International Individual	Instagram	15,300,000
Afghanistan	Unicef afghanistan	Local Branch	International Organization	Instagram	126,000
Afghanistan	OCHA Afghanistan	Local Branch	International Organization	Instagram	221
Afghanistan	Afshinismaeli	Journalist	International Individual	Instagram	129,000
Afghanistan	Qasim Mirzaie	Photographer	Local Individual	Instagram	5,565
Afghanistan	RukshanaMedia	News	Local Organization	X	146,000
Afghanistan	BBCYaldaHakim	Journalist	International Individual	X	374
Afghanistan	DrSimasamar	Political/Activist	Local Individual	X	41,700
Afghanistan	AhmadShuja	Activist	Local Individual	X	47,300
Afghanistan	ShaharzadAkbar	Activist	Local Individual	X	174,800
Afghanistan	TOLOnews	News	Local Organization	X	1,600,000
Afghanistan	RAWA	Nonprofit	Local Organization	X	3,929
Bangladesh	ro_yassin_abdumonab	Photographer/Journalist	Local Individual	Instagram	2,957
Bangladesh	Ziahero	Photographer/Editor	Local Individual	Instagram	3,350
Bangladesh	Mdimranpho	Photographer/Editor	Local Individual	Instagram	2,163
Bangladesh	unhcr_bgd	Local Branch	International Organization	Instagram	3,707
Bangladesh	rohingyatographer	Photographers	Local Organization	Instagram	2,998
Bangladesh	UNHCR, the UN Refugee Agency	International Organization	International Organization	YouTube	196,000
Bangladesh	Mijanur32462757	Photographer	Local Individual	X	789
Bangladesh	RohingyaResp	Nonprofit	Local Organization	X	9,046
Bangladesh	Anuwar_Sadek47	Photographer	Local Individual	X	959
Bangladesh	rbhafizu	Photographer/Videographer	Local Individual	X	276
Bangladesh	mdhossain5101	Photographer	Local Individual	X	560
Bangladesh	ayubkhan_dkl	Artist	Local Individual	X	1,279
Bangladesh	Md Jamal Photography	Photographer	Local Individual	Facebook	8,200
Bangladesh	Myanmar Now - English Version	News	Local Organization	Facebook	186,000
Bangladesh	Largest Refugee Camp BD	Independent	Local Organization	Facebook	3,500
Colombia	Villalonsantamaria	Photographer	Local Individual	Instagram	4,707
Colombia	Manuelmonterrosa	Youtuber	Local Individual	Instagram	38,700
Colombia	Lynseyaddario	Photographer/Journalist	International Individual	Facebook	19,000
Colombia	Aljazeeraenglish	News	International Organization	Instagram	5,100,000
Colombia	Semana	News	Local Organization	Instagram	2,200,000
Colombia	Hias	Nonprofit	International Organization	Instagram	20,300
Colombia	Realbaldandbankrupt	Youtuber	International Individual	Instagram	370,000
Colombia	Timmy.karter	Youtuber	International Individual	Instagram	123,000
Colombia	Arte	News	International Organization	YouTube	3,780,000
Colombia	Al Bavers	Journalist	International Individual	Facebook	474
Colombia	Human Rights Watch	Activist	International Organization	Facebook	2,900,000
DRC	Focuscongo	Nonprofit	Local Organization	Instagram	101,000
DRC	Pappyorion	Videographer	Local Individual	Instagram	25,500
DRC	Gomactif	Activist	Local Organization	Instagram	11,800
DRC	Freecongodrc	Activist	Local Individual	Instagram	26,300
DRC	DRdenismukwege	Doctor/Nobel Peace Prize	Local Organization	Instagram	103,000
DRC	Philemon.barbier	Photographer/Journalist	International Individual	Instagram	2,340
DRC	Johnbehets	Photographer	International Individual	Instagram	7,539
DRC	Congolibarary	Nonprofit	Local Organization	Instagram	144
DRC	Ntibonerafoundation	Foundation	International Organization	Instagram	4,673
DRC	Isaac__jimmy	Journalist	Local Organization	Instagram	11,200
DRC	A.c.h65	Nonprofit	Local Organization	Instagram	1,683
DRC	Djuniomar	International Dancer	International Individual	Instagram	2,269
DRC	Juliah Muthoni	Activist	Local Individual	Facebook	3,998
DRC	Laurie Kelley	Public Person	International Individual	Facebook	1,200
DRC	PK Kabubu	Activist	Local Individual	Facebook	43
Greece	Silaszinder	Photographer	International Individual	Instagram	2,253
Greece	now_you_see_me_moria	Artist	Local Individual	Instagram	40,700
Greece	by.milene	Photographer	International Individual	Instagram	11,100
Greece	the_human_of_moria	Community	Local Organization	Instagram	5,566
Greece	aris.messinis	Photographer	Local Individual	Instagram	73,900
Greece	panagiotis_balaskas	Photographer/Journalist	Local Individual	Instagram	988
Greece	yousif_alshewaili	Journalist	International Individual	Instagram	11,700
Greece	unpreparedformoria	Book	Local Individual	Instagram	1,354
Greece	tita_mavro	Photographer	International Individual	Instagram	12,800
Greece	stichtingbootvluchteling	Nonprofit	International Organization	Instagram	5,992
Greece	theunheardrefugees	Community	Local Organization	Instagram	897
Greece	no.more.moria	Organization	Local Organization	Instagram	1,223
Greece	Drapen i Havet	Organization	International Organization	Facebook	30,000
Greece	toddrigosphotography	Photographer	International Individual	Instagram	3,261
Greece	Euro Relief	Nonprofit	Local Organization	Instagram	5,947
Haiti	Wyclef	Artist	Local Individual	X	36,000
Haiti	HaitiHumanitar1	Nonprofit	Local Organization	X	20
Haiti	HaitiInfoProj	News	Local Organization	X	34,600
Haiti	HaitiAction1	Activist	Local Organization	X	1,014
Haiti	USAID_Haiti	Local Branch	International Organization	X	107,500
Haiti	laloidemabouche	Activist	Local Individual	X	70,100
Haiti	Haitifutur75	Nonprofit	International Organization	Facebook	29,000
Haiti	missiontohaitiorg	Activist	International Organization	Facebook	3,800
Haiti	haiticommunitere	Nonprofit	Local Organization	Facebook	3,100
Haiti	ONUHaiti	Local Branch	International Organization	Facebook	5,400
Haiti	hopeforhaiti	Nonprofit	International Organization	Facebook	33,000
Haiti	alex.morel.01	Artist	International Individual	Instagram	487
Haiti	foh2010inc	Nonprofit	International Organization	X	552
Haiti	haitijustice	Activist	Local Individual	X	11,500
Haiti	CAREHaiti20	Nonprofit	Local Organization	Facebook	10,000
Iran	Everydayiran	Activist	Local Organization	Instagram	153,000
Iran	officiallyjoko	Public Person	Local Individual	Instagram	1,100,000
Iran	azamjangravi	Public Person	Local Individual	Instagram	9,888
Iran	un_iran	Local Branch	International Organization	Instagram	1,318
Iran	iranlovers.to	Activist	Local Organization	Instagram	9,350
Iran	awvageravand_	Activist	Local Individual	Instagram	15,000

Country	Name	Role	Classification	Platform	Followers
Iran	vahidmirzaeii	Photographer	Local Individual	Instagram	3,694
Iran	middleeastimages	News	Local Organization	Instagram	12,400
Iran	centerforhumanrights	Nonprofit	Local Organization	Instagram	47,000
Iran	narges_mohamadi_51	Public Person	Local Individual	Instagram	259,000
Iran	sepidehmoafi	Artist	Local Individual	Instagram	225,000
Iran	masih.alinejad	Journalist	Local Individual	Instagram	8,600,000
Iran	PahlaviReza	Crownprince	Local Individual	X	1,400,000
Iran	pasgad72	Influencer	Local Individual	TikTok	9,170
Iran	ozi_ozar	Activist	International Individual	TikTok	30,600
Jordan	Zaatari refugee camp	Nonprofit	Local Organization	Instagram	1,111
Jordan	Qs youth center	Nonprofit	Local Organization	Instagram	563
Jordan	Dream Day Foundation	Nonprofit	International Organization	Instagram	101
Jordan	Aziz Aldamkh	Influencer	Local Individual	Instagram	556
Jordan	Chef Mary Sue Milliken	Public Person	International Individual	Instagram	18,700
Jordan	Zaatari and Azraq Refugee Camps	Nonprofit	Local Organization	X	21,100
Jordan	Roberto Zichitella	Journalist	International Individual	Instagram	1,438
Jordan	Melissa Jun Rowley	Independent	International Individual	Instagram	86.7000
Jordan	Michelle Miller	Journalist	International Individual	Instagram	59,700
Jordan	Yoshitomo Nara	Artist	International Individual	Instagram	543,000
Jordan	Steve Pannells	Journalist	International Individual	Instagram	128,000
Jordan	UN refugee Agency	International Organization	International Organization	Instagram	2,000,000
Jordan	Ayman Halaseh	Activist	Local Individual	Instagram	293
Jordan	Alsarh Constructing	Private company	Local Organization	Instagram	199
Jordan	Anna Maria Corazza Bildt	Politician	International Individual	Instagram	1,415
Jordan	The United Nations Population Fund Office in Jordan	Nonprofit	Local Organization	X	4,057
Jordan	Official English account of the Saudi Press Agency	Press Agency	International Organization	X	102,800
Jordan	Embassy of France in Jordan	Embassy	International Organization	X	9,373
Kenya	UNHCRKenya	Local Branch	International Organization	Instagram	41,400
Kenya	Abdullahi Mire	Journalist	Local Individual	Instagram	8,585
Kenya	Francesca Mannocchi	Journalist	International Individual	Instagram	13,900
Kenya	The One Armed Chef	Photographer	International Individual	Instagram	15,000
Kenya	Kristin Davis	UNHCR Goodwill Ambassador	International Individual	Instagram	1,600,000
Kenya	Refugee Consortium of Kenya RCK	Nonprofit	Local Organization	Instagram	113
Kenya	Lillian Muli	Journalist	International Individual	Instagram	1,600,000
Kenya	Somali Forgotten Minds	Nonprofit	International Organization	Instagram	25,600
Kenya	Inzone Practise	Activist	Local Organization	Instagram	87
Kenya	My Start Project	Artist	Local Organization	Instagram	1,124
Kenya	Brian Inganga	Photographer	International Individual	Instagram	3,148
Kenya	Tdh Kenya	Local Branch	Local Organization	Instagram	304
Kenya	UNICEF Kenya	Local Branch	International Organization	Instagram	60,500
Kenya	UK in Kenya	Local Branch	International Organization	Instagram	8,685
Kenya	Refugee Easthorn	International Organization	International Organization	Instagram	6,659
Kenya	Kakuma Co	Nonprofit	Local Organization	Instagram	77
Kenya	The Most Of Us	Nonprofit	Local Organization	Instagram	217
Lebanon	AssociatedPress	News	International Organization	YouTube	3,280,000
Lebanon	RawReporting	News	Local Organization	Twitch	14,000
Lebanon	Ilredalert	News	Local Individual	X	17,000
Lebanon	Eyeonpalestine	Activist	Local Organization	X	230,000
Lebanon	Eye.on.llebanon	Activist	Local Organization	Instagram	363,000
Lebanon	Southern.libanon	Activist	Local Organization	Instagram	106,000
Lebanon	Sallyhayd	Photographer	Local Individual	Instagram	5,468
Lebanon	Danielcardephtos	Photographer	Local Individual	Instagram	3,131
Lebanon	Myriamboulos	Photographer	International Individual	Instagram	55,300
Lebanon	Basmehzeitooneh	Nonprofit	Local Organization	Instagram	5,865
Lebanon	Rescuing_in_lebanon	Nonprofit	Local Organization	Instagram	13,500
Lebanon	UNHCRlebanon	International Organization	International Organization	Instagram	25,900
Lebanon	Lorienttoday	News	Local Organization	X	22,500
Lebanon	Lebanontimes	News	Local Organization	Instagram	378,000
Lebanon	Houssein_almahadi	Influencer	Local Individual	Instagram	16,000
Lebanon	Ahmad_ihjaber	Influencer	Local Individual	Instagram	29,100
Lebanon	Zainab.5alil	Influencer	Local Individual	Instagram	19,600
Sudan	guy_peterson	Photographer	International Individual	Instagram	2,951
Sudan	unhcrsudan	Organization	International Organization	Instagram	68
Sudan	walad.kosti	News	Local Organization	Instagram	2,453
Sudan	mazinalzain	Photographer	Local Individual	Instagram	3,019
Sudan	sudan.updates	News	Local Organization	Instagram	119,000
Sudan	Alaska Sudan Medical Project	Nonprofit	Local Organization	X	249
Sudan	ala.kheir	Photographer	Local Individual	Instagram	5,983
Sudan	khalid_alarabi	Photographer	Local Individual	Instagram	4,066
Sudan	hopefocus	Photographer	International Individual	Instagram	7,100
Sudan	unicefssudan	Local Branch	International Organization	Instagram	64,700
Sudan	wenyengabriel	Public Person	Local Individual	Instagram	168,000
Sudan	amelpain	Photographer	Local Individual	Instagram	588
Sudan	johnbehets	Photographer	International Individual	Instagram	7,545
Sudan	almigdadhassan0	Journalist	Local Individual	Instagram	47,100
Sudan	zohrabensemra	Photographer	International Individual	Instagram	15,200
Sudan	gabrielavivacqua	Photographer	International Individual	Instagram	27,100
Sudan	حرب السودان	News	Local Organization	X	984
Sudan	Sudan War Monitor	News	Local Organization	X	18,000
Ukraine	Evgenymaloletka	Photographer	Local Individual	Instagram	1,600,000
Ukraine	Zelenskyy	Ukraine President	Local Individual	Instagram	15,700,000
Ukraine	Angelina Jolie	Celebrity	International Organization	Instagram	15,300,000
Ukraine	Red cross Ulraine	Nonprofit	International Organization	Instagram	39,400
Ukraine	nuttty_art	Artist	Local Individual	Instagram	567
Ukraine	Stop War Ukraine	News	Local Organization	Facebook	42,327
Ukraine	UN	International Organization	International Organization	Instagram	8,000,000
Ukraine	UAWeapons	News	Local Organization	X	851,000
Ukraine	banderafell	Writer	Local Individual	X	273,000
Ukraine	kharkiv.vibe	Activist	Local Individual	Instagram	62,800
Ukraine	an_magerramova	Journalist	Local Individual	Instagram	3,844
Ukraine	Ukraine Army	Activist	Local Individual	Facebook	58,733
Ukraine	klitschko	Celebrity	Local Individual	Instagram	945,000
Ukraine	warzorussia	Activist	International Organization	Telegram	459
Ukraine	dsns_ukraine	State Emergency Service	Local Organization	Instagram	96,200
Ukraine	Ukraine_defence	Activist	Local Organization	Instagram	541,000

Ukraine	Ukrainecrisisnews	Journalism	Local Organization	Instagram	2,019
Ukraine	Mykhaylo Palinchak	Photographer	Local Individual	Instagram	24,200
Ukraine	Sasha Maslov	Photographer	Local Individual	Instagram	18,200
Ukraine	Felipe Dana	Photographer	International Individual	Instagram	135,000
Ukraine	Slava Ucraini	Activist	Local Organization	X	3,881
Ukraine	Ukrainian Squad	Activist	Local Organization	X	208,800
Ukraine	Worldnews264	News	Local Organization	TikTok	74,400
Ukraine	ukraine_vs_russia2022	Activist	Local Organization	TikTok	49,100
Ukraine	Lynsey Addario	Photographer	International Individual	Instagram	42,700
Ukraine	Julia Kochetova	Photographer	Local Organization	Instagram	47,500
Ukraine	Justyna Mielnikiewicz	Photographer	Local Organization	Instagram	8,846
Ukraine	Edward Kaprov	Photographer	Local Organization	Instagram	5,111
West Sahel	Michele Cattani	Photographer	International Individual	Instagram	2,789
West Sahel	Fatoumata Diabatè	Journalist	Local Individual	Instagram	3,105
West Sahel	Unicef	Nonprofit	International Organization	Instagram	10,500
West Sahel	Fatoumata Diawara	Artist	Local Individual	Instagram	198,000
West Sahel	Burkina24	News	Local Organization	Instagram	5,743
West Sahel	Ibrahim Traorè	Politician	Local Individual	Instagram	4,866
West Sahel	Goita Assimi	Politician	Local Individual	Instagram	10,600
West Sahel	Marco Gualazzini	Photographer	International Individual	Instagram	24,800
West Sahel	Fada Collective	News	International Individual	Instagram	5,437
West Sahel	Marco Simoncelli	Photographer	International Individual	Instagram	1,010
West Sahel	Maliweb	News	Local Organization	Instagram	1,947
West Sahel	Intersos	International Organization	International Organization	Instagram	11,800

Figure 5.22 *Humanitarianism and Social Media.* Analyzed accounts, October 2024

This chapter was previously published on *e-flux Architecture* (November 2025). It was produced as part of *The Future of Humanitarian Design (HUD),* a research program that explores how space design and political science can jointly address the increasing challenges of humanitarian action, jointly run by HEAD – Genève (HES-SO), the Geneva Graduate Institute, the University of Copenhagen, and the EssentialTech Center at EPFL, with support from SNSF Sinergia.

Analysis conducted as part of the *Humanitarianism and Social Media* module HEAD – Genève (HES-SO). Fall semester 2024
Professor: Javier Fernández Contreras; PhD candidate: Damien Greder
Data Analytics (MAIA students in Interior Architecture): Matilde Arletti, Martino De Grandis, Maxime Joost, Lina Laube, Bianca Longoni, Hugo Maia Schmitt, Letizia Milone, Ailyn Pieyre, Célestine Potin, Paul Rigal, Lisa Schober, Kim Schönauer, Karol Szmigielski, and Mariannina Thielemans
Crises analyzed, as of October 2024:
—Afghanistan: 656 images from 15 accounts on Instagram and X (by Lina Laube)
—Kutupalong camp, Bangladesh: 503 images from 15 accounts on Facebook, Instagram, and X (by Hugo Maia Schmitt)
—Darién Gap: 358 images from 11 accounts on Facebook, Instagram, and YouTube (by Ailyn Pieyre)
—Democratic Republic of the Congo: 360 images from 15 accounts on Facebook and Instagram (by Mariannina Thielemans)
—Lesvos, Greece: 146 images from 15 accounts on Facebook and Instagram (by Célestine Potin)
—Haiti: 239 images from 15 accounts on Facebook and X (by Karol Szmigielski)
—Iran: 662 images from 15 accounts on Instagram, TikTok, and X (by Kim Schönauer)
—Za'atari camp, Jordan: 277 images from 18 accounts on Instagram and X (by Martino De Grandis)

- —Dadaab camp, Kenya: 206 images from 17 accounts on Instagram (by Letizia Milone)
- —Lebanon: 632 images from 17 accounts on Instagram, Twitch, YouTube, and X (by Matilde Arletti)
- —Ukraine: 1,008 images from 28 accounts on Facebook, Instagram, Telegram TikTok, and X (by Lisa Schober and Paul Rigal)
- —West Sahel: 394 images from 12 accounts on Instagram (by Bianca Longoni)

Notes

1 Susan Sontag, *Regarding the Pain of Others* (London: Penguin Books, 2019), 42. First published: New York: Picador, 2003.

2 Harmeet Kaur, "Palestinians are documenting the war for millions on social media. Their followers have come to see them as family," *CNN*, January 19, 2024 (accessed July 20, 2025), https://edition.cnn.com/2024/01/19/world/palestinians-x-tiktok-instagram-gaza-cec/index.html

3 Imago, "Imago was the ordinary Latin word used to signify the copy or likeness of anything ('Imago ab imitatione dicta,' Festus, 112); and, as applied to copies of nature, it includes pictures, statues, busts, or any mode of artistic representation," in *A Dictionary of Greek and Roman Antiquities,* ed. William Smith, William Wayte, and George E. Marindin (London: John Murray, Albemarle Street, 1890).

4 Chiara Bottici, "Imagination, Imaginary, Imaginal: Towards a New Social Ontology?" *Social Epistemology*, no. 33(5) (2019), 433–441, https://doi.org/10.1080/02691728.2019.1652861

5 Lilie Chouliaraki, *The Ironic Spectator: Solidarity in the Age of Post-humanitarianism* (Malden, MA: Polity Press, 2013), 45.

6 Susan Sontag, *Regarding the Pain of Others*, 16.

7 Barbie Zelizer, "CNN, the Gulf War, and Journalistic Practice," *Journal of Communication*, no. 42(1) (March 1992), 66–81, https://doi.org/10.1111/j.1460-2466.1992.tb00769.x

8 Lilie Chouliaraki, *The Ironic Spectator*, 134.

9 Jeff Jarvis, "How Katrina humbled the American news machine," *The Guardian,* September 12, 2005 (accessed July 20, 2025), https://www.theguardian.com/media/2005/sep/12/pressandpublishing.hurricanekatrina1

10 See: Sarah Shamim, "What is 'All eyes on Rafah'? Decoding a viral social trend on Israel's war," *Al Jazeera*, May 29, 2024 (accessed July 20, 2025), https://www.aljazeera.com/news/2024/5/29/what-is-all-eyes-on-rafah-decoding-the-latest-viral-social-trend; Kat Tenbarge, "'All Eyes on Rafah'

image shared by millions on Instagram following Israeli airstrike," *NBC News*, May 29, 2024 (accessed July 20, 2025), https://www.nbcnews.com/tech/internet/all-eyes-rafah-image-shared-millions-instagram-rcna154380

11　The average is first calculated by category within each crisis. The total maximum deviation of the content classified by category and crisis is 9 percent.

12　"Darién Gap: The Jungle Where Poor Migration Policies Meet," *Human Rights Watch* (accessed July 20, 2025), https://www.hrw.org/feature/2024/09/11/darien-gap/the-jungle-where-poor-migration-policies-meet

13　See channels: @baldandbankrupt, @manuelmonterrosa, @TimmyKarter.

14　Andrew Herscher, *Displacements: Architecture and Refugee* (Berlin: Sternberg Press, 2017), 6.

15　See: Susan Sontag, *Regarding the Pain of Others*. See also: Luc Boltanski, *Distant Suffering: Morality, Media and Politics*, trans. Graham Burchell (Cambridge: Cambridge University Press, 1999). First published in French as *La Souffrance à distance : Morale humanitaire, médias et politique* (Paris: Métaillé, 1993).

6

PET INFLUENCERS: ANIMAL PORTRAITURE AND MEDIATED DOMESTICITIES

Javier Fernández Contreras

What is a pet?

In 1980, art critic and novelist John Berger defined a pet as an animal "either sterilised or sexually isolated, extremely limited in its exercise, deprived of almost all other animal contact, and fed with artificial foods."[1] In 1987, the European Convention for the Protection of Pet Animals stipulated that "[b]y pet animal is meant any animal kept or intended to be kept by man in particular in his household for private enjoyment and companionship."[2] More recently, in 2023, François Gemenne, a member of the Intergovernmental Panel on Climate Change (IPCC), declared that "the cat is a disaster for biodiversity, the dog is a disaster for the climate,"[3] referring to cats' feral behavior after captivity and to the pollution caused by pet feed.

The definitions above are all both scientifically and culturally constructed. Pets have lived alongside humans since antiquity: indeed, influential contemporary scholars such as Donna Haraway argue that relationships between companion species (both human and nonhuman) are co-constitutive.[4] The exponential growth in pet ownership observed in recent decades is typical of postmodern societies, and it indeed

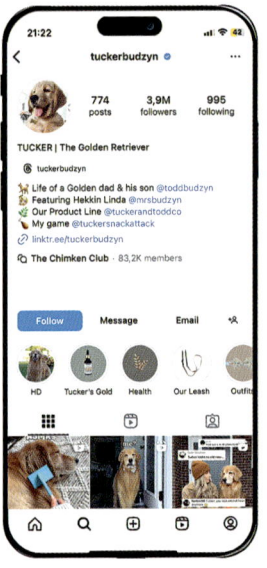

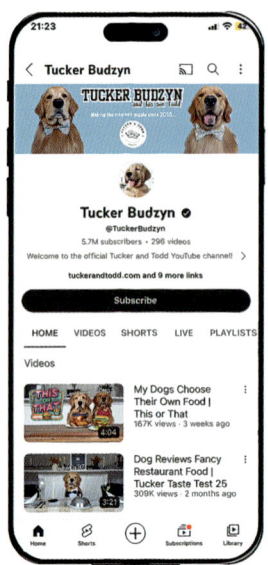

raises questions about animal rights, climate change, and human identity at large. What is less studied is the fact that pets mostly exist as a by-product of space design and interior architecture. While other forms of animal confinement, such as the farm, the zoo, or the circus, have been both spatially studied and ethically contested in recent years, critical surveys of domesticity from the perspective of pets are relatively scarce.[5]

Even less analyzed is the phenomenon of "pet influencers," that is, domesticated animals whose very existence is mediated and monetized by their owners, mainly on social media platforms. The phenomenon itself is recent. Even though Wikipedia contains numerous profiles of animal celebrities such as Doug the Pug or Grumpy Cat, as of April 2024, the entry "pet influencer" lacked a proper definition, instead redirecting toward the broader entry "internet celebrity." Whereas online celebrities exist in front of the camera, their portraits becoming the avatars of their mediated personas, pet influencers belong to the tradition of animal portraits, with the camera always pointing at them from the human's side. From the mansion of Nala Cat to the pictures of celebrities posing with Jiffpom the dog, and from the multi-platform influence of Tucker Budzyn to the anthropomorphized behavior of the Floofnoodles ferrets, what emerges from this study is a new way of

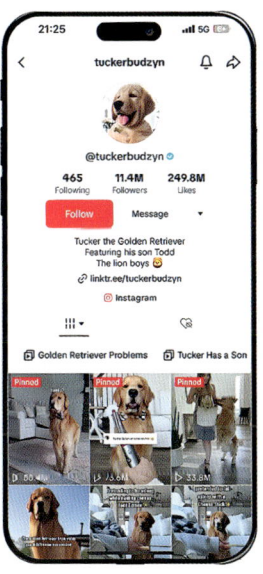

Figure 6.1 Tucker Budzyn. Impact on social media platforms as of January 2025. From left to right: Instagram (3.9 million followers), Facebook (4.7 million), YouTube (5.7 million), TikTok (11.4 million), X (62,000)

understanding the contemporary home as a place of animal domestication, online mediatization, and, ultimately, domination.

Profile vs. Portrait: The Genealogy of Animal Representation

The depiction of animals in images runs through human history. From cave art to deified animals in Egypt, and from the Nazca lines to Roman mosaics, their representation has evolved along with human civilization. However, the question of pet portraiture is of a different nature. Whether portrayed in isolation or staged with their human companions, the inclusion of animals within interior spaces—and, more specifically, the moment when they begin looking straight into the eyes of spectators, establishing a precise empathy through images—has a different genealogy. In the book *Medieval Pets* (2012), writer Kathleen Walker-Meikle overturns traditional perceptions of animals' roles in the Middle Ages by emphasizing their status as beloved household pets, exploring their acquisition, care, and depiction in art and literature, and covering species such as dogs, cats, monkeys, squirrels, and parrots.[6]

This shifting bond may have paved the way not only for a new relationship with domesticated animals but also for a new means of perceiving them through images. While the perspectival incorporation of the viewer into the space of the painting in Jan van Eyck's *The Arnolfini Portrait* (1434) has been widely discussed, less attention has been paid to the fact that the only sentient being looking into the eyes of the audience is actually the dog, thereby breaking through the space of representation.[7] In the ensuing decades and centuries, other artists, including Leonardo da Vinci, Diego Velázquez, and Sofonisba Anguisola, would also incorporate pets within the representation of portrait and domesticity.

In the 18th century, animal portraiture would be taken to a different level with the individualization of feelings within the frame, as clearly exposed by artist Jacques Laurent Agasse, a trained veterinarian who would move from the picturesque, object status of the animal to a more in-depth exploration of its psyche through portraits made in British menageries, such as that of the orangutan Joko (1819). At the end of the 19th century, the relationship between pets and domestic interiors would take on its modern, pre-social media shape through the work of Cassius M. Coolidge, who popularized the genre of anthropomorphized animals performing human social behavior for advertising purposes, as can be seen in *Dogs Playing Poker* (1894–1910), a series of paintings where dogs are seen smoking and playing cards.

The invention of photography—and, later, the development of cinema—further increased the reification of animals through images in the 19th and 20th centuries. Pets have played significant roles in the history of both mediums, with iconic figures like Lassie, Rin Tin Tin, and Terry capturing the hearts of audiences. This historical trend has been exacerbated in the 21st century with the institutionalization of the internet and the rise of social media platforms. At the basis of animals' circulation on media is, often, the monetization of their behavior.

Pet Influencers: New Celebrities, New Domesticities

The show features contestants called "pet influencers" who live together in a specially constructed house that is isolated from the

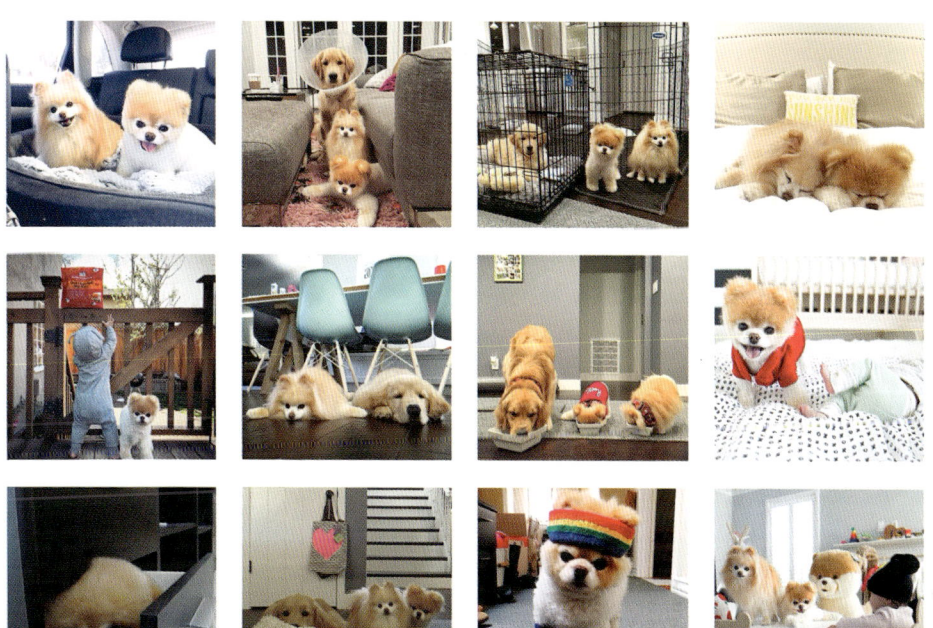

Figure 6.2 Buddy and Boo. Space types where the pets were normally portrayed. From left to right, top to bottom: car, living room, kitchen, bedroom, terrace, dining room, corridor, kids' bed, furniture (inside), staircase, corridor, kids' bedroom

outside world. The name is inspired by Big Brother from George Orwell's novel *Nineteen Eighty-Four,* and the pet influencers are continuously monitored during their stay in the house by live television cameras as well as personal audio microphones.[8]

Wikipedia, "Big Brother (franchise)" (edited by the author), 2024

The Wikipedia description of the TV show *Big Brother* is interesting. A literary exercise in replacing the word "housemates" in the original text with "pet influencers" reveals new forms of domesticity—specially constructed (or technically equipped) houses where animals remain physically isolated while maintaining connections with the outside world through social media. Can this be considered a new form of online celebrity and staged domesticity?

This appears to be the case with some of the most notable pet influencers of recent decades, such as Buddy and Boo, Jiffpom,[9] and Grumpy Cat, who have already passed away, as well as Nala Cat and Doug the Pug, who, at the time of writing, are still alive and broadcasting. These are mostly US-based profiles which, beyond their shared celebrity status, tell the story of American pet life. A brief analysis of each reveals how their biographies are entwined with their environments—hybrids of domestic spaces and production studios—and especially with their online personas as anthropomorphized versions of their animal selves.

An analysis of the domesticities of some of the most-followed pet influencers up to 2024 reveals that their mediated existence is intricately linked with their living environments. Despite variations in the portrayal of their habitats, certain patterns emerge, offering insight into how these animals are presented to their audiences and the ethical implications this entails. For instance, Buddy and Boo, two Pomeranian Spitzes born in 2003 and 2006 respectively, rose to fame when Boo's Facebook page, created by his owner in 2009, garnered public attention after endorsements from celebrities like Khloé Kardashian. They were mainly depicted with other dogs within the family, either at home or on vacation, and were also occasionally shown outdoors, on trips, or simply in their yard or garden. In their images, they appeared in various rooms within the house, mainly the living room, and their small size and full-body photography centered the visibility of their surroundings, creating an intimate atmosphere of architectural rooms. Similarly, Jiffpom, a Pomeranian born in 2010 in Illinois, gained recognition through social media engagement with human celebrities, as well as by featuring as an actor in films and video clips such as Katy Perry's *Dark Horse* (2014), turning a profit through public appearances and merchandise. With a preference for a dressed body and close-ups, Jiffpom's online presence reveals fewer glimpses of his owner's apartment, showcasing specific areas like the bedroom and living room while leaving others hidden from public view. This selective portrayal suggests a curated narrative that emphasizes certain aspects of his living environment while concealing others. In a more camouflaged domestic set, Grumpy Cat, a pet with feline dwarfism born in Arizona in 2012, regularly featured in compositions with her body disguised in costumes or domestic paraphernalia, and even against collaged backgrounds and in studio settings, obscuring the visibility of her actual living space.

The account of Doug the Pug, a celebrity dog born in 2012 in Tennessee, follows a similar pattern, with a focus on portraits and close-ups that render interior spaces secondary to the composition, where

Figure 6.3 Jiffpom. Analysis of the latest posts on Jiffpom's Instagram account (as of March 2024), including pictures with human celebrities. All celebrities have at least 1 million followers

only fragments of walls, sofas, or bed linen are visible as simple backgrounds, with a preference for white and gray tones. His economic model extends beyond domesticity, encompassing public ceremonies and charitable endeavors through the Doug the Pug Foundation to help children battling cancer and other life-threatening diseases. In contrast, the account of Nala Cat, a Siamese and Tabby mix born in 2010, displays a wider visibility of domestic spaces, her body regularly undressed and framed within the interior spaces of her owners' mansion in California. She is consistently presented in specific domestic spaces such as the living room, the kitchen, or the bedroom, and is notably absent from outdoor spaces, which she cannot access as all windows have mosquito nets to prevent her from fleeing. The deliberate confinement of her living environment suggests a conscious effort to maintain a particular image of domesticity for media consumption, expanding into television appearances and lucrative endorsements, making her the most valuable cat profile worldwide, with a net worth exceeding $100 million by 2023.[10]

From events to merchandising, and from video clips to charity, the public images of these pet influencers seem to differ little from those of their human counterparts. Converted into digital avatars of themselves,

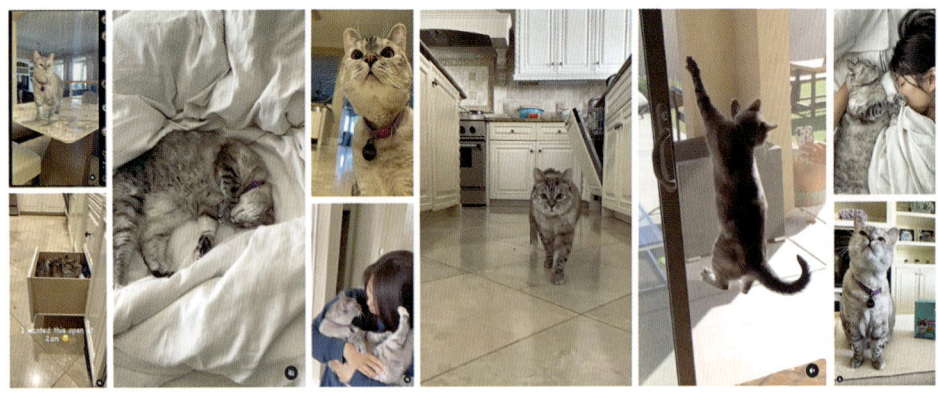

Figure 6.4 Nala Cat. Space types where the pet is normally portrayed: living room 43%; kitchen 10%; bedroom 7%; other 40%; outdoor 0% (mosquito screens in all windows to avoid Nala from fleeing the mansion)

their online celebrity remains active beyond their lifespan. A comparative analysis of these profiles unveils multifaceted dimensions of their virtual presence, the business strategies employed by their owners, and the lifestyles they project. In terms of popularity and reach, Jiffpom and Tucker Budzyn, a Golden Retriever born in 2018 in Michigan, stand out with the highest combined follower counts across platforms, surpassing 31 million and 25 million, respectively. Jiffpom's dominance is particularly evident on TikTok with over 20 million followers, while Nala Cat holds the record for being the most-followed cat on Instagram with 4.5 million followers. Buddy and Boo have a substantial following, peaking at 14 million on Facebook and 500,000 on Instagram, while Grumpy Cat maintains a considerable following with millions of followers across platforms, including 7.6 million on Facebook, 2.6 million on Instagram, and 1.5 million on X.[11]

Like the sets of *Big Brother*, where environments are meticulously designed to evoke certain emotions and interactions, the domesticities of these pet influencers can be seen as curated stages for their online personas. Just as the *Big Brother* house served as a backdrop for drama and narrative development, the living environments of these pets shape the narratives constructed around them, affecting how their bodies and lives are inserted within the space and the camera. They all communicate during the daytime, the nocturnal dimension of their animality being adjusted to the circadian rhythm of their owners. While these pet influencers offer entertainment and joy to their audiences, the

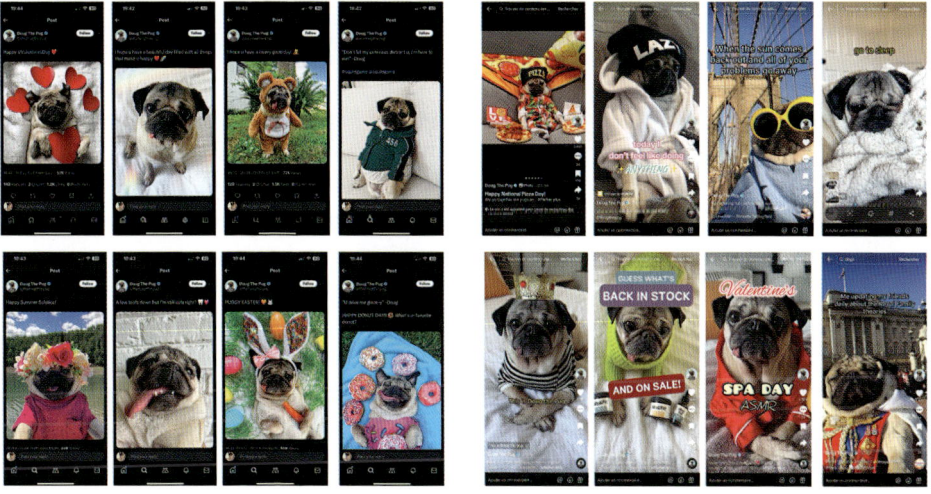

Figure 6.5 Doug the Pug. Comparison between the pet's X (Twitter) and TikTok accounts, as per total data available as of March 2024. X (Twitter): 2.7 million followers; Dominant viewpoint: full-body portrait; Activity: wearing a suit, lying down, listening to his mistress sing; Interior: 43% Day: 93%; Human presence (visible): 38%. TikTok: 5.9 million followers; Dominant viewpoint: full-body; Activity: lying down, walking, listening to his mistress sing; Interior: 56%; Day: 89%; Human presence (visible): 45%

commodification of their behavior and the mediatization of their domestic lives raise concerns about the boundaries between public spectacle and private space, between lack of consent and animal rights. These animals are thrust into the spotlight of social media, where selected aspects of their lives are subject to scrutiny and commodification. All pet influencers have leveraged their online presence for monetization through merchandising, brand partnerships, sponsored posts, and appearances. The business models pursued by the owners of the Jiffpom and Nala Cat accounts involve a wide range of merchandise and sponsored events, indicating diversified revenue streams. Beyond partnerships with companies and sponsored posts, Tucker Budzyn also offers products for pets and humans on Amazon, while most of his $2 million annual revenue comes from social media.[12] Buddy and Boo generated significant profits primarily through brand partnerships, with Boo's owner authoring a bestselling book about the pet's cuteness. Doug the Pug's business model extends to philanthropy, with the establishment of his foundation.[13] Finally, Grumpy Cat's legacy continues through licensed products even after her passing, highlighting the enduring nature of her business model.

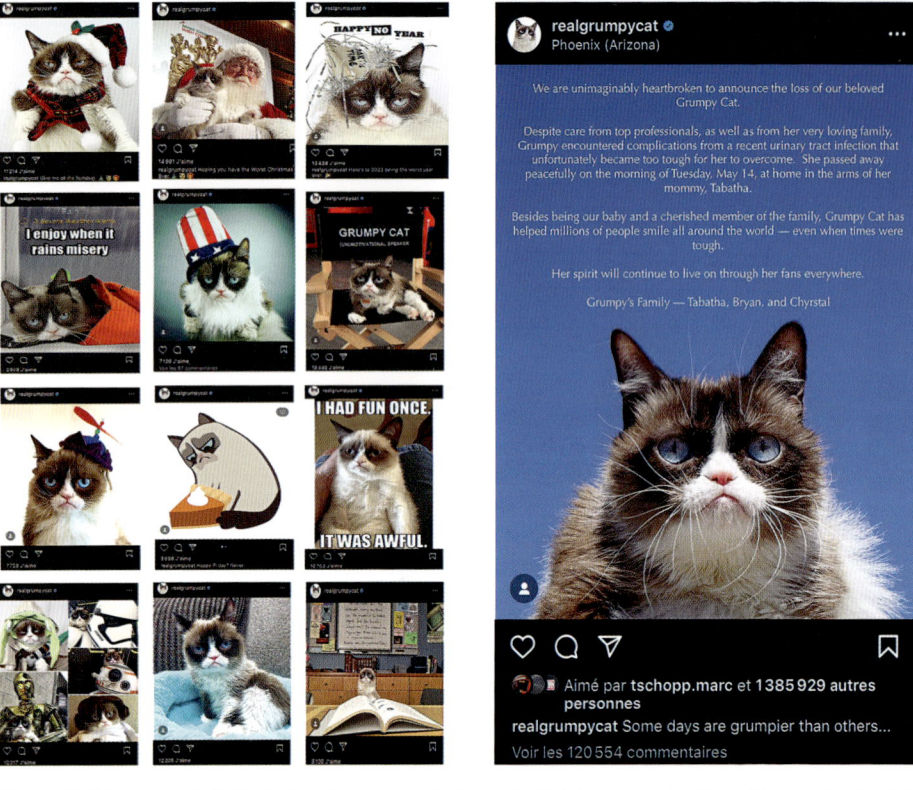

Figure 6.6 Grumpy Cat. Typical Instagram portrait, and official communication of the pet's death in May 2019. The official Instagram account (@realgrumpycat) continues to regularly communicate on the animal's legacy and memory

Pet Close-ups: The Hands of the Ventriloquist

Ventriloquism, the art of making inanimate puppets appear alive, has a long history dating back centuries. However, it was not until the 20th century that animal figures began to take center stage, bringing a new dimension to the act. It is interesting to note that these animal puppets became influential mainly through their audiovisual impact via TV broadcasting. Unlike the theaters and other entertainment venues of the 18th and 19th centuries, where ventriloquism thrived with large, child-sized anthropomorphic dummies visible from afar, the 20th-century television format made it possible to use smaller puppets—such as Lamb Chop or Topo Gigio (a lamb and a mouse, respectively)—allowing for close-ups that emphasized their disproportionately large faces. It is therefore no coincidence that some of the pet influencers discussed above have disproportionately small bodies in relation to the size of their heads. Of the top ten most-followed pet accounts worldwide, two feature Pomeranians, compact, sturdy dogs weighing 2–3 kilograms and measuring 20–35 cm high at the withers; one centers on a pug, a dog with cobby body proportions; and another revolves around a cat with feline dwarfism.

The first pet celebrities were mainly dogs and cats that did not require human hands to scaffold their postures. However, recent years have seen the rise of a new generation of pet influencers whose anthropomorphizing goes beyond simple dressing up and human-like activities and behavior. This is the case with. That Little Puff and Floofnoodles, profiles based respectively on a cat and ferrets, which have become celebrities since 2020. Their owners are post-COVID ventriloquists, and their pets are online dummies. Interestingly, they mostly communicate through native video platforms like TikTok (where they respectively boast 33.4 million and 17.4 million followers as of April 2024), and the editing of their videos is fast-paced, with shots often under one second long, in which their postures are stop-motioned without showing the in-between tempo of the human hands that position them.

The phenomenon of That Little Puff, under the ownership of Lynch Zhang from Puff Media Group, exemplifies the confluence of pet ownership, social media, and commercialization. During the pandemic, the closure of restaurants prompted Zhang and his family to explore homemade cuisine, inadvertently sparking interest in their cat, who, through curated content primarily featuring cooking demonstrations and life hacks, amassed a significant following across platforms like TikTok and YouTube. While predominantly featured alone in videos, often engaging in human-like activities, the cat is largely assisted by humans, his body strategically edited to create the illusion of independence.

In the case of Floofnoodles, human intervention is even more obvious because of the very animal morphology and size of ferrets. The entire strategy is built around the plurality of animals under one brand. Floofnoodles is a TikTok and Instagram profile featuring the staging of various ferrets: Lucas (deceased at 6 in 2021), Drixie (deceased at 3 in 2022), and Matthew, Daisy, and Mathilda, who are still alive.

Figure 6.7 That Little Puff. Portraiture and communication style of the official TikTok account (@thatlittlepuff): About 200 videos/year; Portrait: tabletop to bust level; Activities: Life hacks/cooking; Indoors: 100%; Daytime: 100%, with artificial light support; Human presence (non-visible): 100%

Controversies arose over the owner's portrayal of the ferrets' lives. In 2022, there were allegations that mistreatment led to the premature deaths of two ferrets, sparking the *@justice4lucas* movement.[14] There have also been claims that Drixie died of starvation after two days without food. These controversies are entangled with the owner's bodily presence, as he is visible in many videos controlling the animals' postures. Completely disconnected from outdoor environments and any visible circadian rhythm, the ferrets of Floofnoodles are never shown interacting naturally; instead, they are constantly staged by their owner, even when they are sleeping. Because of their size, the type of framing is not portraiture but rather full-body presence, whether propped up ("dancing") or "lying" on the bed. The distance between the camera and their faces ensures the longevity and continued renewal of their brand, which does not have to rely on just one ferret.

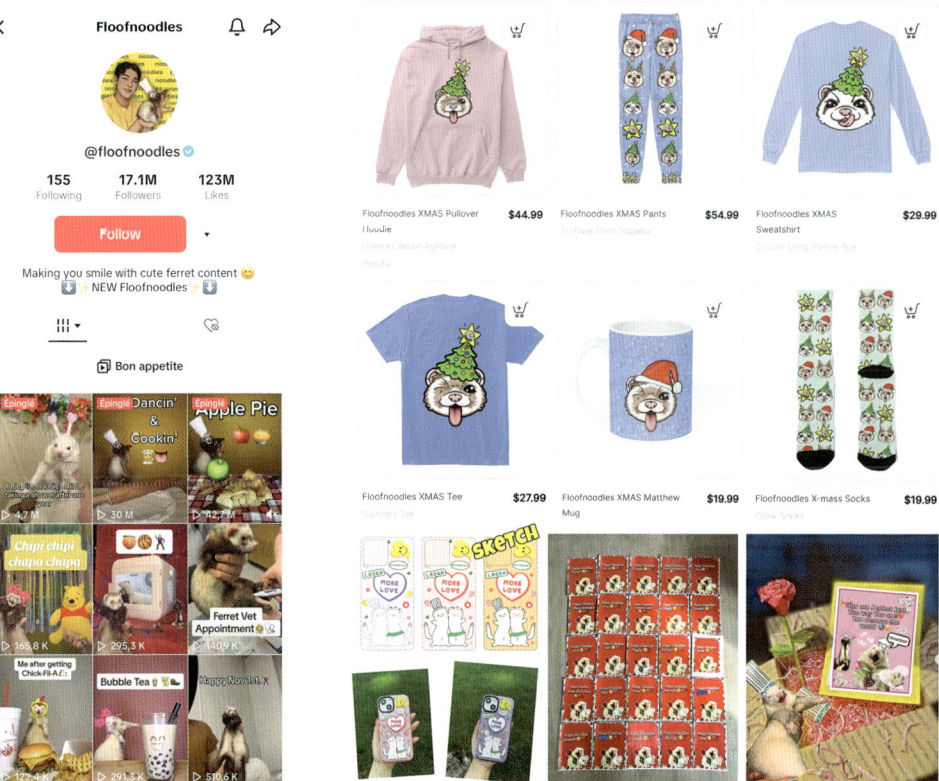

Figure 6.8 Floofnoodles. Official TikTok account (@floofnoodles) and merchandizing products, March 2024

A comparison of the domestic spaces utilized as production studios by That Little Puff and Floofnoodles reveals distinct approaches regarding the integration of pets within the narrative framework. That Little Puff predominantly employs a fixed indoor setting, notably the kitchen, with the occasional incorporation of a background setting for video collages, emphasizing an anthropomorphized portrayal of the cat without distracting image changes. This strategy centralizes the cat as the focal point, facilitated by the features of the TikTok platform, where the majority of That Little Puff's content is posted. It is characterized by frontal, interior shots with consistent lighting, mainly depicting "manual" activities and cooking. Conversely, Floofnoodles showcases the dynamic utilization of various household spaces, predominantly featuring the ferrets' activities, such as cooking scenes in the kitchen, playful interactions on stairs, or showering moments in the bathroom.

The focus is on the bodies of the ferrets, with only partial visibility of the interior spaces as a result of the chosen camera angles, creating a more fragmentary and episodic representation.

Coda: Animals, Selfies, and the Right to the Image

> The trial judge dismissed the action on the basis that even if Naruto had taken the pictures by "independent, autonomous action," the suit could not continue as animals do not have standing in a court of law and therefore cannot sue for copyright infringement.[15]
>
> ANDRES GUADAMUZ, *WIPO Magazine*, 2018

In 2011, nature photographer David Slater published portraits of Naruto, a crested macaque in Sulawesi, claiming they were self-portraits taken by the animal himself, sparking copyright disputes over whether the images belonged to the photographer or to the primate.[16] Beyond legal implications, the dispute spurred discussions on the ethical treatment of animals and on their agency, which are especially relevant in the context of the pet influencers analyzed in this chapter. Philosophical inquiries into the nature of representation further complicate the debate surrounding animals' rights: advocates for recognizing nonhuman agency align with principles of nonanthropocentric ethics and political ecology;[17] conversely, some thinkers contest that the attribution of partial legal protection to nonhumans (particularly in the context of animal welfare) is often counterproductive, as it regularly justifies "necessary" abuses, whether for dietary or scientific reasons.[18]

Except for cases such as the monkey selfie copyright dispute, the question of animals' right to their own visual representation is often marginal in these debates. Animal portraiture has intensified in the 21st century with the rise of social media. With smartphones, humans have also diversified the portrait range, adding the selfie to the most circulated image types. Even though the self-portrait belongs to the history of pictures, the temporal relationship between the subject and the object (the body as an image) has traditionally been asynchronous in this format. Yet in the selfie, this tempo is synchronous, therefore blurring the line between subject and object, and further reinforcing human exceptionalism in the creation of pictures. Because, even though cases of selfies taken by animals such as Naruto have been reported, most nonhuman species cannot shoot them owing to the configuration of their extremities and, therefore, have limited control concerning both the production and—more importantly—the distribution of their own images.

The proliferation of pet photographs in recent years, particularly through online social networks, raises important questions. When placed in front of the camera, pets—both anonymous and influencers—are actively used and objectified through image production, their pictures competing for likes and comments on their cuteness. Their corporality, constrained by human intervention, blurs the lines between subject and object. Since pets primarily exist within interior spaces, particularly in confined domestic environments, it follows that further architectural, ethical, and philosophical reflection is needed in order to understand the implications of animal representation in the digital age, ultimately questioning the role of architecture and social media in the perpetuation of human domination over nonhuman beings.

This chapter was previously published on: *KoozArch*, May 24, 2024.

Analysis conducted as part of the *Theory of Mediated Spaces* module
HEAD – Genève (HES-SO). Spring Semester 2024
Professor: Javier Fernández Contreras
Data Analytics (BA students in Interior Architecture):
— Buddy and Boo: Alexis Lang, Manon Lebon, and Maelle Mabru
— Doug the Pug: Cléa Bertossa, Aurore Biache, and Alexia Dahman
— Floofnoodles: Marie Mamou Blanché, Elise Mathis, and Missilia Mendy
— Grumpy Cat: Yan Vasquez, Nina Wallimann, and Jiwon Yuk
— Jiffpom: Benjamin Dohollou, Tiago Dos Santos Pinto, and Carla Ferey
— Juniper and Friends: Zoé Mettraux, Luca Negro, and Norah Pittet
— Nala Cat: Martin Annen, Nassim Baron, and Giona Leo Baumann
— That Little Puff: Mireille Gidi, Hippolyte Giraud, and Ambre Gravina
— Tucker Budzyn: Bryan Jefferson Reyes, Anna Smiian, and Kateryna
Sushynska

Notes

1 John Berger, "Why Look at Animals?," in *About Looking* (New York:
Pantheon Books, 1980), 12.

2 Council of Europe, "European Convention for the Protection of Pet Animals"
(adopted November 13, 1987), ETS No. 125, Article 1: "Definitions,"
https://rm.coe.int/168007a67d

3 Armêl Balogog, "Vrai ou faux: Les chiens et les chats sont-ils des
'catastrophes' pour la biodiversité et le climat?," *Radio France*, December
15, 2023 (accessed April 5, 2024), https://www.francetvinfo.fr/replay-radio/
le-vrai-du-faux/vrai-ou-faux-les-chiens-et-les-chats-sont-ilsdes-
catastrophes-pour-la-biodiversite-et-le-climat_6216132.html

4 See: Donna Haraway, *The Companion Species Manifesto: Dogs, People,
and Significant Otherness* (Chicago: Paradigm, 2003).

5 Jack Halberstam, "Zombie Antihumanism at the End of the World," in *Wild
Things: The Disorder of Desire* (Durham: Duke University Press, 2020),
147–174.

6 Kathleen Walker-Meikle, *Medieval Pets* (Woodbridge: Boydell Press, 2012).

7 At least until the interesting hypothesis of the physician Jean-Philippe
Postel, who interprets the invisibility of the dog reflection in the mirror and
the frontality of its gaze as a dual form of absence and presence, a
simulacrum that pierces the surface of representation. See: Jean-Philippe
Postel, *L'Affaire Arnolfini : Les secrets du tableau de Van Eyck* (Arles:
Éditions Actes Sud, 2016).

8 "Big Brother (franchise)," *Wikipedia*, last edited on March 27, 2024, 01:27 (UTC), https://en.wikipedia.org/wiki/Big_Brother_(franchise)

9 Although not officially communicated, information about the death of Jiffpom spread on mass media in 2022. See: Leda Manos, "Is Jiffpom Dead? Investigating Rumours About the Beloved Pomeranian and Dog Influencer," *LA Weekly*, November 29, 2022 (accessed April 5, 2024), https://www.laweekly.com/is-jiffpom-dead-rumors-swirl-online-about-the-beloved-pomeranian-and-dog-influencer/

10 "Here are the richest cats in the world in 2023," *The Economic Times*, August 10, 2023 (accessed April 5, 2024), https://economictimes.indiatimes.com/industry/miscellaneous/here-are-the-richest-cats-in-theworld-in-2023/nala-cat/slideshow/102613326.cms

11 Follower count as of April 2024.

12 Trisha Sengupta. "Meet Tucker Budzyn, Golden Retriever earning millions as influencer," *Hindustan Times*, May 24, 2023 (accessed April 5, 2024), https://www.hindustantimes.com/trending/meet-tucker-budzyn-golden-retriever-earning-millions-as-influencer-101684942117153.html

13 See: Doug the Pug Foundation, https://www.dougthepugfoundation.org

14 @justice4lucas: 3,665 followers and 142.4K likes on TikTok as of April 2024.

15 Andres Guadamuz, "Can the monkey selfie case teach us anything about copyright law?" *WIPO Magazine*, February 21, 2018 (accessed April 5, 2024), https://www.wipo.int/en/web/wipo-magazine/articles/can-the-monkey-selfie-case-teach-us-anything-about-copyright-law-40287

16 "Monkey selfie copyright dispute," *Wikipedia*, last edited on April 5, 2024, 02:09 (UTC), https://en.wikipedia.org/wiki/Monkey_selfie_copyright_dispute

17 See: Bruno Latour, "Esquisse d'un parlement des choses," *Écologie politique*, no. 10 (summer 1994), 97–115. See also: Bruno Latour, *Politics of Nature: How to Bring the Sciences into Democracy*, trans. Catherine Porter (Cambridge: Harvard University Press, 2004). First published in French as *Politiques de la nature : Comment faire entrer les sciences en démocratie* (Paris: La Découverte, 1999).

18 See: Gary Francione, *Animals, Property, and the Law* (Philadelphia: Temple University Press, 1995); Gary Francione and Robert Garner, *The Animal Rights Debate: Abolition or Regulation?* (New York: Columbia University Press, 2010); Florence Burgat, *Les animaux ont-ils des droits ?* (Paris: La Documentation française, 2022).

7

UNBOXING ROBLOX: ARCHITECTURE, URBANISM, AND VIDEO GAMES

Javier Fernández Contreras

Can Roblox be considered a social media platform? Launched in 2006, Roblox is an online gaming ecosystem where users can both create and play video games—called "experiences"—designed by other users. Initially a platform for game creation and sharing, it has evolved into a virtual universe with millions of user-generated experiences. According to classic definitions, social media are "a group of Internet-based applications that build on the ideological and technological foundations of Web 2.0, and that allow the creation and exchange of user-generated content."[1] What sets Roblox apart is that it is the main platform merging social media, user-created content, and interaction through gameplay. Unlike traditional social networks, where content creation is typically limited to posts, images, and videos, Roblox enables users to design immersive 3D environments and games. This integration of social networking and gaming provides a unique space where players not only interact and share content but also collaborate on game development, participate in virtual events, and form communities around shared interests within the virtual worlds they conceive and explore. As of 2024, Roblox boasts over 40 million experiences and more than 210 million active monthly users, with

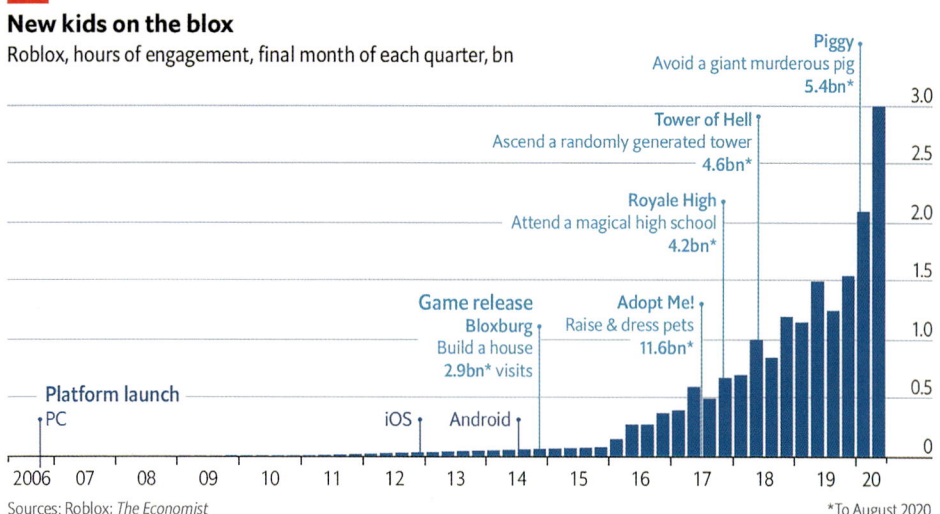

New kids on the blox
Roblox, hours of engagement, final month of each quarter, bn

Piggy
Avoid a giant murderous pig
5.4bn*

Tower of Hell
Ascend a randomly generated tower
4.6bn*

Royale High
Attend a magical high school
4.2bn*

Game release
Bloxburg
Build a house
2.9bn* visits

Adopt Me!
Raise & dress pets
11.6bn*

Platform launch
PC

iOS

Android

Sources: Roblox; *The Economist*

*To August 2020

Figure 7.1 Roblox: Hours of engagement, final month of each quarter, billions, to August 2020. Courtesy of *The Economist*

approximately 40 percent of its players being under 13, although it also has a significant number of adult users.[2]

According to an essay published in 2023 by *The Economist*, titled "The rise of user-created video games,"[3] the revolution of amateur user-generated content that has transformed the TV industry—with Americans under 18 spending twice as much time on TikTok and YouTube as on Netflix and Disney+—is now reaching the video game sector. The essay suggests that Roblox might soon become "the YouTube of gaming."[4] This shared agency and DIY spirit belongs to the history of the medium itself. Already in 1973, the book *101 BASIC Computer Games*, compiled by engineer David Ahl, was a seminal collection of simple games written by anonymous users in the BASIC programming language, designed to run on early microcomputers.[5] The book reflects a time when gamers were creators, modifying and improving code to personalize their gaming experiences. This ethos of modification, or "modding," has since become a cornerstone of gaming culture, allowing players to extend the life and breadth of their favorite games by creating new content, improving graphics, or adding features, fostering a participatory community.

When it comes to Roblox, what are the implications of user-created video games for architecture? Many of the experiences on the platform are multiplayer online games that feature various architectural styles, including modern, suburban, rustic, medieval, fantastic, and pirate-themed, each with its own unique aesthetic and atmosphere. With the platform already acting as a full 2D metaverse on screens and, progressively, 3D in virtual reality (VR) headsets, this chapter analyzes the architecture of the most-played video games on Roblox, as well as the insertion of avatars in the spaces where users socialize, play, chat, and buy products with Robux, Roblox's virtual currency. From the streets of *Brookhaven RP* to the stairs of *Tower of Hell*, and from the pets of *Adopt Me!* to the humans of *Murder Mystery 2*, what emerges from this study is a new way of understanding virtual architecture as a place where the evolution of contemporary society, particularly generations Z and Alpha, is played out.

Roblox Studio: Cartesian Geometry and Figurative Architecture

In the history of space design in video games, it is possible to trace an evolution from the abstract, diagrammatic scenes of the first video games to the figurative, perspectival, and photorealistic ones of today. In the 1960s and 1970s, early titles such as *Spacewar!* (1962), *Pong* (1972), and *Breakout* (1976) featured basic, non-perspectival spaces. In 1974, *Maze War* became the first game to feature three-dimensional space and first-person perspective inside a wireframe architecture of lines and corridors. In the 1980s, *Donkey Kong* (1981) and *Super Mario Bros.* (1985) played pivotal roles; while these games did not feature 3D environments, *Donkey Kong* introduced vertical platforming and *Super Mario Bros.* pioneered side-scrolling levels with distinct spatial layouts, establishing core conventions of the platformer genre where movement occurs primarily within a shallow space. In the 1990s, the transition to full 3D gaming began with titles like *Doom* (1993), which utilized simple, textured environments. This breakthrough was confirmed with *Quake* (1996), offering fully three-dimensional spaces with first-person shooter navigation—a graphical perspective seen from the viewpoint of the player character, with its hands (and weapons) incorporated onto the screen.[6]

The spaces of these early video games coincided with the call of the postmodern architects of the time for a semantic readability of architectural elements, a phenomenon that was coined "Figurative Architecture." As Michael Graves would claim, "[a]rchitectural elements require this distinction, one from another, in much the same way as language requires syntax; without variations among architectural elements, we will lose the anthropomorphic or figurative meaning."[7] This is to say that walls, floors, ceilings, columns, and doors should be recognized as independent components with their own texture and material identity. As Graves pointed out, "[i]t might be wondered why these elements, given their geometric similarity in some cases (for example, floor and ceiling) must be understood differently."[8] While it is unlikely that postmodern architectural theory influenced Roblox, the buildings, cities, and landscapes of its most-played video games seem to adhere to these principles. Architectural elements are readable as autonomous entities, recognizable by their colors, textures, and volumes, albeit with a certain preference for low-poly geometry—a style of 3D computer graphics where models are created with a relatively small number of polygons (or faces). Roblox allows players to create their own games using its proprietary engine, Roblox Studio, which is built with a derivative of the scripting language Lua, named Luau. This platform is based on the X, Y, and Z axes, originating from the coordinate system developed by René Descartes in the 17th century. Beyond freeform or sculpting software, Roblox Studio and 3D modeling software like 3D Studio, Maya, and Rhinoceros mainly use the three perpendicular axes to position points in space: the X-axis represents width, the Y-axis represents height, and the Z-axis represents depth. Objects are modeled and positioned using these coordinates, enabling precise movement, rotation, and scaling.

The grid, and the modeling it makes possible, construct a certain idea of architectural space that belongs to a specific historical lineage. It is interesting to note that, before Cartesian coordinates were invented, 15th-century Renaissance Italy saw the coexistence of various perspectival systems, as explained by architect and historian Robin Evans in the book *The Projective Cast* (2000).[9] While the linear perspective developed by Filippo Brunelleschi and documented by Leon Battista Alberti in the treatise *De pictura* (1435) was a technique in graphical projection where parallel lines converge at one or more vanishing points on the horizon line, creating the illusion of depth and distance on the picture plane, *De prospectiva pingendi* (1474–1482) by Piero della Francesca was a method based on the accurate placement of discrete points in space, without relying on them being aligned to lines

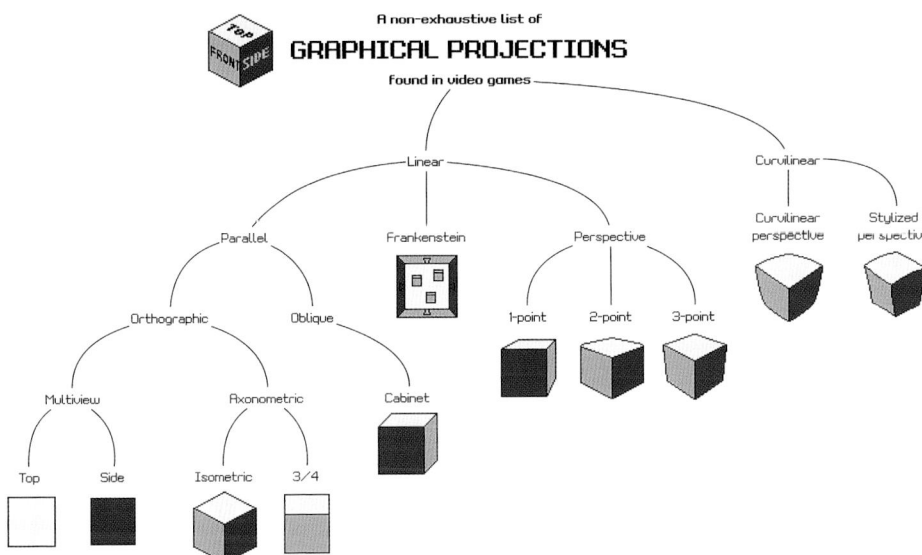

Figure 7.2 Graphical projections found in video games. Courtesy of Matej 'Retro' Jan

converging at vanishing points. This method allowed for the precise and detailed representation of complex objects by projecting their dimensions and "point cloud" directly onto the picture plane. Despite its failure to become a new standard, possibly owing to its complexity, it might have altered the course of history by allowing for greater formal freedom and geometric complexity in architectural design. With the triumph of linear perspective as the new default for representing (and thinking about) space in Western painting, it is no coincidence that the 15th century witnessed the emergence of a new kind of space, with architecture becoming somewhat box-like and its points gridded into parallel lines meant to meet at vanishing points. This is the space of paintings like Perugino's *The Delivery of the Keys* (1481–1482), with bodies inserted like avatars in different positions, thanks to a grid of coordinates.

The representation system of most perspectival video games can be traced back to linear perspective and Cartesian geometry. In a seminal essay on graphical projections in video games, entitled "Game developer's guide to graphical projections,"[10] Matej 'Retro' Jan develops a taxonomy of space types according to the projective mechanisms developed to represent them within the screen (the classification does not include virtual reality). Isometric video games like *Syndicate* (1993) belong to linear parallel projections, as do platformer games such as

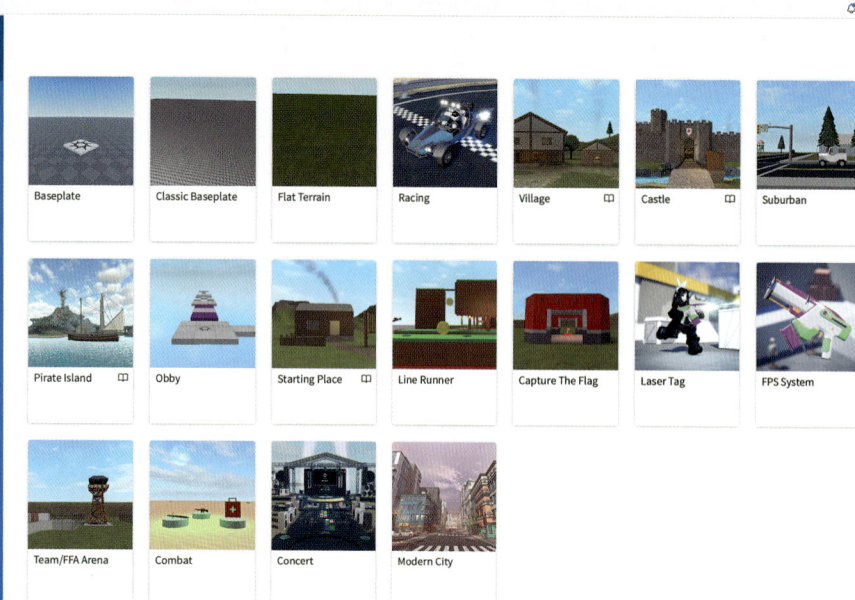

Figure 7.3 Roblox Studio: Templates, June 2024

Gods (1991). Within this scheme, Roblox would fall into the category of "Projection/Linear/Perspective/3-point" video games. The space in the most-played Roblox experiences typically involves low-poly spatial design with interactive third-person views and dynamic camera systems. In these games, linear projection plays a significant role, prompting dynamic three-point perspectives to enhance depth and orientation. Buildings, roads, and structures converge toward multiple, mobile vanishing points, creating a realistic depiction of the game world.

While Roblox Studio is not figurative by default, its Cartesian geometry encourages a preference for regular, standardized architecture. Designers can choose from various project templates, which have evolved over the years—some have been removed, revamped, or added based on user statistics and feedback. By the early 2010s, Roblox began including basic templates such as *Baseplate* and *Flat Terrain*, which respectively offer a blank horizontal grid and a classic textured terrain, providing abstract, simple starting points for new projects. Between 2015 and 2018, the variety of templates expanded to include pre-made game options like *Obby* and *Racing*, catering to popular game genres such as obstacle courses and car races within

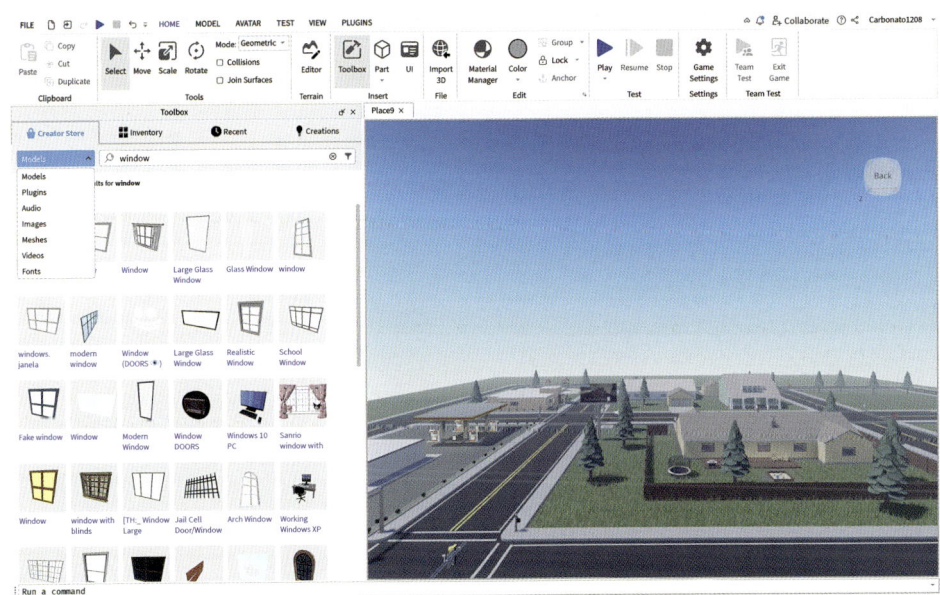

Figure 7.4 Roblox Studio: Suburban template. Displayed menu: Windows, June 2024

the Roblox community. Interestingly, recent years have seen a trend toward offering worlds with prebuilt architectures and cities, which are highly figurative and archetypal in their styles.[11] Examples of these templates include *Village*, *Suburban*, *Modern City*, *Castle*, and *Pirate Island*, each characterized by thematic elements. For instance, *Village* typically features rustic cottages, winding paths, and communal spaces such as a marketplace or town square, evoking a quaint rural setting. In contrast, the *Suburban* template depicts low-density neighborhoods with houses, yards, and streets, aiming for a residential feel. On a larger scale, the *Modern City* template showcases skyscrapers, roads, parks, and bustling urban environments, aiming to replicate a metropolitan area with a blend of residential, commercial, and recreational spaces. Catering to different epochs and geographies, the *Castle* template often includes grand stone walls, towers, and a throne room designed to emulate a medieval fortress, while *Pirate Island* focuses on tropical landscapes with sandy beaches, palm trees, hidden coves, and pirate-themed structures such as docks and ships.

Each template is designed to provide a distinct virtual environment tailored to its specific theme, offering users diverse settings to explore and interact with on the Roblox platform. While designing, gamers can insert objects and effects from the Roblox toolbox, grouped into key categories: Models (3D objects like buildings, furniture, or vehicles), Plugins (tools and scripts for additional functionality), Audio (sound effects and music), Images (decals and textures for surfaces), Meshes (custom 3D shapes), Videos (multimedia files), and Fonts (typefaces for in-game menus like signage and UI). These assets are contributed by the Roblox Corporation and, mainly, by the gaming community. Both in templates and in objects from the toolbox, architecture becomes both the subject and the icon of its figurative representation. Buildings look like buildings, walls look like walls, and windows look like windows. Architecture, ultimately, looks like Roblox architecture.

Avatar, Space, Time: The Most-Played Roblox Experiences

The relationship between avatars, space, and camera position traverses the history of video games. In the case of Roblox, while its architecture is modeled in the Studio, the menu allows each player to customize their virtual body as an avatar to be inserted into the platform's spaces. Roblox avatars have evolved significantly over the years, transitioning from a blocky, LEGO-like design to more figurative models. Launched in 2006, the early R6 avatar consisted of only six body parts or joints, closely resembling the blocky LEGO universe, an aesthetic affinity that was confirmed with the launch of the Man and Woman characters in 2012. This style suited the platform's young audience and made it easy to navigate. In 2016, the R15 avatar update introduced a more humanoid design, enhancing customization with fifteen body parts instead of six.[12] Since then, Roblox has expanded customization options, which have increased the platform's appeal and diversified its business model, allowing for buyable personalized clothing and accessories in regular collaborations with brands.[13] Avatar customization is a common feature in many games, varying in complexity. Some experiences, like *Brookhaven RP*, are sensitive to inclusivity issues such as impairment, allowing users to select a variety of objects, including wheelchairs. However, other games still include default models with a high degree of normativity. For example, *Adopt Me!* invites users to choose between

Figure 7.5 *Brookhaven RP*: Wheelchair chosen from the Vehicles menu

gendered styles, and *Tower of Hell* reinforces ableism by offering non-accessible routes based on jumping across platforms and stairs. While the range of bodies included in the menu is extensive—encompassing human, humanoid, animal, robotic, and extraterrestrial species—some body types are less represented and harder to customize, such as those of overweight or elderly people, as well as individuals with certain impairments, such as one-legged avatars, whose customization can imply buying expensive accessories.[14] Nonetheless, in recent years, corporalities have been diversified, and the option to unselect gender binary on the account settings has been added.[15]

While Roblox constructs perspectivism in its avatar customization options, the gameplay styles of its most-played experiences[16] reinforce the changeability and constraints of these perspectives. These video games feature diverse genres that can be categorized into social simulation, role-playing game (RPG), horror and mystery, obstacle challenges, and pet-centric simulation. Social simulation games include *Brookhaven RP*, a life simulation game where players can explore a virtual city, own homes, and interact with others; *MeepCity*, which offers social interactions, home decoration, and mini-games played alongside object-like creatures called "meeps"; and *Royale High*, a fantasy high

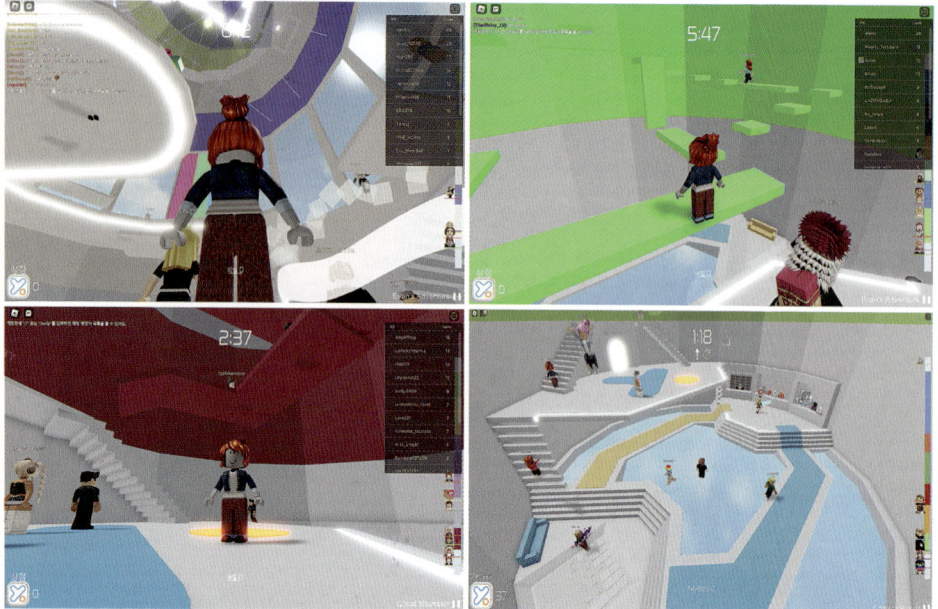

Figure 7.6 *Tower of Hell*: Different camera types including first- and third-person views. Perspectives can be chosen, no elevator visible

school game, inspired by the animated series *Winx Club*, where players can participate in events and competitions, attend classes, and teleport between different universes. In the horror category, *Murder Mystery 2* is a whodunit experience where users are randomly assigned roles of Innocent, Sheriff, or Murderer, with the goal of either solving or committing a murder; and *Piggy* is a survival horror game where players must solve puzzles and escape from an eponymous zombie creature. Adventure and RPG games like *Blox Fruits* immerse users in a world inspired by anime, forcing them to choose between being pirates or marines, master various fighting styles, and explore islands in search of fruits that grant special abilities. Obstacle challenges are represented by *Tower of Hell*, an obby game with no checkpoints, requiring players to navigate vertically through difficult towers. Finally, pet-centric games like *Adopt Me!* and *Pet Simulator X!* focus on collecting, trading, and nurturing pets. As a sign of societal evolution, *Adopt Me!* was originally launched in 2017 as a role-playing experience where players could pretend to adopt or be adopted as babies. In 2019, it introduced the option of adopting and caring for virtual pets, a change that has significantly boosted the game's popularity.

Figure 7.7 *Adopt Me!* game sequence: What's your style?; Furnish your own home; On the way to the nursery; Adoption choice: babies or pets

These scenarios are mediated through architecture. Roblox video games can be grouped according to their architectural styles. *Brookhaven RP* features a contemporary suburban design with simple, functional buildings, while *Adopt Me!*, *MeepCity*, and *Pet Simulator X!* have whimsical, cartoonish styles characterized by colorful, customizable home designs. *Pet Simulator X!* includes themed areas, also known as biomes, ranging from urban environments to enchanted forests and beach landscapes, providing diverse experiences where players can collect and trade pets. *Tower of Hell* adopts a minimalist, functional style focused on raised platforms differentiated by colors, and *Blox Fruits* blends pirate-themed buildings, ancient ruins, and futuristic structures. *Piggy* presents a dark, eerie style creating suspense, with various abandoned places such as train stations, houses, refineries, ports, and factories, while *Murder Mystery 2* employs a realistic, immersive style with detailed environments reflecting specific interiors such as office buildings, mansions, and military bases. *Royale High* boasts a fantasy-inspired, ornate style with grand structures reminiscent of fairy tales. In cartographic terms, games like *Adopt Me!* simulate mini cities, whereas *Blox Fruits* recreates the world of pirate anime with islands spanning different seas. Some experiences

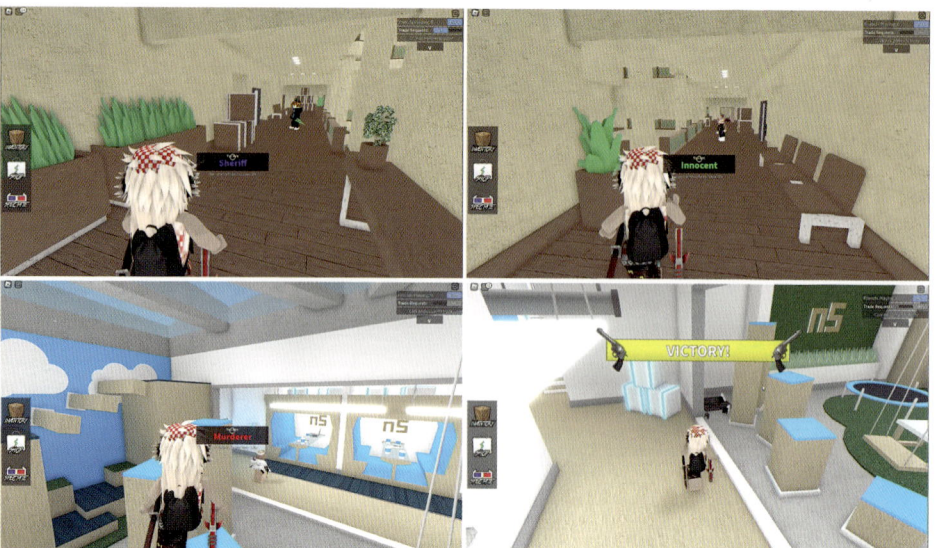

Figure 7.8 *Murder Mystery 2*: Different gameplay scenes, assigning Sheriff, Innocent, or Murderer identities randomly

feature various maps unlocked as players progress, such as *Murder Mystery 2*, which offers around ten different worlds. In most cases, inspiration is drawn from anonymous architecture, like the rural styles in *Adopt Me!* and the generic modernist constructions in *Brookhaven RP*. Stereotypical and magical architectures are also prominent, with *Pet Simulator X!* featuring archetypal city and beach worlds, and *Royale High* showcasing references from popular culture in settings merging medieval castles and Disneyland architecture.

The perception of these architectures is linked to the avatar's position and camera type. The camera in Roblox experiences is highly interactive, capable of rapidly shifting from first-person to third-person view, pivoting and rotating around the avatar, and tracking it while moving. Although there are no precise statistics about the most commonly used camera types on the platform, both anonymous players and influential Roblox streamers such as Mayrushart, Auiciq, and Janet and Kate show a preference for third-person view while moving. In this view, users see their character from an external perspective, usually from behind and slightly above, similar to the ActiveTrack feature found in modern drones, which allows for autonomous following and filming of a subject without manual control. This tracking camera generally maintains a diagonal top-down view, ensuring the avatar is always in sight and creating a sense of distortion. In Roblox, the camera angles often make the avatar's head

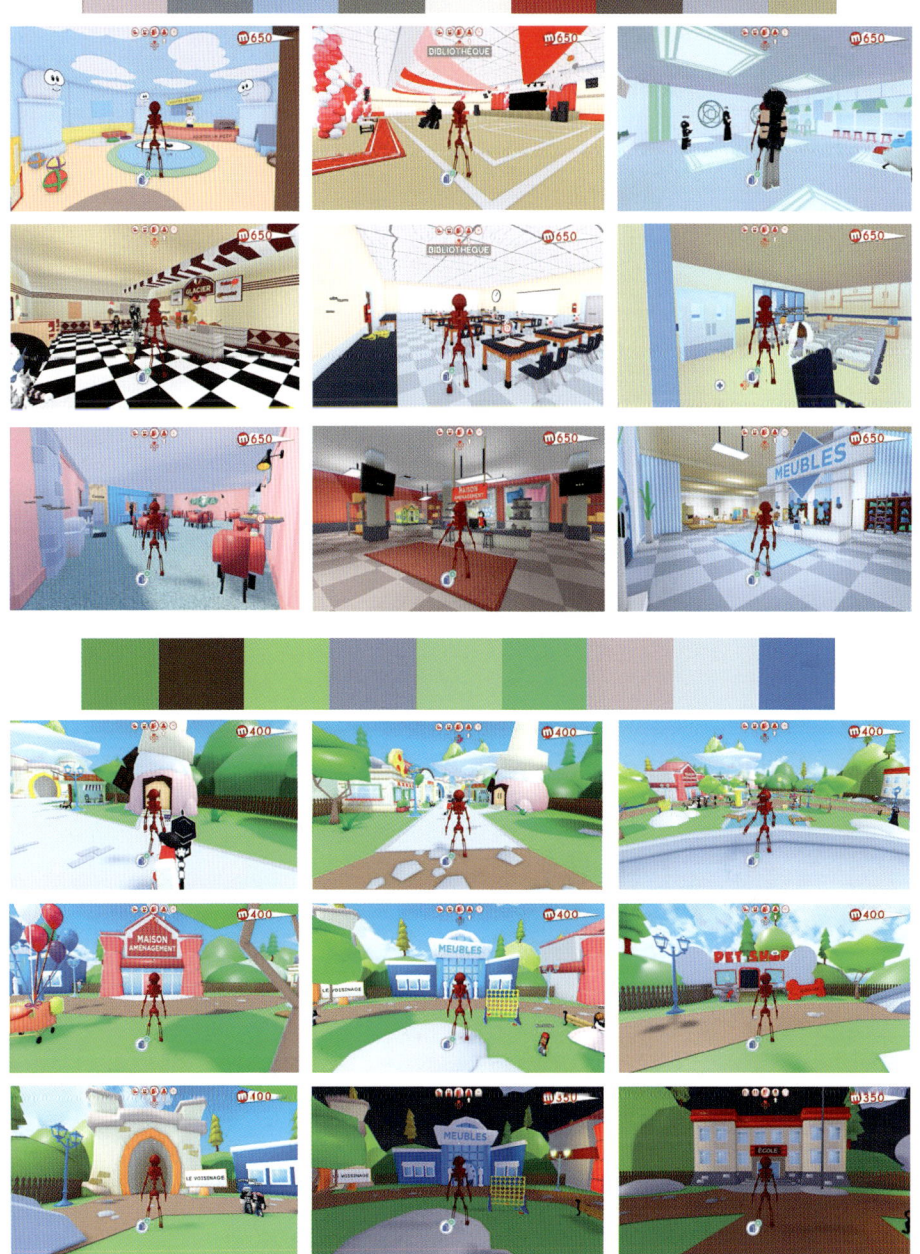

Figure 7.9 *MeepCity*: Comparison between interior and exterior spaces, including different chromatic palettes

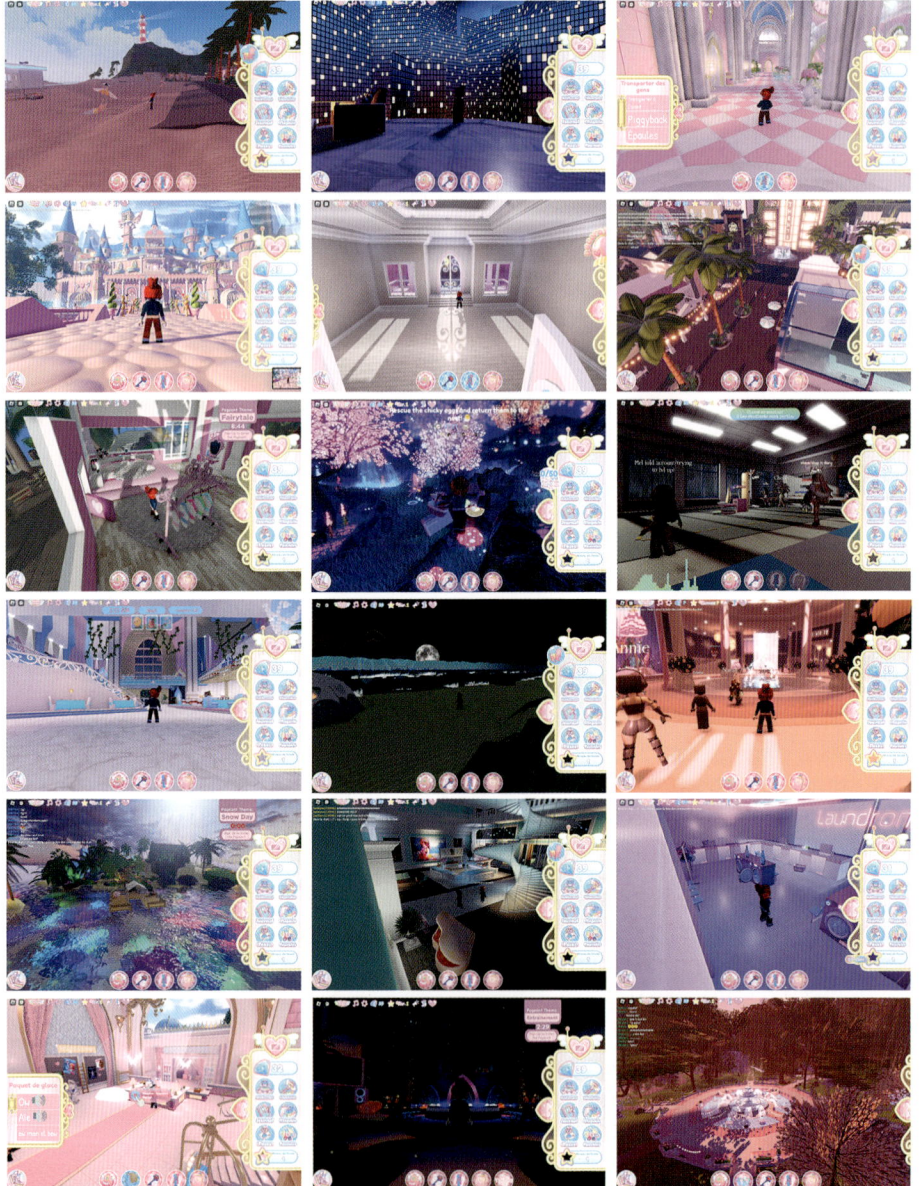

Figure 7.10 *Royale High*: Gameplay sequence traversing interior and exterior spaces. Homogeneous chromatic palette based on pink and purple tones

appear larger relative to the rest of the body, and the ground more visually prominent compared with the ceiling or sky (which, even in outdoor spaces, is sometimes not visible). The elevated and rotating camera angle often creates a three-point linear perspective with two vanishing points on the horizon sides, and one above or below it, eliminating parallel lines on the screen and exaggerating proportions. In the history of art, the illusion of distorted objects in space is called "foreshortening," a means of rendering depth through the compression of form. While foreshortening has been fundamental to understanding the placement of bodies within pictorial space since the Renaissance—especially in the works of Masaccio and Mantegna in the 15th century—there have been few significant examples depicting foreshortened spaces using three-point perspective in art. The most famous case is probably M.C. Escher's *Ascending and Descending*, a lithograph from 1960 that foreshadows the perspectival spaces found in video games. In Roblox's architecture, buildings, roads, and structures converge toward multiple, mobile vanishing points, creating an idea of the world built from the designed and behavioral movements of its avatars.

Intimacy is constructed both digitally and architecturally. Some experiences offer personal spaces for players, such as houses, studios, rooms, or dormitories. These are mainly found in simulation and virtual world exploration genres. In *Brookhaven RP*, players have houses, while *Adopt Me!* begins within interior domestic spaces that they can customize and furnish before starting to adopt pets. Similarly, *MeepCity* allows its users to furnish their spaces with furniture and decorations, while *Royale High* also offers personal spaces. Although experiences like *Brookhaven RP*, *Adopt Me!*, *Royale High*, and *Pet Simulator X!* lack strong storylines or quests, they allow gamers to freely explore, socialize, and customize their rooms. Other games feature clear scenarios involving survival, cooperation, or progression through levels by completing various tasks and quests. Some focus on generating adrenaline, offering short, time-limited sessions, as seen in *Tower of Hell* and horror titles like *Murder Mystery 2*. As a form of collective interaction, gamers regularly traverse public and private programs, indoor and outdoor spaces. One game offers exclusively interior spaces—*Tower of Hell*—while two are mainly played outdoors: *Pet Simulator X!* and *Blox Fruits*. *Murder Mystery 2* is primarily an indoor experience, enacting the cinematographic relationship between interiors and horror. Simulation and role-playing titles regularly

Figure 7.11 *Pet Simulator X!* Mostly diurnal, outdoor, and above-ground. The three bottom images represent the only underwater world, following the same composition principles

offer recognizable spaces associated with city lifestyles, such as shops, parks, and public facilities, as well as residential areas. *Brookhaven RP*, *Adopt Me!*, *MeepCity*, and *Royale High* all feature these elements. These games are mostly multiplayer, though some offer solo modes. Multiplayer modes may be limited to a maximum number of people, such as *Tower of Hell's* twenty-player limit and *Blox Fruits'* twelve-player limit. As of April 2024, all titles in the ten most-played Roblox games (by all-time visits) had over a billion connections, with *Brookhaven RP* leading at over 45 billion and *Pet Simulator X!* closing the list with over 8 billion.[17]

As an epitome of the construction of parallel space–time, the day/night cycle is never maintained in a circadian rhythm. Some games have longer days than nights, while others invert or obliterate these cycles. For instance, *Murder Mystery 2* features 100 percent daytime with changing weather, while *Royale High* and *Blox Fruits* have a ratio of daytime to nighttime of approximately 65 percent. In *Brookhaven RP*, the time and day of the week are displayed at the top right of the game screen, with approximately two cycles completed in one hour of real-time play. The horror game *Piggy* reverses this trend with 25 percent daytime and 75 percent nighttime to enhance the fear factor. *Pet Simulator X!* does not have a night mode, although it displays one world out of eleven that is exclusively nocturnal, called *Tech World*, embodying the idea that technological environments are artificially lit. In the non-circadian spaces of Roblox, all experiences feature synchronous chat conversations, sometimes including voice chat for collaboration in horror genres like *Piggy*, and both public and private chat options in titles like *Royale High*. In *Murder Mystery 2*, players use the chat to devise strategies to avoid in-game death, whereas in *Adopt Me!*, it facilitates collaboration on quests, the creation of virtual families, and pet trading. This digital trust is monetized, with strategies to engage users that include virtual shops for purchasing items with in-game money as well as events, temporary worlds, regular updates, quests, and new levels that are collectively discussed.

Designers use specific color palettes to reflect these universes: *Royale High* uses pink, pastel, and warm tones for its fairy world, while *Murder Mystery 2* and *Piggy* use dark palettes for a sinister atmosphere. Some games propose brighter, more diverse colors, as seen in *Adopt Me!*, *Brookhaven RP*, and *Blox Fruits*. *Tower of Hell* functionally uses colors as markers to help the player navigate through the platforms. Imaginaries such as the prevalence of above-ground spaces and the invisibility of ancillary areas, which are very prevalent in traditional architectural representation, are also recognizable in Roblox, although with some exceptions. A few experiences display underground spaces in small proportions, including *Brookhaven RP*, *Adopt Me!*, *Blox Fruits*, *MeepCity*, and *Piggy*, while *Pet Simulator X!* also features one underwater world. Some show annexes and ancillary spaces: *Adopt Me!* can include a storage room in the player's house; *MeepCity* include technical facilities, and *Royale High* has auxiliary rooms for relaxation and conversation. In titles like *Tower of Hell* and *Blox Fruits*, players must complete quests or unlock levels to access new areas. Some games have private spaces accessible only to the player, while others, like *Brookhaven RP*, allow free access to other users' houses, blurring the line between public and private in a non-circadian, artificially intimate, digital world.

Figure 7.12 *Piggy*: Mostly nocturnal, indoor, and above-ground

Multiplayer Surveillance: Customized Cameras, Perspectives, and Control Rooms

> For the past few months, I, along with my development team, have been working on an ambitious MMORPG project on the Roblox platform. A key theme we decided early on was to focus on immersion and realism, and as a result, I decided to create a custom camera system that serves that purpose.[18]
>
> LUGICAL, "CameraService: A New Camera for a New Roblox," 2022

The Roblox Creator Hub is the platform's user guide, providing tutorials, tools, and resources for creators to design video games on the platform. Under the title "Customizing the Camera," designers can learn about Roblox's built-in camera, which shifts between a default third-person mode and an optional first-person mode. For more customized scenarios, it is possible to adjust the properties in Camera or replace it entirely for views such as over-the-shoulder, isometric, and weapon scoping.[19] These options are complemented by solutions provided in the Roblox Developer Forum, a blog-based platform that allows game designers to chat with other creators, learn about updates, and report issues with the platform. In a blog started in 2022, Lugical, a programmer, shares details of a new CameraService, stating, "I've decided to open-source it, allowing developers of all kinds to implement new, breathtaking camera views into their games and experiences with just a few lines of code!"[20] Fellow programmers show their enthusiasm and share their questions about the new resource. "Great work, my man, keep it up!" exclaims Ayden. "In shift lock view, if you move your mouse over a proximity prompt, you are not able to use your mouse anymore," complains Helyras after thanking Lugical for sharing. "The idea of a cinematic camera just gave me a ton of inspiration to implement more immersive cutscenes in my games," concludes Astra.

In the seven-second launch video shared by Lugical, an R15 Roblox avatar with an intellectual look smiles confidently amid a green pasture. He turns around and walks past different labels carrying the names Tilt Camera, Cinematic Camera, Shake Camera, Shift Lock, and Third Person. At the end of the video, he stops alone in the middle of the greenery and seems to look at the horizon. We can only see his body from behind, but it is possible to imagine his perpetual smile, as Roblox characters do not normally change expressions. This is a world in which the camera type, viewpoint, focal length, depth of field, and related attributes are decided by individual creators and used in shifting modes by anonymous users. Underneath rigid facial expressions lies a world of multiple, malleable perspectives. Unsurprisingly, while navigating, the character is seen from above, and the video ends with a shot in which the horizon line is dramatically tilted diagonally.

In the foreshortened architecture of Roblox, three-point perspectives create the visual impression that the walls, doors, and objects with which the avatars interact come closer. In psychology, it is commonly accepted that humans have a vertical attention bias that directs their focus toward the tops of objects and the bottoms of scenes, generally favoring a downward gaze.[21] In Roblox, players can interact with objects (such as doors, buttons, or NPCs) by clicking on them or pressing a designated key when close enough. This interaction may trigger an animation, open a dialogue, or perform an action like picking up an item. Since these are multiplayer games with individual screens per

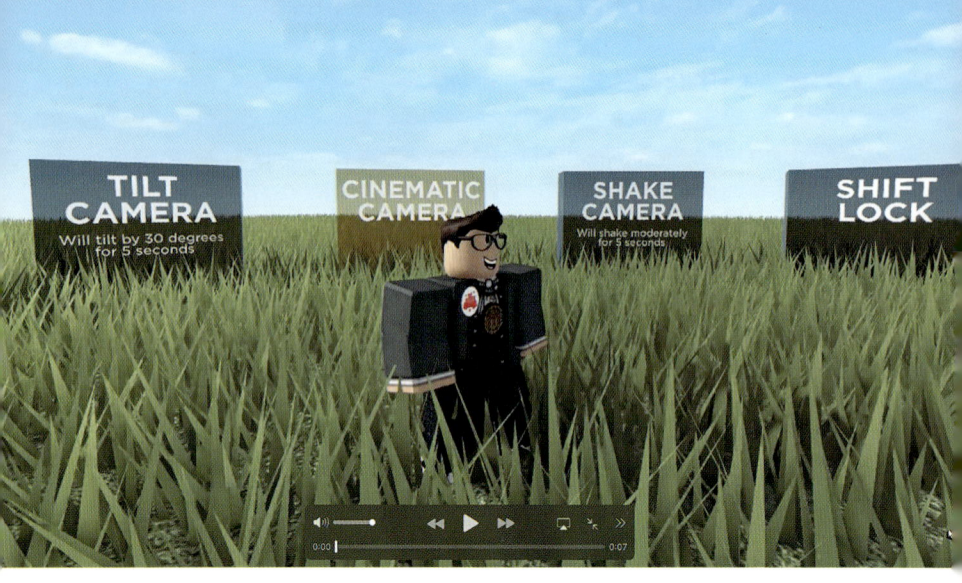

Figure 7.13 Lugical, "CameraService: A New Camera for a New Roblox," 2022

user, the perspective is rendered differently for each one, always ensuring they are drawn to the game mechanics of continuous stimulation, framed within architectural spaces.

If Roblox is considered a form of social media, then interactions occur directly within its experiences. Players can meet each other in virtual spaces such as shops, resting areas, meeting spots, and lobbies. Chat becomes an essential tool for collaboration and can exert a real influence on the platform, both in designers' forums and in gaming discussions. Communities can converse while playing, collaborate on coding and design, help each other out, or simply socialize. They are also often active on other platforms outside Roblox, such as Discord, Twitter, Reddit, Facebook, and YouTube, where they livestream and comment on their gameplay. This normalizes an aesthetic of surveillance where gamers and creators interact through chats and tracking cameras that prompt CCTV-like perspectives. In the case of Roblox, the most commonly used device for gaming across all experiences is the smartphone (80%), followed by the desktop computer (20%) and sometimes the console.[22] The platform is used by various age groups, although it is noteworthy that the most-played experiences target a child or adolescent audience, with adults rarely exceeding 18 or 20 years old. Since every player has a different screen, this architecture features fragmented, elevated viewpoints, similar to the perception of multiple distant spaces in the control rooms used to monitor contemporary cities.

This is significant, since no other space better epitomizes the relationship between screen, space, and surveillance than the control room. Originally conceived as centralized facilities for monitoring dispersed activities in factories in the 1920s, later scaled up to territorial scale after the experiments of the Architecture Machine Group and the Aspen Movie Map in the 1970s, control rooms have nowadays colonized cities and architecture worldwide as multiscreen spaces where categories such as traffic, environment, and security are monitored. As authors such as Orit Halpern have explained, the amount of information visualized in control rooms escapes human cognition; instead, it is directly analyzed computationally: "These architectures are performances, demonstrations of big data enacted for individuals who can neither see nor directly analyze the images."[23] Referring to the total alienation of human presence within space, Halpern further notes that "[t]hese gleaming rooms are merely the flagship displays for vast infrastructures of computing, performances of control and surveillance on ever larger and increasingly global networks."[24]

Interestingly, Roblox proposes an inverted model. While contemporary cities are monitored from centralized control rooms, in-game architectures are seen from decentralized, individualized screens where camera types and viewpoints can be adjusted at will. The controllers are both creators and gamers, who serve as both observers and the observed through multiple CCTV perspectives. This fragmented and deterritorialized system of surveillance reflects a broader shift toward distributed forms of control, mirroring trends in digital technologies. In these virtual environments, the multiplicity of perspectives, akin to countless cameras, allows players to engage with the game world from multiple angles. This setup creates a complex web of interactions that is continually monitored and adjusted in real time. The Roblox model exemplifies how modern digital landscapes function through dispersed yet interconnected devices, reshaping traditional notions of surveillance. Ultimately, the evolution from centralized control rooms in physical cities to fragmented, player-centric control screens in games like Roblox highlights a shift toward simultaneously computational and individualized forms of seeing, reflective of broader societal changes in how we interact with, trust, and distrust our environments.

Analysis conducted as part of the *Theory of Mediated Spaces* module
HEAD – Genève (HES-SO). Spring Semester 2024
Professor: Javier Fernández Contreras
Data Analytics (BA students in Interior Architecture):
  —*Piggy*: Alexis Lang, Manon Lebon, and Maelle Mabru
  —*Pet Simulator X!*: Cléa Bertossa, Aurore Biache, and Alexia Dahman
  —*Royale High*: Marie Mamou Blanché, Elise Mathis, and Missilia
  Mendy
  —*Tower of Hell*: Yan Vasquez, Nina Wallimann, and Jiwon Yuk
  —*Adopt Me!*: Benjamin Dohollou, Tiago Dos Santos Pinto, and Carla
  Ferey
  —*Brookhaven RP*: Zoé Mettraux, Luca Negro, and Norah Pittet
  —*MeepCity*: Martin Annen, Nassim Baron, and Giona Leo Baumann
  —*Murder Mystery 2*: Mireille Gidi, Hippolyte Giraud, and Ambre
  Gravina
  —*Blox Fruits*: Bryan Jefferson Reyes, Anna Smiian, and Kateryna
  Sushynska.

Notes

1 Andreas M. Kaplan and Michael Haenlein, "Users of the world, unite! The
 challenges and opportunities of Social Media," *Business Horizons*,
 no. 53(1) (January–February 2010), 59–68.

2 Rohit Shewale, "Roblox Statistics For 2024 (Active Players, Revenue
 & Usage)," *Demandsage*, January 15, 2024 (accessed June 21,
 2024), https://www.demandsage.com/how-many-people-play-
 roblox/

3 "The rise of user-created video games," *The Economist*, March 25, 2023
 (accessed June 21, 2024), https://www.economist.com/special-
 report/2023/03/20/the-rise-of-user-created-video-games

4 Ibid.

5 David H. Ahl, ed., *101 BASIC Computer Games* (Maynard, MA: Digital
 Equipment Corporation, 1973). The second edition, published in 1978,
 sold over
 1 million copies, becoming the first computer book to do so and attesting
 to the impact of collaborative video game coding on society.

6 For a history of the evolution of video games until 2010, see: Mathieu
 Triclot, *Philosophie des jeux vidéo* (Paris: Éditions Zones, 2011).

7 Michael Graves, "A Case for Figurative Architecture," in Peter Arnell, Ted
 Bickford, and Karen Vogel Wheeler (eds.), *Michael Graves: Buildings and
 Projects 1966–1981* (New York: Rizzoli, 1982), 11–13.

8 Ibid.

9 Robin Evans, "Piero's Heads," in *The Projective Cast: Architecture and Its Three Geometries* (Cambridge: MIT Press, 2000), 123–178. First published: Cambridge: MIT Press, 1995.

10 Matej 'Retro' Jan, "Game developer's guide to graphical projections (with video game examples), Part 1: Introduction," *Medium*, November 2, 2017 (accessed June 21, 2024), https://medium.com/retronator-magazine/game-developers-guide-to-graphical-projections-with-video-game-examples-part-1-introduction-aa3d051c137d

11 For a history of Roblox, see:
– *Wikipedia*, last edited on July 19, 2024, 18:40 (UTC), https://en.wikipedia.org/wiki/Roblox
– toastedcherries, "the history of roblox, i guess (part 1)," YouTube, July 19, 2021 (accessed June 21, 2024), https://www.youtube.com/watch?v=n-9llr9xsys&t=259s
– toastedcherries, "the history of roblox, i guess (part 2)," YouTube, August 2, 2021 (accessed June 21, 2024), https://youtu.be/lDSOrb-aJ-0?si=ToewacWPISMcXYIB

12 "Avatar," *Roblox Wiki* (accessed June 21, 2024), https://roblox.fandom.com/wiki/Avatar#2004-2005

13 *Roblox for Brands* is a dedicated space for brands to sell their virtual products on the platform, https://brands.roblox.com. Iconic brands selling their products on Roblox include Gucci, Samsung, and Nike, to name a few. See: Webb Wright, "From Nikeland to Gucci Town: The Top 5 Branded Roblox Activations," *The Drum*, November 11, 2022 (accessed June 21, 2024), https://www.thedrum.com/news/2022/11/11/the-top-5-branded-roblox-activations-2022-luxury-shopping-sustainable-farming

14 Named "Korblox Deathspeaker Leg," alternatives for acquiring similar items without payment by following online videos and tutorials can also be found.

15 "Stop Giving Two Gender Options; Acknowledge Non-Binary Users," *Roblox Creator Hub*, July 2020–June 2022 (accessed June 21, 2024), https://devforum.roblox.com/t/stop-giving-two-gender-options-acknowledge-non-binary-users/700782

16 Most-played Roblox games worldwide as of April 2024, by all-time visits, in order from most to least visited: *Brookhaven RP*, *Adopt Me!*, *Tower of Hell*, *Blox Fruits*, *MeepCity*, *Piggy*, *Murder Mystery 2*, *Royale High*, *Pet Simulator X!* See: "Most-played Roblox games worldwide as of April 2024, by all-time visits (in billions)," *Statista*, April 8, 2024 (accessed June 21, 2024), https://www.statista.com/statistics/1220905/roblox-most-visited-games/

17 Ibid.

18 Lugical, "CameraService: A New Camera for a New Roblox," *Roblox Developer Forum*, September 2022 (accessed June 21, 2024), https://devforum.roblox.com/t/cameraservice-a-new-camera-for-a-new-roblox/1988655

19 "Customizing the Camera," *Roblox Creator Hub* (accessed June 21, 2024), https://create.roblox.com/docs/workspace/camera

20 Lugical, "CameraService: A New Camera for a New Roblox."

21 Matthew D. Langley, Kaitlin Van Houghton, Michael K. McBeath, and Kelsey Lucca, "Children and adults exhibit a common vertical attention bias for object tops and scene bottoms," *Developmental Psychology*, no. 59(8) (2023), 1377–1388, https://doi.org/10.1037/dev0001553

22 "Distribution of Roblox audiences worldwide as of December 2023, by platform," *Statista*, December 2023 (accessed June 21, 2024), https://www.statista.com/statistics/1190919/roblox-games-users-global-distribution-platform/

23 Orit Halpern, "Architecture as Machine: The Smart City Deconstructed," in Andrew Goodhouse (ed.), *When Is the Digital in Architecture?* (Montreal: CCA; Berlin: Sternberg Press, 2017), 125–126.

24 Ibid.

8
PORN ROOMS: ULTIMATE INTERIORITY

*Javier Fernández Contreras and
Vytautas Jankauskas*

The relationship between pornography and interior spaces spans the history of humankind, reflecting societal, technological, and aesthetic shifts. From ancient erotic frescoes in Pompeii to lavishly decorated 19th-century Parisian brothels, the spaces of intimacy have long been intertwined with the representation of sexuality. The emergence of photography and cinema further reinforced this relationship, bringing staged eroticism into controlled studio environments. With the advent of smartphones in the 21st century, the widespread availability of mobile cameras connected to the internet has transformed the audiovisual industry of pornography. Cinematic productions once defined by high-budget film aesthetics have largely given way to tube sites—a shorthand term for pornographic websites. A significant shift accompanying this transition has been the amateurization of online production, meaning that content creators now operate outside the mainstream industry, engaging in a precarious gig-economy model where individuals create and distribute their own material.[1]

Pornhub, the most-visited porn site in the world as of February 2025,[2] exemplifies this shift by mixing professional and user-generated content. Its amateur section can be considered a form of social media, as it allows creators to upload, share, and monetize their videos while engaging with an audience through comments, rankings, and personalized profiles. With content produced by virtually anyone, anywhere, interior spaces have become essential sites of sexually explicit performance—physically private yet digitally exposed. By and large, most porn content on the internet is shot indoors, as these spaces provide both discretion and controlled environments for recording. Far from being neutral, interior architecture is therefore implicated as a profession in the ethical, intellectual, political, and sociological concerns of porn. The seclusion and visual autonomy of interiors can reinforce power asymmetries between those on camera and those watching, making it important to identify the archetypes and design strategies of these rooms.

This analysis examines the role of interior spaces in the porn industry, identifying archetypes whose aesthetics, furnishing, and filming techniques serve as props in the erotization of space, shaping how bodies interact with their environments. The result of an interdisciplinary workshop with participants from the arts, cinema, and design departments at HEAD – Genève, the study explores the interplay between performed spaces and the bodies that perform them, analyzing how different elements, decor, and settings appear in audiovisual frames. Using visual research and digital tools, participants individually identified recurring patterns and examined the relationship between architecture and content creation. The research focused on user-generated content, often filtered by "most viewed," with options to analyze various subtags such as setting type, decor, gender, sexual practice, and filming style. Visual templates accompanied the research, featuring a grid-based overview. A central hypothesis and takeaway from the workshop was that, in the space of the internet, different architectural rooms are "pornified" through varying sexual performances, depending on their spatial design and configuration.

The types of interior spaces identified included those classified by elements such as artworks (cheap, generic paintings positioned to be visible behind performers), plush toys (associated with Asian-inspired aesthetics), chairs (centrally placed within the frame, typically captured in limited shots without further editing), and windows (often showing gray days to avoid direct sunlight, with skyscrapers evoking a corporate or luxurious setting for lovemaking). Similarly, different space types contribute to the sensualized environment—gyms emphasize hypersexualized bodies using workout equipment as erotic props, while cars, often filmed vertically with smartphones, reflect a mobile, voyeuristic aesthetic. Filming technology also shapes the medium, with night-vision devices creating a hidden-camera aesthetic—bodies entwined in bed linen reminiscent of reality TV shows such as *Big Brother*. Seasonal themes influence search trends, as seen in Christmas-related content, where specific decorative motifs and Santa-like apparel appear. Inversely, a non-seasonal, year-long trend involves the visual appropriation of religious spaces such as churches for sex performances: here, the original interior design is preserved to create a stark figure–background contrast. The representation of different body types also informs the visual language of space, with content featuring trans women showing differences in terms of subject matter, agency, and interior design when they curate their own accounts versus when these are controlled by men. Finally, specific formats like sex vlogs structure content in a particular sequence, typically starting outdoors before transitioning into interior spaces, with edited cuts replacing long takes.

While the traditional, pre-internet audiovisual porn industry was characterized by extensive film editing and professional set design—as exemplified in photographic works like Larry Sultan's *The Valley* (2004) or Jo Broughton's *Empty Porn Sets* (2001–2007)—the contemporary era might suggest that the democratization of porn has expanded the variety of interiors represented in these videos. However, an analysis of highly ranked content instead suggests a standardization of the most-watched spaces. While the professional porn industry frequently staged its productions in aestheticized interiors such as those featuring Le Corbusier and Charlotte Perriand's LC4 chaise longue[3] or the high-end furniture often showcased in Hugh Hefner's *Playboy* domesticities,[4] amateur porn tends to be produced in generic and economically accessible environments. Many videos are shot in spaces furnished with mass-market items from IKEA, Amazon, or Alibaba, using decor that is widely available and easily replaceable. Additionally, the rise of short-term rental platforms such as Airbnb has made it possible for performers to shoot in ever-updated interiors that are curated to evoke an aspirational yet relatable indoors. These spaces balance a "XX-next-door" appeal with a neutral, depersonalized design, enabling viewers to project themselves as virtual voyeurs inhabiting similar, standardized interiors.

Beyond spatial analysis, the workshop also raised ethical concerns regarding the content itself. Participants critically engaged with the often-problematic nature of so-called amateur material, questioning the agency of the performers, potential exploitative dynamics, and the broader implications of analyzing user-generated pornography. Findings revealed spatial trends such as gendered associations with specific settings and the repeated use of rented properties. Additionally, the project confronted issues of consent, commercialization, and the opacity of Pornhub's data practices, prompting reflections on the methods of studying such material. By integrating critical inquiry with digital tools, the workshop examined how interior spaces both reflect and shape porn content creation while problematizing the ethical complexities embedded in the platform's ecosystem. The visual material is not published out of consideration for sex workers, whose online self-representation often stems from structurally marginalized contexts.

To all performers whose bodies float on the internet, we express our utmost respect.

Analysis conducted as part of *The Interiors of Porn* workshop
HEAD – Genève (HES-SO). February 2025
Tutors: Javier F. Contreras, Vytautas Jankauskas; Assistant: Lola Jutzeler
Analysis (students):
  —Paintings: Antonin Ricou
  —Chairs: Emilie Rau and Nicolas Ulrich
  —Plushies: Delia Aeberli and Carla Plan
  —Windows: Ileana Leveuf Feliz
  —Gyms: Léo Dorner
  —Churches and cemeteries: Lelia Quero and Caïque Interlandi
  —Cars: Louisa Azzouz and Denis Désir
  —Night-vision: Léo Dorner
  —Christmas: Lelia Quero and Caïque Interlandi
  —Trans women portrayed by men: Jaeggi Sky and Fatana Mia Paris
  —Trans women owning their images: Jaeggi Sky and Fatana Mia Paris
  —Sex vlogs: Emeline Mermoud

Notes

1 For a general overview of the evolution of the porn industry from cinema
   production to tube sites, with a particular focus on Pornhub, see: Ovidie,
   Pornocracy: The New Sex Multinationals (Production: Magneto Presse,
   Fatalitas Productions, 2017).

2 "List of most-visited websites," *Wikipedia*, last edited on February 17, 2025,
   15:52 (UTC), https://en.wikipedia.org/wiki/List_of_most_visited_websites

3 Augustine Rockebrune and Josephine Rockebrune, *We Don't Embroider
   Cushions Here* (Paris: Sammlung Preislos, 2015).

4 See: Paul Preciado, *Pornotopia: An Essay on Playboy's Architecture and
   Biopolitics* (New York: Zone Books, 2019). First published in Spanish as
   Pornotopía: Arquitectura y sexualidad en "Playboy" durante la Guerra Fría
   (Barcelona: Anagrama, 2010). See also: Beatriz Colomina and Nikola
   Jankovic, *L'Univers Playboy* (Paris: Éditions B2, 2016).

AFTERWORD

Marina Otero Verzier

In *The Interiors of Social Media*, Javier Fernández Contreras navigates the convergence of architecture and digital platforms, highlighting how social media produces, circulates, and reconfigures space—particularly interiors. The book makes a case for why architects and spatial practitioners must engage with these dynamics as active participants in an unfolding transformation that is reshaping the discipline.

Architecture has always been entangled with media, as scholars such as Beatriz Colomina have extensively investigated. Yet never before have its representation, practice, and experience been so deeply mediated by digital networks. The proliferation of screens, interfaces, and algorithmic curation has multiplied the realms of spatial entanglements and their forms of visibility, shaped by engagement metrics, attention economies, and the demands of digital consumption. In this matrix, digital platforms do not merely document space; they generate it.

Think of the project *Pornified Homes* (2016) by Andrés Jaque/Office for Political Innovation. The film examines the constellations of online male prostitution and the transnational, transmedia architectures that enable them to exist. Jaque argues for the emergence of a distinct urbanism enabled by the convergence of digital platforms and domestic environments—one that results from the coordination of escort apartments, online profiles, and district transformations.

Building upon these and other explorations—including the historical trajectory of architectural mediation and the study of representation techniques from 17th-century Dutch paintings, Grand Tour sketches, early cinema, and television sets—Fernández Contreras unpacks the contemporary interiors circulated on platforms such as Pinterest, Twitch, TikTok, and Roblox. These digital environments and their encoded logics establish conventions that shape specific aesthetics and architectures, creating feedback loops between the screen and the analog world.

Consider the endlessly re-pinned interiors of Pinterest. They result from processes of visual compilation, where users organize eclectic collections of images, textures, and colors. These constellations— sourced from different origins and periods—are decontextualized. In their circulation, these amnesic mood boards enable feedback loops between the binary language of 0s and 1s on a screen and the spatial structures in the analog world that either inspire them or are inspired by them.

Fernández Contreras analyzes the relationships between screens and rooms, as well as the processes of standardization, pattern recognition, and typological consolidation that facilitate their circulation— from the staged intimacy of influencer bedrooms to the algorithmically optimized set designs of amateur porn. These interiors are often hyper-visible yet paradoxically placeless stages. They exist as templates, mostly designed as smooth surfaces optimized for scrolling and sharing, produced for circulation.

Staging for an audience is not new; architects and scholars such as Ignacio G. Galán have analyzed how power regimes have depended on design practices as part of larger political projects, using popular magazines, department stores, and film sets as spaces for producing a totalizing image. However, as the book contends, what is new is the scale and speed at which these processes now unfold. Their impact can be seen in how domestic spaces are furnished, how real estate is marketed, how cities brand themselves, and how architecture is taught and practiced—influencing not only how we interact with the world but also the limits of our imagination.

The possibilities these platforms offer for user interaction are predetermined. The lack of transparency regarding the materials and algorithms used to train these models raises further questions about the ideologies embedded within them. The companies behind these platforms control and profit from a vast catalog of textual and visual knowledge—both human and synthetic—delivered to users through algorithms that channel the sale of experiences and commodities. As the book shows, these platforms function as arenas of economic extraction while also perpetuating biases, exclusions, and privileges.

Similarly, the resource consumption of these systems is immense and growing. The infrastructure required for data production, storage, and circulation demands significant energy for its operation and, often, potable water for cooling, contributing to CO_2 emissions.

In this context, Fernández Contreras asks: How can architects intervene in this space—not simply by critiquing its effects but by actively shaping its futures? The book offers a way forward in this era of digital mediation. It lays the foundation for new lines of research, new pedagogical approaches, and new ways of practicing architecture that critically engage with the spatial logics of social media as an integral part of contemporary architectural culture. Instead of treating digital space as a service we passively consume as "users," the book invites us to recognize it as an intrinsic part of our lives—one over which we must assume active responsibility—transcending its limits to imagine alternative ways of inhabiting digital space.

CONTRIBUTORS

Javier Fernández Contreras (PhD) is an architect and architectural theorist, and the head of the Department of Space Design/Interior Architecture at HEAD – Genève (HES-SO). His work explores the relationship between architecture, representation, and media, with a specific focus on the role of interiors in the construction of contemporaneity. He is the author of the books *The Miralles Projection* (2020) and *Manifesto of Interiors: Thinking in the Expanded Media* (2021), and the co-editor of *Scènes de Nuit: Night & Architecture* (2021), *Intimacy Exposed: Toilet, Bathroom, Restroom* (2023), *A Nocturnal History of Architecture* (2024), and *Nothing About Interior Architecture* (2025).

Michela Bassanelli is a senior lecturer in interior architecture and exhibition design at the Department of Architecture and Urban Studies, Politecnico di Milano. In 2023, she was an associate researcher at HEAD – Genève (HES-SO). She has recently been examining the effects of the COVID-19 pandemic on changes in contemporary living. She has authored monographs and numerous papers published in peer-reviewed international journals. Her most recent book is *Dispositivi e Architettura. Lo spazio dinamico dell'abitare* (2024).

Damien Greder is a PhD candidate in international relations and political science and a doctoral researcher for *The Future of Humanitarian Design (HUD)* research project at the Geneva Graduate Institute and HEAD – Genève (HES-SO). He is the co-founder of Hypothesis atelier, which engages with social structures, and of data-room.xyz, which explores connections between material and digital spaces. His work has been recognized notably in the *Swiss Publication Building Culture: Quality and Critique. 13 Projects Under Scrutiny* (2022). Greder's PhD research "Political Housing: Toghether*less*" explores how collective housing can materialize sufficiency principles.

Vytautas Jankauskas is a lecturer in media art and design and the director of the Digital Pool at HEAD – Genève (HES-SO). His research and creative practice explore connected domestic devices, social networks, and artificial intelligence, with a particular emphasis on speech synthesis and voice agents. His recent project, *Latent Intimacies* (2024), investigates human–machine relationships through localized, open-source large language models.

Marina Otero Verzier (PhD) is Dean's Visiting Professor at the Columbia University Graduate School of Architecture, Planning and Preservation (GSAPP), where she leads the "Data Mourning" initiative on digital infrastructures and climate catastrophe. In 2022, she received Harvard's Wheelwright Prize for her research on future data storage. She collaborates with scientific institutions to develop alternative models for data storage, such as Computational Compost. Otero was invited by the Chilean Government to help develop its first National Data Centers Plan. She authored "En las Profundidades de la Nube" (2024), proposing new paradigms and aesthetics for data storage, integrating architecture, preservation, and digital culture.

Paule Perron is an architect and lecturer at the Department of Space Design/Interior Architecture at HEAD – Genève (HES-SO). She develops a practice between research and project to question the perpetuation of domination patterns through the study of mutual influences between spaces and bodies. Through the conception and representation of alternative narratives, she hopes to open up new possibilities for caring architectures. Her work has been published and exhibited in various books, magazines, and exhibitions such as *Plan Libre*, the *Villa Noailles*, the *Maison de l'architecture Île-de-France*, and *Archizoom*.

CONTRIBUTORS (FULL CREDITS PER CHAPTER)

Foreword

Javier Fernández Contreras

1 Instagram, Typology, and Architecture

Javier Fernández Contreras and Paule Perron

—Data Analytics: Paule Perron

2 Screens Within Screens: The Interiors of Twitch

Javier Fernández Contreras

—Data Analytics: BA students in Interior Architecture, HEAD – Genève (HES-SO): Charlene Claveria, Lisa Divorne, and Noémie Castella.

3 Rooms, Pins, and Boards: The Hyper-interiors of Pinterest

Javier Fernández Contreras and Michela Bassanelli

—Data Analytics: BA students in Interior Architecture, HEAD – Genève (HES-SO): Martin Annen, Nassim Baron, Giona Leo Baumann, Cléa Bertossa, Aurore Biache, Alexia Dahman, Benjamin Dohollou, Tiago Dos Santos Pinto, Carla Ferey, Mirellle Gldi, Hippolyte Giraud, Ambre Gravina, Bryan Jefferson Reyes, Alexis Lang, Manon Lebon, Marie Mamou Blanché, Elise Mathis, Missilia Mendy, Zoé Mettraux, Luca Negro, Norah Pittet, Anna Smiian, Kateryna Sushynska, Yan Vasquez, Nina Wallimann, and Jiwon Yuk.

4 TikTok: Vertical Editing

Javier Fernández Contreras

—Data Analytics: BA students in Interior Architecture, HEAD – Genève (HES-SO): Camille Bodin, Annie Bornet, and Taiana Broillet.

5 Architecture, Humanitarianism, and Social Media

Javier Fernández Contreras and Damien Greder

—Data Analytics: MAIA students in Interior Architecture, HEAD – Genève (HES-SO): Matilde Arletti, Martino De Grandis, Maxime Joost, Lina Laube, Bianca Longoni, Hugo Maia Schmitt, Letizia Milone, Ailyn Pieyre, Célestine Potin, Paul Rigal, Lisa Schober, Kim Schönauer, Karol Szmigielski, and Mariannina Thielemans.

6 Pet Influencers: Animal Portraiture and Mediated Domesticities

Javier Fernández Contreras

—Data Analytics: BA students in Interior Architecture, HEAD – Genève (HES-SO): Martin Annen, Nassim Baron, Giona Leo Baumann, Cléa Bertossa, Aurore Biache, Alexia Dahman, Benjamin Dohollou, Tiago Dos Santos Pinto, Carla Ferey, Mireille Gidi, Hippolyte Giraud, Ambre Gravina, Bryan Jefferson Reyes, Alexis Lang, Manon Lebon, Marie Mamou Blanché, Elise Mathis, Missilia Mendy, Zoé Mettraux, Luca Negro, Norah Pittet, Anna Smiian, Kateryna Sushynska, Yan Vasquez, Nina Wallimann, and Jiwon Yuk.

7 Unboxing Roblox: Architecture, Urbanism, and Video Games

Javier Fernández Contreras

—Data analytics: BA students in Interior Architecture, HEAD – Genève (HES-SO): Martin Annen, Nassim Baron, Giona Leo Baumann, Cléa Bertossa, Aurore Biache, Alexia Dahman, Benjamin Dohollou, Tiago Dos Santos Pinto, Carla Ferey, Mireille Gidi, Hippolyte Giraud, Ambre Gravina, Bryan Jefferson Reyes, Alexis Lang, Manon Lebon, Marie Mamou Blanché, Elise Mathis, Missilia Mendy, Zoé Mettraux, Luca Negro, Norah Pittet, Anna Smiian, Kateryna Sushynska, Yan Vasquez, Nina Wallimann, and Jiwon Yuk.

8 Porn Rooms: Ultimate Interiority

Javier Fernández Contreras and Vytautas Jankauskas

Assistant: Lola Jutzeler

   —Data analytics: Students, HEAD – Genève (HES-SO): Delia
Aeberli, Louisa Azzouz, Léo Dorner, Denis Désir, Caïque Interlandi,
Ileana Leveuf Feliz, Emeline Mermoud, Fatana Mia Paris, Carla
Plan, Lelia Quero, Antonin Ricou, Emilie Rau, Jaeggi Sky, and
Nicolas Ulrich.

Afterword

Marina Otero Verzier

Book package coordinator: Alexandra Miskufova

FIGURES

1.1 Analysis of posts without explicit commercial purpose published by the eleven most-followed Instagram accounts worldwide in 2022   2

1.2 The private gym: Posts published in 2022 by the most-followed Instagram accounts worldwide   13

1.3 The sofa: Posts published in 2022 by the most-followed Instagram accounts worldwide   15

1.4 The bed: Posts published in 2022 by the most-followed Instagram accounts worldwide   17

1.5 The dressing room: Posts published in 2022 by the most-followed Instagram accounts worldwide   18

1.6 The bathroom: Posts published in 2022 by the most-followed Instagram accounts worldwide   19

1.7 Private transport: Posts published in 2022 by the most-followed Instagram accounts worldwide   22

2.1 Justin.tv. Lifecast. May 22, 2007, 12:09:01 (PST)   26

2.2 *Mystery Science Theater 3000*. Episode 12: "Fugitive Alien." February 5, 1989   29

2.3 The ten most-followed streamers on Twitch in 2022   32

2.4 Ninja. Streaming room in 2022   34

2.5 Ninja's room during the thirty most-watched streams of 2022   36

2.6 Pokimane's room during the thirty most-watched streams of 2022   38

2.7 Emilycc's subathon on Twitch, November 2, 2023   40

2.8 IKEA. Matchspel, gaming chair, 2023   42

3.1 Oh Joy! Pinterest boards, April 2024   46

3.2 Poppy Talk. Pinterest boards, April 2024   50

3.3   Jane Wang. Pinterest boards, April 2024   54
3.4   Maryann Rizzo. "Laundry Rooms" board, April 2024   58
3.5   Bonnie Tsang. "Living Spaces" board, fragment, April 2024   60
3.6   HonestlyWTF. "Doors" board, April 2024   62
3.7   Pejper. "Green Interior" board, April 2024   63
3.8   Cathie Hong. "Cathie Hong Interiors" board, April 2024   64
3.9   Mamas Uncut. "Home Hacks and Decor Ideas" board,
      April 2024   66
4.1   Khabane Lame. Thirty most-watched videos posted on
      his TikTok account in 2022   76
4.2   Charli D'Amelio. Thirty most-watched videos posted
      on her TikTok account in 2022   77
4.3   Denarie Taylor/Bella Poarch. Thirty most-watched videos
      posted on her TikTok account in 2022   78
4.4   Addison Rae. Thirty most-watched videos posted on
      her TikTok account in 2022   79
4.5   Zachary Michael King. Thirty most-watched videos
      posted on his TikTok account in 2022   80
4.6   Kimberly Guadalupe Loaiza Martinez. Thirty most-watched
      videos posted on her TikTok account in 2022   81
4.7   Dixie D'Amelio. Thirty most-watched videos posted on
      her TikTok account in 2022   82
4.8   Spencer Polanco Knight. Thirty most-watched videos
      posted on his TikTok account in 2022   83
4.9   Loren Gray. Thirty most-watched videos posted on her
      TikTok account in 2022   84
4.10 Michael Le/Justmaiko. Thirty most-watched videos posted
      on his TikTok account in 2022   85
5.1   Self-organizing map based on the 7,559 images collected
      on social media platforms through October 2024   88
5.2   Global humanitarian images. Exterior spaces in 5,653 of
      the images collected from social media platforms through
      October 2024   89
5.3   Global humanitarian images. Interior spaces in 1,446 of
      the images collected from social media platforms through
      October 2024   90
5.4   Global humanitarian images. Subject: group of people in
      3,212 of the images collected from social media platforms
      through October 2024   92

5.5 Global humanitarian images. Subject: individual subject in 1,691 of the images collected from social media platforms through October 2024   94

5.6 Global humanitarian images. Viewpoint: eye level in 5,470 of the images collected from social media platforms through October 2024   96

5.7 Global humanitarian images. Viewpoint: bird's-eye view in 595 of the images collected from social media platforms through October 2024   97

5.8 Global humanitarian images. Time: daytime in 5,305 of the images collected from social media platforms through October 2024   98

5.9 Global humanitarian images. Time: nighttime in 374 of the images collected from social media platforms through October 2024   100

5.10 Average humanitarian picture (diurnal, group-based, color photograph, eye-level perspective, shared by a local organization or individual) in twenty representative examples from the dataset of 7,559 images collected on social media platforms through October 2024   101

5.11 Iran. Portraits within interiors. Posts through October 2024   102

5.12 Darién Gap. Landscape views. Posts through October 2024   103

5.13 Ukraine. Bird's-eye views. Posts through October 2024   104

5.14 Lebanon. Nocturnal images. Posts through October 2024   105

5.15 Afghanistan. Gendered interiors. Data visualization from social media posts through October 2024   106

5.16 DRC. Gendered spaces. Data visualization from social media posts through October 2024   107

5.17 Dadaab camp, Kenya. Places of transience. Data visualization from social media posts through October 2024   108

5.18 Moria–Mavrovouni camps, Greece. From left to right: Progression from improvised tents to stable shelters. Posts through October 2024   109

5.19 Kutupalong camp, Bangladesh. Narratives of resilience. Posts through October 2024   110

5.20 Sudan. Activities amid the crisis. Data visualization from social media posts through October 2024   112

5.21 Haiti. Humanitarian images. Platform-specific focus: Facebook: group-based humanitarian work; X: institutional representation; Instagram: artistic storytelling, independent projects. Data visualization from social media posts through October 2024   114

5.22 *Humanitarianism and Social Media*. Analyzed accounts, October 2024   116

6.1 Tucker Budzyn, Impact on social media platforms as of January 2025   122

6.2 Buddy and Boo. Space types where the pets were normally portrayed   126

6.3 Jiffpom. Analysis of the latest posts on Jiffpom's Instagram account (as of March 2024)   127

6.4 Nala Cat. Space types where the pet is normally portrayed   128

6.5 Doug the Pug. Comparison between the pet's X (Twitter) and TikTok accounts, as per total data available as of March 2024   129

6.6 Grumpy Cat. Typical Instagram portrait, and official communication of the pet's death in May 2019   131

6.7 That Little Puff. Portraiture and communication style of the official TikTok account   132

6.8 Floofnoodles. Official TikTok account (@floofnoodles) and merchandizing products, March 2024   133

7.1 Roblox: Hours of engagement, final month of each quarter, billions, to August 2020   140

7.2 Graphical projections found in video games   143

7.3 Roblox Studio: Templates, June 2024   144

7.4 Roblox Studio: Suburban template, June 2024   145

7.5 *Brookhaven RP*: Wheelchair chosen from the Vehicles menu   147

7.6 *Tower of Hell*: Different camera types including first- and third-person views. Perspectives can be chosen, no elevator visible   148

7.7 *Adopt Me!* Game sequence: What's your style?; Furnish your own home; On the way to the nursery; Adoption choice: babies or pets   149

7.8   *Murder Mystery 2*: Different gameplay scenes, assigning
Sheriff, Innocent, or Murderer identities randomly   150

7.9   *MeepCity*: Comparison between interior and exterior
spaces, including different chromatic palettes   151

7.10 *Royale High*: Gameplay sequence traversing interior and
exterior spaces. Homogeneous chromatic palette based
on pink and purple tones   152

7.11 *Pet Simulator X!* Mostly diurnal, outdoor, and above-
ground. The three bottom images represent the only
underwater world, following the same composition
principles   154

7.12 *Piggy*: Mostly nocturnal, indoor, and above-ground   156

7.13 Lugical, "CameraService: A New Camera for a New
Roblox," 2022   158

INDEX

Note: Page numbers in *italics* refer to figures. References to endnotes show both the page number and the note number (43n.6).

abolitionism 91
Adopt Me! (game) 148, 154, 155
    architectural style 149, *150*
    avatars 146–7
    game sequence *149*
    interior domestic spaces 153
Afghanistan 93, 114
    gendered usage of space 102–3, *106*
Agasse, Jacques Laurent 124
Ahl, David 140
Alberti, Leon Battista 142
algorithms 87–8
All Eyes on Rafah (computer-generated image) 92
American National Exhibition, Moscow (1959) 52
Amini, Mahsa 103
animal puppets 130–1
animals
    genealogy of representation of 123–4
    portraits of 134
anime 148
Architectural Digest 56
architectural styles, of Roblox video games 140–1, 149–50
architecture
    and digital platforms 169
    as situated asymmetry 102–12
    typology in 1, 11
Archizoom (Italian group) 66
armed conflicts 93
Arnolfini Portrait, The (van Eyck) 124
Ascending and Descending (Escher) 153
avatars
    Roblox 146, 147, 150–3, 157
    Twitch 35

Bangladesh
    Kutupalong refugee camp 106, 107–8, *110*
    Rohingya refugee camp 107
bathrooms, Instagram posts from *19*, 20
Baudrillard, Jean 45, 48
Beavis and Butt-Head (TV series) 28, 43n.6
beds, Instagram posts from *17*, 18–19
Benetton 91
Berger, John 121
Beyoncé, use of elevators in Instagram posts 21
Bieber, Justin
    Instagram posts
        beds in *17*, 18
        dressing rooms in *18*

sofas in *15*
use of private transportation in 21, *22*
Big Brother (TV series) 125, 128
Blox Fruits (game) 148, 149, 153, 154, 155
Boltanski, Luc 113
Bottici, Chiara 89
Brookhaven RP (game) 146, 147, 149, 150, 154, 155
architectural style 149
personal spaces for players 153
wheelchair from Vehicles menu *147*
Broughton, Jo 165
Brunelleschi, Filippo 142
Buddy and Boo (celebrity dogs) 125, *125*, 126, 128, 129

Capa, Robert 90
celebrity pets. *see* pet influencers
Cho, Joy 56
Chouliaraki, Lilie 89–90
circulation spaces 21
closed *poché* 20
CNN (news channel) 88, 91
Coffman, Erica Chan 59
Colombia 93, 100
Colomina, Beatriz 52
control rooms 159
Coolidge, Cassius M. 124
Crimean War 87, 90
Crystal Palace 66

D'Amelio, Charli 73
TikTok videos *77*
D'Amelio, Dixie 74
TikTok videos *82*
Darién Gap 100, 111–12
landscape views 97, *103*
Dark Horse (Perry) 126
Delivery of the Keys, The (Perugino) 143
della Francesca, Piero 142

Democratic Republic of the Congo (DRC) 104
gendered usage of space 102, 104–5, *107*
internal displacement in 93
De pictura (Alberti) 142
De prospectiva pingendi (della Francesca) 142
diffuse houses 65, 66, 67
Digital Millennium Copyright Act (DMCA) claim 36
digital platforms, architecture and 169
digital spaces 171
distant suffering 90, 113
Dogs Playing Poker (Coolidge) (paintings) 124
domesticity, mediated 12–14
domestic spaces 12, 20, 170
Donkey Kong (game) 141
Doug the Pug (celebrity dog) 125, 126–7
business model 129
X (Twitter) and TikTok accounts *129*
dressing rooms, in Instagram posts *18*, 21
drone snapshots, of Ukraine 100–1

Eames, Charles and Ray 49
Economist, The 140
e-flux Architecture 118
elevators, in Instagram posts 21
Emilycc (Twitch streamer) 27, 34, *40*
Empty Porn Sets (Broughton) 165
Escher, M.C. 153
European Convention for the Protection of Pet Animals 121
Evans, Robin 142
Evans, Walker 91
Exodus, or the Voluntary Prisoners of Architecture (Koolhaas) 66

Facebook 11, 107
    humanitarian content 111, 112,
        114
family photographs 16
Fenton, Roger 87, 90
ferrets. *see* Floofnoodles (celebrity
    ferrets)
Figurative Architecture 141–2
films 20, 28
    frame-within-frame compositions
        28, 43
Floofnoodles (celebrity ferrets) 122,
    131–2
    domestic spaces utilized as
        production studios 133–4
    TikTok account *133*
Forbes 71 n.7
foreshortening 153
Foucault, Michel, notion of utopian
    corporality 15
fundraising events 91
*Future of Humanitarian Design
    (HUD), The* (research
    program) 118

Gaza War, use of social media
    in 88
Gemenne, François 121
Gen Z 71n.14
Glimpses of the USA (film) 52
global *poché* 20
Gogglebox (TV show) 28–9
Gomez, Selena
    Instagram posts
        bathrooms in *19*, 20
        hotel hallways in 21
        sofas in *15*
Grande, Ariana
    Instagram posts 23n.6
        bathrooms in *19*
        dressing rooms in *18*, 21
        hotel hallways in 21
        private gyms in *13*
Graves, Michael 141–2
Gray, Loren 75, *84*

Greece, Moria–Mavrovouni refugee
    camps 106, 107, *109*
Grumpy Cat (celebrity cat) 125, 126,
    128, 129, *130*
Guadamuz, Andres 134
Gulf War (1990–1991) 91
gyms
    in Instagram posts *13*
    role in porn industry 164

Haiti 93, 111
    humanitarian images *114–15*
Halpern, Orit 159
Halvarson, Jan 56
Hammershøi, Vilhelm 28, 43
Hefner, Hugh 14
Hepburn, Audrey 91
Herscher, Andrew 106
hidden-camera aesthetic 165
Hockney, David 28
Hong, Cathie 57, 68
hotel hallways, in Instagram posts 21
humanitarian images
    average/typical 97, *101*
    bird's-eye view in *97*
    daytime in *97–9*
    diurnal 101
    exterior spaces in *89*
    eye level viewpoint in *96*
    genealogy of 89–93
    group pictures 97
    groups of people in *92*
    individual subjects in *93–5*
    interior spaces in *90*
    nighttime in *100*
    presence of the human body in
        96
    role in the narration of conflict 90
    self-organizing map based on *88*
humanitarian imaginary 89
humanitarianism 88
    social media and 87
humanitarian narratives, eye level
    construction 100
Hurricane Katrina 92

hyperconnectivity 48
hyper-interior spaces 48
hyper-personalization 48
hyperreal 48
hypertext 48

IKEA
    catalog of interiors for gamers 40,
        41–2
    gaming chair *42*
    Republic of Gamers (ROG) 40,
        41
Instagram 1–24, 93, 107, 111, 112
    hierarchies 11, 12
    humanitarian images 111, 112
        Dadaab refugee camp, Kenya
            106
        Haiti 111, *114*
        Kutupalong camp,
            Bangladesh 107–8
        Lesvos (Greek island) 107
        Sudanese conflict 108
    most-followed accounts 11
        analysis of posts *2–10*
        bathrooms in *19*, 20
        beds in *17*, 18–19
        dressing rooms in *18*, 21
        private gyms in *13*
        private transport in *22*
        sofas in *15*, 16–17
    pet influencers 128
        Grumpy Cat 128, *130*
        Jiffpom *127*
        Tucker Budzyn 122, *122–3*
interior spaces 12
    definition of 23n.4
    frames as a way of seeing
        through 28
    functional 20
    in global humanitarian images
        90
    on Pinterest 53–6
    pornography and 163, 164,
        166
    on Roblox 153

internal displacements 93
Iran 93, 102, 103–4, 114
    portraits within interiors 97,
        102
Isaacs, Ken 52
Israel–Lebanon conflict 93

Jan, Matej 'Retro' 143
Jaque, Andres 169
Jebb, Eglantyne 91
Jenner, Caitlyn Marie 23n.6
Jenner, Kendall 13, 20
Jenner, Kylie 20
Jiffpom (celebrity dog) 122, 125,
    126, 128
    business model 129
    Instagram account *127*
    TikTok followers 128
@justice4lucas movement 132
Justin.tv 25, 29
    livecast *26*

Kan, Justin 25, 29
Kardashian family 21
Kardashian–Jenner family 11, 18
Kardashian, Kim 13, 20
Karin, Anna 59
Keeping Up with the Kardashians
    (TV show) 11
Kenya, Dadaab refugee camp 106,
    108
King, Zachary Michael 74, *80*
Knight, Spencer Polanco 74
    TikTok videos *83*
Knowledge Box 52
Koolhaas, Rem 66

Lame, Khabane 73, *76*
Lange, Dorothea 91
Lebanon
    Israel–Hezbollah conflict in 109,
        110–11
    Israeli attacks over 101
    nocturnal images 97, *105*
Le, Michael (Justmaiko) 75, *85*

Lesvos (Greek island), refugee camps 107
lifecasting 29
Live Aid (1985) 91
Loaiza Martinez, Kimberly Guadalupe 74, *81*
Luau (scripting language) 142
Lucan, Jacques 20

MAIO 65, 66
Mayolo, Carlos 91
Medieval Pets (Walker-Meikle) 123
MeepCity (game) 147, 149, 153, 154, 155
    interior and exterior spaces *151*
Messi, Leo 17, 18
    Instagram posts
        beds in *17*
        gyms in *13*
        private transport in 21, *22*
        sofas in *15*, 16, 17
Met Gala (2017) 20
mirrored rooms 40–3
Moneo, Rafael 1
multiscreen mediated rooms 49
Murder Mystery 2 (game) 148, 150, 153, 154, 155
    architectural style 149
    gameplay scenes *150*
Mystery Science Theater 3000 (TV series) 28, *29*, 43n.5

Nala Cat (celebrity cat) 122, 125, 127, 128
    business model 129
    space types where the pet is portrayed *128*
Naruto (crested macaque) 134
natural disasters 93
Nelson, Ted 48
New Babylon (Nieuwenhuys) 66
Nieuwenhuys, Constant 66
night-vision devices 165
Nolli, Giambattista 67

No-Stop City (project by Archizoom) 66

Office for Political Innovation 169
101 BASIC Computer Games (Ahl) 140
online celebrities 122
open/urban *poché* 20
Ospina, Luis 91
Ozu, Yasujiro 28, 43

paintings, frame-within-frame compositions 28
Panama 93, 100
Perry, Katy 126
perspectival systems 142
Perugino, Pietro 143
pet influencers 122, 124–6
    Buddy and Boo 125, *125*, 126, 128, 129
    Doug the Pug 125, 126–7, 129, *129*
    Floofnoodles 122, 131–4
    Grumpy Cat 125, 126, 128, 129, *130*
    Jiffpom 122, 125, 126, *127*, 128, 129
    Nala Cat 122, 125, 127, 128, *128*, 129
    popularity and reach 128
    That Little Puff 131, *132*, 133
    Tucker Budzyn 122, *122–3*, 128, 129
pet ownership, growth in 121
pet photographs 123, 135
pets
    definition of 121
    in photography and cinema 124
Pet Simulator X! (game) 148, 149, 153, 154, *154*, 155
Philosophie des jeux vidéo (Triclot) 31
photographs, frame-within-frame compositions 28
Piggy (game) 148, 149, 155, *156*

Pinterest 45–72, 170
   ancillary rooms 56
   architectural genealogy 49–53
   boards 48
      displaying interior spaces
         53–6
      interior design 59
      most followed 49
   business accounts 53
   "Buyable Pins" ("Product Pins")
      53
   history of 45–8
   hyper-interiors of 67
   "Image Search" 69
   "Lens" 53
   mobile device access to 69
   most-followed accounts 48, 53
      Bonnie Tsang 57, 59, *60–1*,
        68
      Cathie Hong 57, *64–5*
      Honestly WTF 57, 59, *62*
      Jane Wang *54–5*, 57, 59
      Mamas Uncut 63, *66–7*
      Maryann Rizzo 57, *58*, 59
      Oh Joy! *46–7*, 49, 56, 59, 68
      Pejper 49, 57, 59, *63*, 68
      Poppytalk *50–1*, 56–7, 68
   outdoor spaces 56
   "Pin it" ("Save") 48
   pins 48
      external 68
      "rich" 68
   "Shop the Look" ("Shop Similar
      Items") 53, 69
   "Visual Search" 53
Plan of Rome (Nolli) 67
Playboy (magazine) 14
Poiret, Anne 92
Pokimane (Twitch streamer) 27,
   32–3, 36, *38*
Pollack, Sara 45
porn 163–7
   amateur productions 165
   content 165–6
   filming technology 164–5
   professional productions 165
   relationship between interior
      spaces and 163
   representation of different body
      types 165
   role of interior spaces in 164
   seasonal themes 165
   spatial trends 166
   traditional, pre-internet
      audiovisual 165
   types of interior spaces in 164
Pornhub 163–4
Pornified Homes (film) 169
pornomiseria 91
Pornotopia (Preciado) 14, 21
portraits 96
Preciado, Paul 14, 21
private transportation spaces, in
        Instagram posts 21, *22*
Projective Cast, The (Evans) 142

Quake (game) 141
Quan-Haase, Anabel 48

Rae, Addison 74, *79*
refugee camps 92, 93, 106, 107
resistance movements 93
Riis, Jacob 91
Rizzo, Maryann 57, 59, 68
Roblox 139–62
   adventure and role-playing (RPG)
      games 148
   annexes and ancillary spaces
      155
   architectural styles of video
      games 140–1, 149–50
   avatars 143, 146–7, 150
   cameras 150–3, 156
   "CameraService" (Lugical) 157,
      158
   chat 155, 158
   color palettes 155
   Creator Hub 156
   day/night cycles 154–5
   Developer Forum 157

devices used for gaming 158
horror games 148
hours of engagement on *140*
interactions between players 153,
    158
objects and effects for designing
    games 146
obstacle challenges 148
personal spaces for players 153
pot-centric games 148
simulation and role-playing
    games 154–5
social simulation games 147
solo and multi-player modes 154
templates 144–6, *144*
    Castle 145
    Modern City 145
    Pirate Island 145
    Suburban 145, *145*
    Village 145
underground spaces 155
Roblox Studio 142
Cartesian geometry 144
Rock, the
Instagram posts
    beds in *17*
    elevators in 21
    private transport in 21, *22*
    sofas in *13*
Ronaldo, Cristiano
Instagram posts 13
    bathrooms in *19*
    beds in *17*, 18
    dressing rooms in *18*
    gyms in *13*
    private transport in *22*
    sofas in *15*, 16, 17
Rose, Gillian 16
Royale High (game) 147–8, 149,
    150, 154, 155
gameplay sequence *152*
personal spaces for players 153

Save the Children campaign 91
Sciarra, Paul 45

Seiber, Michael 25
selfies 96, 134, 135
servant spaces 20–1
sex vlogs 165
Sharp, Evan 45, 69
Shear, Emmett 25
Silbermann, Ben 45, 59
Slater, David 134
Sloterdijk, Peter 66
smartphones 12, 40, 87, 100, 134,
    163
social imaginary 89
sofas, in Instagram posts *15*,
    16–17
Sontag, Susan 91, 113
space types 143, 164
Spacewar! (game) 31
Spanish Civil War (1936–1939) 90
staged everyday 12–14
Steyerl, Hito 41
Sudan
    civil war 107
    internal displacement in 93
    visual documentation of conflict
        in 108, *112–13*
Sultan, Larry 165
Super Mario Bros. (game) 141
Superstudio, *Continuous Monument*
    66
Syndicate (video game) 143

Taylor, Denarie (Bella Poarch) 73,
    78
tele-intimacy 91
That Little Puff (celebrity cat) 131
    TikTok account *132*, 133
Think (film) 52
TikTok 73–85, 140
    Doug the Pug account *129*
    Floofnoodles account 131, *133*
    Jiffpom account 128
    most-followed accounts (2022)
        73–5
        Addison Rae 74, *79*
        Charli D'Amelio 73, *77*

Denarie Taylor/Bella Poarch 73, *78*
Dixie D'Amelio 74, *82*
Khabane Lame 73, *76*
Kimberly Guadalupe Loaiza Martinez. 74, *81*
Loren Gray *84*
Michael Le/Justmaiko *85*
Spencer Polanco Knight 74, *83*
Zachary Michael King 74, *80*
pet celebrity followers on 131
That Little Puff *132*, 133
total statistics 75
Toscani, Oliviero 91
Tote (app) 45, 52
Tower of Hell (game) 147, 148, 149, 153, 155
camera types and perspectives *148*
multiplayer mode 154
Triclot, Mathieu 30, 31
Tsang, Bonnie 57, 59, 68
Pinterest board *60–1*
tube sites 163
Tucker Budzyn (celebrity dog) 122, *122–3*, 128, 129
TV programs, *mise en abyme* of 26–7
Twitch 25–44, 111
archaeology of 28–30
content 27
digital archives 35–9
free channels and subscriptions 35
influencers' perspective of 35
interface 30
livestreams 27
most-followed streamers (2022) 30–5
Auronplay 27, 31–2, 33, 36
El Rubius 32, 33, 36
Emilycc 27, 34, *40*
Ibai 32, *33*

JuanSGuarnizo 32, 33, 36
Ninja 27, 31, *32*, *34*, 36, *36*
Pokimane 27, 32–3, 36, *38*
Shroud 32, 33, 36
Tfue 27, 32, 33, 36
TheGrefg 32, 33, 36
xQc 27, 32, 33, 36
subathons 27, 34, *40*
views from mobile devices 40

Ukraine
bird's-eye views of war in 100, *104*
portrayal of ruins in 109–10
UNICEF Goodwill Ambassador 91
utopian corporality 15

Valley, The (Sultan) 165
Vampires of Poverty, The (mockumentary) 91
Van Eyck, Jan 124
ventriloquism 130
Vermeer, Johannes 28, 43
video games 25, 29, 139, 140. *see also* Roblox
3D gaming 141
in the 1960s and 1970s 141
ability to disrupt the circadian rhythm 31
graphical projections found in 143
isometric 143
space design in 141
spatialization of 30–1
user-created 140
Vietnam War (1955–1975) 91
Vogt, Kyle 25
V-Tubers 35

Walker-Meikle, Kathleen 123
Wang, Jane 57, 59
Pinterest boards *54–5*
Welcome to Refugeestan (documentary) 92
Wellman, Barry 48

West Sahel 102, 104
    gendered use of space in 105
Winx Club (TV series) 148
World Fair, New York (1964) 52

X (Twitter) 107, 111
    Doug the Pug account *129*

Grumpy Cat followers on 128
humanitarian images from Haiti
    on *114*

YouTube 11, 100, 107, 111, 112

Zhang, Lynch 131